P9-CDI-861

THE SHORT-CUT COOK

ALSO BY JACQUES PEPIN

The Other Half of the Egg (1975)
Jacques Pépin: A French Chef Cooks at Home (1975)
La Technique (1976)
La Méthode (1979)
Everyday Cooking with Jacques Pépin (1982)
The Art of Cooking, Volumes 1 and 2 (1987/1988)
A Fare for the Heart (1988)
A Fare That Fits (1989)

THE SHORT-CUT COOK

JACQUES PEPIN

*Illustrations
by the author*

WILLIAM MORROW AND COMPANY, INC. NEW YORK

Copyright © 1990 by Jacques Pépin, Inc.

All rights reserved. No part of this book may be reproduced or utilized in any form
or by any means, electronic or mechanical, including photocopying, recording or by
any information storage and retrieval system, without permission in writing from the
Publisher. Inquiries should be addressed to Permissions Department, William
Morrow and Company, Inc., 105 Madison Avenue, New York, N.Y. 10016.

Recognizing the importance of preserving what has been written, it is the policy of
William Morrow and Company, Inc., and its imprints and affiliates to have the books
it publishes printed on acid-free paper, and we exert our best efforts to that end.

Library of Congress Cataloging-in-Publication Data

Pépin, Jacques.
     The short-cut cook / Jacques Pépin.
         p.   cm.
     ISBN 0-688-09448-1
     1. Cookery, easy.   2. Convenience foods.   I. Title.
   TX652.P434   1990
   641.5—dc20   90-6306
                                                                          CIP

Printed in the United States of America

First Edition

1 2 3 4 5 6 7 8 9 10

BOOK DESIGN BY KATHLEEN HERLIHY-PAOLI

This book is dedicated to my daughter, Claudine.
May these recipes make your life easier
and your love for cooking even greater.

ACKNOWLEDGMENTS

This book was not a solitary endeavor, and I have many people to thank for it: my wife, Gloria, the best in the world, and, among my many friends, Zimmy, Ben, Charlie, and Priscilla, who dutifully consume my creations. Special thanks to Laurie Orseck for her thorough editing and to my dear friend Ann Bramson, whose idea made my book possible. More than anyone else I want to thank my assistant, Norma Galehouse, whose hard work and reliability I depend on entirely, and whose diligent and meticulous attention to detail brought this project toward completion in record time.

CONTENTS

INTRODUCTION

T his book is intended to make your life easier. In it I share streamlined cooking techniques, teach you how to make use of quality convenience foods, suggest supplies for a well-stocked freezer and pantry, and specify which cooking equipment and utensils are the most useful.

The "short-cut" cuisine that emerges in the two hundred-plus recipes here is one born of necessity to accommodate today's fast-paced lifestyles, a cuisine that is rewarding without being demanding. Although not all the recipes are quick—a few take time, intended for those weekends when you have a free day and want to make a special dish for your family or guests—they're all easy. Essentially, the book celebrates simple, satisfying fare that can be prepared easily and cooked quickly at the end of a busy day.

Many styles of cooking are represented on these pages, with dishes created to satisfy a variety of needs and fit a host of occasions. Just as it's not "right" or "wrong" to eat in the kitchen rather than the dining room, simple food is not "better" than elaborate food: The food and the setting should be compatible with the occasion, and if something tastes good, it doesn't matter whether it is "authentic" or prepared "correctly"—what works, works.

With very little time to cook today, people often eat in fast-food restaurants or buy expensive and often inferior precooked food. My way of cooking—based on years of professional experience—makes use of fresh foods and supermarket convenience foods, to which I apply a personal touch to make them my own.

All supermarkets now feature foods like precut meats and poultry, grated cheeses, presliced mushrooms, and washed spinach. Although it's a bit more expensive to buy these convenience foods, the savings in time and effort make it worth the additional cost—and the quality of your cooking is not diminished because someone else has done some of the preparation for you. Commercial mayonnaise, yogurt, and peeled red peppers are examples of the basic, useful products that can be given your personal signature with a little ingenuity.

Small restaurants—pressed for time and short of skilled hands—often proceed along the same lines. They buy small quantities of prepeeled and prediced fresh vegetables, cleaned salad greens, trimmed lamb racks, and filleted fish. Even though these products are more expensive than when bought in bulk, the savings in time and labor offset the higher cost and often provide the only possible course of action.

During the past several years, the term "homemade" has taken on a righteous tone: In today's terminology, it means better, more virtuous, truer to nature—in short, the proper way to do things. But homemade food is good only when it is superior in taste to its store-bought counterpart. In reality, many so-called homemade breads, cakes, croissants, jams, and condiments are greatly inferior to similar items available at the local supermarket.

In France it is quite common for even great home cooks to buy certain prepared foods—those renowned for their exceptional quality—at the market. Things like breads, pâtés, quenelles, dumplings, basic doughs, jams, and relishes are rarely made at home. The supermarket is a reliable source of supply, and the quality of each brand is determined by trial and error. Making use of proven brands, the resourceful home cook creates her own dishes. To quote Montaigne, a sixteenth-century French writer, "The bees go from flower to flower to gather the pollen but with it they create their own honey." We are proposing the same course of action here: Select superior items at the market and use them in ways that make them your own.

Selectively mixing fresh with canned, bottled, or frozen food can result in great dishes. For example, quickly sauté fresh scallops and toss them in a delicious sauce made of commercial bottled mayonnaise that you've flavored with lemon juice, scallions, Worcestershire sauce, and Tabasco sauce (see Scallops in a Skillet, page 138). Or, for an elegant dessert, mold rectangles of packaged puff pastry around fresh Bartlett pear halves and bake (see Bartlett Pears in Puff Pastry, page 256). Your delighted guests will not know or care that these dishes weren't made exclusively with "fresh" food.

Cooking is not the only aspect of food preparation that can be simplified. Food shopping is a time-consuming activity that benefits from thoughtful advance planning. Even the use and cleaning of cooking utensils can be streamlined. And by having a well-stocked larder (see page 17), you can create meals on short notice. An impromptu visit from friends can often be the occasion for a "cuisine of opportunity," with dishes prepared from what is at hand.

Understanding the mechanics of cooking is helpful also. If you decide to cook a stew, for example, know that although it takes a couple of hours to cook it conventionally on top of the stove, a pressure cooker can reduce the cooking time by half. Double or triple the recipe, and either freeze the leftovers for use later on or refrigerate them to create a soup or a purée for a meal later that week.

Techniques are important, too. Peel vegetables directly into a sink equipped with a garbage disposer, or place an oversize garbage can (my version is on wheels) in a convenient position and let the peels drop directly into it. If neither of these options is feasible, spread newspapers on the work surface to catch the peelings and so simplify the cleanup.

Whenever possible, line baking pans with aluminum foil to eliminate time-consuming cleaning afterward. Fill a dirty pot or roasting pan with water as soon as you have finished using it, to loosen solidified cooking bits and make washing-up easier. Roll dough between sheets of plastic wrap to keep the work surface and rolling pin clean. Cook in gratin dishes attractive enough to go directly from the oven to the table. Freeze food in dishes that can go right from the freezer to the oven to the table. When sautéeing meat—whether it be pork chops or veal scaloppine— sauté a vegetable to serve with it in the unwashed skillet; a cleanup step is eliminated and the juice from the meat will enhance the flavor of the vegetable.

Give some thought beforehand to your use of a food processor. If a menu calls for puréed vegetables and fresh bread crumbs, be sure to process the bread first so the processor won't need washing between the two uses. Merely rinse your pots between uses and progress, whenever possible, from cooking "clean" to sticky foods.

A common mistake people make when preparing a pasta dish is to wait until the sauce is finished before they put the pasta cooking water on to boil. Put the pot on the heat when you begin preparing the meal so it will be ready when you need it. When selecting a menu consisting of three dishes, make sure that one or two of them can be made ahead, or you will be too involved in cooking to create a hospitable atmosphere when your guests arrive. To save on work afterward, whenever possible use wipeable placemats and large good-quality paper napkins instead of cloth ones.

Practice my time-and-labor-saving techniques and come up with some of your own, equip your kitchen with the best possible cooking equipment and utensils to make the work easier, and seek out quality convenience foods that you can combine appetizingly with fresh foods to create sumptuous meals. Simple, speedy, sensible, and smart, this is "short-cut" cooking—ideal for people on the run who demand good food.

THE SHORT-CUT KITCHEN

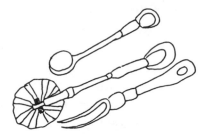

EQUIPMENT

T o be a good short-cut cook, you need high-quality equipment and a well-stocked pantry. Anyone who has attempted to chop vegetables or cut meat with a dull knife, or had to go to the store to buy sugar in the midst of baking a cake, knows how frustrating a poorly organized kitchen can be, even when you're not rushed. But when you don't have much time, inadequate equipment or lack of an ingredient can turn you against cooking altogether. I've taken an inventory at my house and compiled a list of kitchen equipment I find especially useful and pantry items I like to have on hand.

A microwave oven is wonderful, but be discriminating in your use of it. It is good for cooking small portions of vegetables, fish, and fruit and is the best choice for reheating food. Another good feature is that is doesn't require much cleaning.

The pressure cooker is another labor-saving device that is a favorite in my kitchen. A stew can be prepared in half the time that it would take to cook it in a conventional pot, and the quality is not sacrificed. In addition to preserving the nutritional value of foods, the pressure cooker retains their moisture as well, and the modern version of this old invention is completely safe.

A food processor is invaluable. Chopping, puréeing, grating —jobs that used to take hours—are now completed in seconds, thanks to this miraculous machine.

Nonstick pans are essential for most sautéeing, since they are easy to clean. For other cooking needs, select pans made of good, solid stainless steel or thick, heavy copper or aluminum lined with stainless steel; they give an excellent result and clean up easily. Good stainless steel strainers are a must, as are a rubber spatula, high-quality carbon steel knives, and a good knife sharpener, all of which make your job easier.

A salad dryer is indispensable. Use the base of the dryer as a container to wash the salad greens, then lift the greens from the water and place them in the strainer before spinning them dry. Packed in plastic bags and refrigerated, washed greens will keep in the refrigerator for a couple of days.

A mini-chop is also handy. This tiny version of a food processor has a blade that spins much faster than its larger relative and is good for grinding dry ingredients like peppercorns, dried mushrooms, and dried tomatoes and for chopping spices, herbs, and garlic, which in small quantities get lost in a conventional food processor. The mini-chop is easy to clean, too.

An immersion blender is very good to have, also. The shaft of this hand-held appliance goes directly into a soup or vegetable mixture to purée it in seconds, and there is nothing to wash except the shaft, which rinses clean when held under the hot water faucet.

I buy large containers of plastic wrap and aluminum foil, as I use a great deal of both. I find the large rolls are easier to work with and have a better cutting edge than the smaller boxes. Line cookie sheets and pans with aluminum foil to avoid time-consuming cleanups. Plastic wrap seals foods well, preventing spillage from refrigerated leftovers or defrosting foods.

A toaster oven is a wise purchase. It heats very quickly, is big enough for two servings—and sometimes even three or four—and is much more economical to operate than a conventional oven. It's particularly good for toasting nuts, cooking sandwiches, and browning the tops of dishes.

Having a good-size freezer in also vital to short-cut cooking. It enables you to keep soup and sauce bases, ice cream, and frozen fruits and vegetables on hand.

It's fun to cook in a modern, well-equipped kitchen. All these items can do a great many chores for you.

PANTRY

A most important aspect of short-cut cooking is to have a well-stocked larder. If you keep an abundance of dry products, canned goods, frozen food, and fresh ingredients on hand, with a little imagination and help from this book you can easily create terrific meals in no time at all.

Dry products keep for many months. These include dried beans—red, white, and black, as well as chick-peas—pasta, rice, dried tomatoes and mushrooms, and chicken and beef bouillon. I keep a supply of thickeners on hand for soups and stews: flour, oatmeal, farina, couscous, bulgar wheat, and potato flakes are all very useful for this purpose. In the pastry area, keep a stock of cookies, chocolates, cake mixes, and a variety of nuts.

Among the canned products you should have on your pantry shelves are chicken broth, Italian-style tomatoes, tomato paste, smoked mussels, smoked oysters, shrimp, crabmeat, sardines, herring, salmon, ham, beans with pork, corned beef hash, chili, and different types of vegetables, including button mushrooms, sauerkraut, and pumpkin purée.

Products in jars include mayonnaise, various chutneys, Worcestershire sauce, soy sauce, steak sauce, hoisin sauce, chili and garlic sauce, teriyaki sauce, duck sauce, spare rib sauce, fish sauce, and plum sauce. I also keep on hand hot oil, sesame oil, olive oil, vegetable oil, good vinegars, hot salsa, artichoke hearts, caramel sauce, and butterscotch sauce, as well as jars of peperoncini, cherry peppers, sweet peppers, mixed pickles, eggplant in vinegar, marinated mushrooms, an assortment of mustards, cocktail sauce, and horseradish.

If you have enough freezer space, you can stock frozen peeled shrimp, squid, stuffed pasta (manicotti, ravioli, tortellini, lasagna), fruit juice concentrates (orange, pineapple, grapefruit), batters, and of course different dessert products like cakes, brownies, and fruit, a series of ice creams and sherbets, frozen doughs —from crescent dough to bread dough, pie dough, and cookie dough. Frozen strawberries, raspberries, and blueberries, as well as peaches or cherries are very good to have on hand. Very useful, too, are mixed and individually frozen vegetables, from petite peas to corn, tiny pearl onions, sliced mushrooms, French green beans, spinach leaves, cauliflower, and mustard greens. Homemade chicken stock, several types of sausages—from kielbasa to Italian sausage—and chicken breasts are other freezer staples.

When buying fresh products, remember that some items will keep longer than others: garlic, carrots, and eggs keep a long time when stored in the refrigerator; potatoes and onions should be stored in a cool pantry. Take advantage of all the peeled, cleaned, and packaged vegetables, not forgetting to occasionally make use of the salad bar in many supermarkets to pick up ready-to-eat seasonal vegetables. Take advantage, too, of the precut meat and poultry, fish in portion-controlled packages, and the bounty of the supermarket deli departments with their different types of olives, salads—from fish to chicken, to pasta, to potato, to smoked fish—pickles, cold cuts, and sausages.

If you have some or all of the equipment listed here, and know at all times what food items you have in your pantry, refrigerator, and freezer, you can happily and easily accommodate your family and any surprise visitors.

BASICS

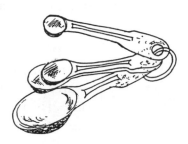

T his chapter contains recipes that are terrific to have on hand; not only can they be used in a variety of ways on their own, but they can be added to other dishes to impart interest and flavor.

Hot Red Salsa, for example—delicious as a dip for corn or potato chips—gives added "zip" to my Chick-pea Salad (page 101), Cheese Tart (page 83), and Broiled Marinated Lamb Chops (page 186). The Mushroom, Tomato, and Nut Mix, great in sandwiches and wonderful as a pasta sauce (see Penne with Mushroom, Tomato, and Nut Sauce, page 116), is also delicious as an appetizer with drinks or as a first course for dinner. And Cranberry Relish with Lime, a natural with Roast Turkey with Garlic (page 171), is versatile enough to go well with most roasts, pâtés, or any type of cold meats.

Once you have made the Mustard Vinaigrette Dressing, you won't buy bottled dressing again—it takes only a few minutes and is wonderful with salad greens, poached fish, or potato salad.

MUSHROOM, TOMATO, AND NUT MIX

This is a great versatile mixture, delicious in salads, sauces, stews, and sandwiches. I use it several times in this book; it helps to season everything from pasta to cheese to salad.

1 ounce dried Polish cèpe
mushrooms
4 ounces sun-dried tomatoes
(not in oil)
¼ cup sunflower seeds
3 small bay leaves
¼ teaspoon red pepper flakes
¼ teaspoon dried tarragon
3 large cloves garlic, peeled and
sliced thin (about 1½
tablespoons)
1 tablespoon thinly sliced
jalapeño pepper
1 cup olive oil, or as needed
½ teaspoon salt (if the tomatoes
are not salted)

Place the mushrooms and tomatoes in a bowl, and add boiling water to cover. Soak for 5 minutes. Drain (reserve the liquid for use in stock or soup).

Place the mushrooms and tomatoes in a jar, and add all the remaining ingredients. Allow the mixture to steep for a few hours before serving. (It will keep in the refrigerator for up to 2 weeks.)

ABOUT 3½ CUPS

HOT CUCUMBER RELISH

This is a staple at our house; we like its hotness and crunchiness. Put it in sandwiches, mix it in salads, and serve it as a condiment with meats. Stored in a jar or bowl in your refrigerator, it will keep for several weeks. Chopped, the cucumbers from the relish make an excellent sauce (see Salmon Croquettes with Hot Cucumber Salsa, page 146).

After you have eaten up all the cucumbers, you can reuse the marinade a couple of times, adding more fresh cucumbers.

1 large cucumber, preferably
    the English-style "seedless"
    variety (about 1¼ pounds)
1 teaspoon salt
2 tablespoons sugar
1 teaspoon crushed red pepper
    flakes
½ cup white or cider vinegar
1 cup boiling water

Peel the cucumber and cut it into very thin slices, by hand or in a food processor fitted with the 1-millimeter blade. Transfer the slices to a bowl and add the remaining ingredients. Mix well, cover, and refrigerate for at least 2 hours before serving.

Note: Add about ¼ cup coarsely chopped cilantro for another taste.

4 CUPS (6 SERVINGS)

HOT RED SALSA

 lthough salsa is readily available at most supermarkets, you might enjoy this homemade version. It will keep for a couple of weeks in the refrigerator.

1 jalapeño pepper, coarsely cut
    (2½ teaspoons)
1 large clove garlic, peeled
1 tablespoon cilantro (coriander
    or Chinese parsley) leaves
2 small plum tomatoes
    (4 ounces total), quartered
1 tablespoon water
1 tablespoon ketchup
⅛ teaspoon salt

Place the hot pepper, garlic, and cilantro in the bowl of a food processor and process for 5 to 10 seconds, until coarsely chopped. Add the tomato pieces, water, ketchup, and salt, and process again until the mixture is chunky, in pieces no larger than ¼ inch. Transfer to a jar and refrigerate until serving time. (This will keep for at least 2 weeks in the refrigerator.)

¾ CUP

USE AS A DIP WITH CHIPS OR ADD TO SALADS AND STEWS.

TAPENADE

T his olive spread is a staple in Provence, where it is usually served with aperitifs or as an appetizer. Try it on pita toasts (see page 84), bagel chips, or *fougasse*, the famous bread of Provence (see page 73). It can also be added to sauces, to ratatouille, or used as a garnish with smoked salmon and other smoked fish or pâtés. Serve a chilled white or rosé wine from Provence with the *tapenade*.

The traditional recipe for *tapenade* doesn't contain dried figs, but I think they are a great addition. Be careful not to overprocess the mixture; it should be chunky, not creamy. Tightly covered, it will keep for up to 2 weeks in the refrigerator.

1 jar (8 ounces) oil-cured olives
    (or another variety of
    olive), pitted (1¼ cups)
1 can (2 ounces) flat anchovy
    fillets in oil
3 tablespoons capers, drained
4 or 5 dried figs (4 ounces
    total), cut into ¼- to ½-inch
    pieces
½ teaspoon freshly ground
    black pepper
¼ cup extra-virgin olive oil
    (best possible quality)

Place all the ingredients in the bowl of a food processor and process for 4 to 5 seconds. Scrape down the sides of the bowl, and process for 7 to 8 seconds longer, until the mixture holds together but is still somewhat chunky. Transfer to a small bowl and serve.

1½ CUPS

HORSERADISH SAUCE

T his is excellent with clams or oysters on the half shell, and it also gives added zip to salad dressings or tomato sauce. It will keep in the refrigerator for a couple of weeks.

½ cup ketchup
½ teaspoon Tabasco sauce
4 tablespoons grated fresh
    horseradish, or 6
    tablespoons bottled
4 teaspoons cider vinegar
2 tablespoons corn oil
2 tablespoons water

Combine all the ingredients and mix thoroughly. Store, refrigerated, in a jar with a tight-fitting lid until ready to use.

1 CUP (6 SERVINGS)

THIS VERSATILE SAUCE KEEPS IN THE REFRIGERATOR. ADD SOME TO YOUR BARBECUE SAUCES FOR MORE ZIP.

EGGPLANT CAVIAR

This delicious spread can be served as an appetizer or as an hors d'oeuvre with aperitifs. Easy to make, it is particularly good on pita toasts (see page 84) or black pumpernickel bread, and it will keep for a week in the refrigerator. You can use it as a pasta sauce, too. Or serve it hot as a side dish with meat or fish.

1 eggplant (1 pound)
1 tablespoon corn or canola oil
2 onions (about 6 ounces total),
    peeled and chopped (1½
    cups)
3 large cloves garlic, peeled,
    crushed, and chopped
    (2 teaspoons)
2 ripe tomatoes (about 12
    ounces total), halved,
    seeded, and cut into ¼-inch
    dice (1½ cups)
2 tablespoons olive oil

½ teaspoon freshly ground
    black pepper
1 teaspoon salt
½ teaspoon Tabasco sauce
½ teaspoon sugar
1 tablespoon cider vinegar
1½ tablespoons chopped
    cilantro (coriander or
    Chinese parsley)

Place the eggplant, whole and untrimmed, on a cookie sheet lined with aluminum foil, and bake it

(continued)

Eggplant Caviar (continued)

in a 400-degree oven for 45 minutes or until soft.

While the eggplant is cooking, heat the corn oil in a skillet, then add the onion and sauté over medium heat for 3 to 4 minutes. Stir in the garlic, then transfer the mixture to a bowl. Add the diced tomato, olive oil, pepper, salt, Tabasco, sugar, vinegar, and cilantro. Stir to combine.

When the eggplant has cooled enough to handle, peel off and discard the skin, and mince the flesh by hand or in a food processor (you should have 1¾ to 2 cups). Add to the ingredients in the bowl, and mix well.

3 CUPS

MUSTARD VINAIGRETTE DRESSING

At our house, we eat salad with almost every meal, and nine out of ten times the dressing is a standard vinaigrette. I make the vinaigrette in a jar with a tight-fitting lid and store it in the refrigerator so it is available when I need it—it will keep for up to 2 weeks.

Occasionally, if I want to vary the taste, I add some pounded garlic to the dressing in the salad (but not to the dressing in the jar, because the garlic will lose its fresh taste after a few days and adversely affect the flavor). I use a tarragon-flavored vinegar. You might want to try another type for a different taste.

This dressing is not homogenized because the oil is added with the other ingredients, not whisked in at the end. So no matter how long or how hard you shake the jar, the dressing won't become creamy. It will blend somewhat, which is what you want—then it will separate again. This means that the salad greens will be glossy and flavorful without being heavily coated with a sauce. Just shake the jar briefly before each use to partially blend the ingredients.

1½ tablespoons Dijon-style
    mustard (preferably "hot")
2 tablespoons tarragon red wine
    vinegar
½ teaspoon salt
½ teaspoon freshly ground
    black pepper
1 cup oil (preferably half virgin
    olive oil and half peanut,
    canola, or corn oil)

Place all the ingredients in a 12-ounce glass jar, cover tightly, and shake well to mix. Refrigerate until ready to use.

When you are ready to use the dressing, shake the jar briefly to recombine the ingredients.

ABOUT 1¼ CUPS (20 PORTIONS)

THIS DRESSING IS MADE AND STORED IN A JAR, READY FOR IMMEDIATE USE.

STEWED TOMATO SAUCE

The tomatoes are not cooked much here—the other ingredients are cooked first and the tomatoes added later and just heated briefly—so the sauce has a very fresh, mild taste.

Tomato paste gives color, texture, and flavor to the tomatoes—especially valuable out of season, when fresh tomatoes tend to be watery and bland. I suggest you use the paste that comes in a tube; you can squeeze out only as much as you need and then recap it, so the remainder doesn't dry out, and it keeps for a long time in the refrigerator.

In addition to serving as a delicious topping for pasta (see page 113), the sauce can be used as a vegetable or as a garnish for fish or broiled meats. You can even mix it into vegetable soup (see Cold Raw Tomato Soup, page 64, and Tomato Soup with Chives, page 63).

(continued)

Stewed Tomato Sauce (continued)

2½ pounds very ripe tomatoes
3 tablespoons olive oil
1 onion (4 to 5 ounces), peeled
    and chopped fine (1 cup)
1 teaspoon herbes de Provence
    (see Note, page 48), or fresh
    thyme leaves
3 cloves garlic, peeled, crushed,
    and chopped very fine
    (about 1½ teaspoons)
1 teaspoon salt
½ teaspoon freshly ground
    black pepper
½ teaspoon sugar
1 tablespoon tomato paste

Plunge the tomatoes into a pot of boiling water for 10 to 15 seconds. Drain, and cool under cold water. Peel off the skin and cut the tomatoes in half parallel to the stem. Squeeze gently, pressing out the seeds and excess juice. Cut the tomato flesh into ½-inch pieces (you should have 4 cups).

Heat the olive oil in a skillet or saucepan (preferably stainless steel to prevent discoloration). When it is hot, add the onion and herbes de Provence, and sauté for about 1½ minutes. Add the garlic and stir it into the onions. Then add the tomatoes, salt, pepper, sugar, and tomato paste. Bring the mixture to a strong boil, reduce the heat, and boil gently for 1 to 2 minutes.

4 CUPS (6 SERVINGS)

CRANBERRY RELISH WITH LIME

This is delicious with turkey (see page 171) and also with game, roast chicken, and roast pork. The relish has a spicy but sweet citrus flavor that goes well with rich food such as pâtés. It takes only a few minutes to make and will keep for weeks in the refrigerator.

1 small lime (about 3 ounces)
1 package (12 ounces) fresh
    cranberries
1 cup light maple syrup
¼ teaspoon cayenne pepper

¼ teaspoon ground ginger
¼ teaspoon ground mace

Cut the lime lengthwise into quarters, then cut each quarter into thin triangular slices. Place them in a stainless steel saucepan and add the remaining ingredients. Stir well, cover, and bring to a boil over high heat. Mix thoroughly, cover again, reduce the heat, and boil gently over medium heat for about 5 minutes. All the cranberries should be broken and the mixture well combined. Transfer the relish to a bowl and allow it to cool. Refrigerate until serving time.

2½ CUPS (8 SERVINGS)

PACKAGED CRANBERRIES COME CLEANED, SO THEY NEEDN'T BE WASHED BEFORE YOU USE THEM.

APPETIZERS
AND FIRST
COURSES

Many of the recipes here make wonderful appetizers for large parties: Tuna Tartare on Daikon Radish, Potatoes and Red Caviar, and Guacamole Piquante, for example, all lend themselves to presentation on big platters or trays. The Red Pepper Dip, in addition to making a great hors d'oeuvre, is good as a pasta sauce (see Rigatoni with Red Pepper Sauce, page 116). Most of these recipes, such as the Black Bean Hummus and the Fondue au Fromage, can, of course, be served as a first course, as well as the two egg recipes: my Mom's Cheese Soufflé, especially easy because you don't have to beat the egg whites independently, and the tasty Eggs in a Spinach Nest. Other first-course recipes can be found throughout the book; and consult the index.

RED PEPPER DIP

This dip has a fresh, interesting taste and is easy to make when you use pimentos or sweet roasted peppers that come in jars or cans. I add pecans, which makes for a somewhat unusual combination. This is a big hit at parties, served with bagel chips, melba toast, fresh toast, or Pita and Cheese Toasts (page 84). It also makes a great pasta sauce (see page 116).

2 cloves garlic, peeled
½ jalapeño pepper (about 1 tablespoon), seeded, or to taste
⅓ cup pecan pieces
1 cup drained sweet roasted or pimento peppers
⅓ cup virgin olive oil
¼ teaspoon salt

Place the garlic and jalapeño pepper in the bowl of a food processor and process for about 10 to 15 seconds, until puréed. Add the remainder of the ingredients and process until the mixture is smooth. Serve as a dip with crispy chips or toast.

ABOUT 2 CUPS (4 SERVINGS)

> RED PEPPERS FROM A JAR OR CAN ARE THE MAIN INGREDIENT IN THIS DELICIOUS, PIQUANT, EASY-TO-MAKE DIP.

SALMON–CREAM CHEESE ROLL-UPS

If you prepare these roll-ups ahead of time and place them in the freezer for a few hours, slicing them will be much easier.

> **USE A SMALL HORS D'OEUVRE LOAF OF BREAD, OR CUT ROUNDS OUT OF LARGER SLICES WITH A 2-INCH COOKIE CUTTER.**

*1 package (8 ounces) cream
    cheese, cold
5 or 6 slices smoked salmon
    (about 5 ounces)
½ teaspoon freshly ground
    black pepper
About 25 small round slices
    pumpernickel or other dark
    bread*

Place the cream cheese on a 12-inch square of plastic wrap. Cover it with another 12-inch square, and with a rolling pin, roll the cream cheese out to form a square approximately 8 by 8 inches.

Peel off and discard the top piece of plastic wrap, and arrange the salmon over the cheese. Sprinkle the pepper evenly over the salmon. Holding the plastic wrap underneath, roll the cream cheese up tightly, enclosing the salmon. (Don't let the plastic get rolled up inside as well.) Use the plastic wrap to help tighten the roll; it should measure about 9 inches by 1½ inches. Seal it well in the plastic wrap and place in the freezer for 1½ to 2 hours.

Remove the partially frozen roll from the plastic wrap, and using a sharp thin-bladed knife, cut it into ⅜-inch slices. Place the slices on the bread rounds. Work quickly while the mixture is cold, so that it doesn't stick too much to your fingers or to the knife. If it gets sticky, return it to the freezer for a few minutes to harden. Arrange the hors d'oeuvre on a large serving plate, and serve cold.

> **ROLLING CREAM CHEESE OUT BE-TWEEN LAYERS OF PLASTIC WRAP ELIMINATES A MESSY CLEANUP CHORE.**

Vegetable~Cream Cheese Roll-Ups In place of the salmon, substitute 1 large carrot, peeled and sliced into thin strips with a vegetable peeler, 8 sun-dried tomatoes from the Mushroom, Tomato, and Nut Mix on page 22, and 12 fresh mint leaves. Arrange the vegetables and mint over the cheese (omit the pepper), and roll up as described.

Note: If you don't have any tomato mix, you can use sun-dried tomatoes packed in oil or reconstituted dehydrated tomatoes.

Try other vegetables as well, for variations in flavor and color.

ABOUT 25 HORS D'OEUVRE

ANCHOVY, PARSLEY, AND CARROT SALAD IN TOMATO BARQUETTES

T his salad is often served with toast as a first course at our house. When serving it as an hors d'oeuvre, I either mound it in hollowed plum tomato halves, as I have here, or present it as a dip with toast, bagel chips, or pita toasts (see page 84). It even makes a delicious sauce for hot pasta.

The salad will keep in the refrigerator for as long as 2 weeks.

4 canned anchovy fillets (see Note)
4 cups flat parsley leaves
8 to 10 cloves garlic, peeled and chopped fine (3 tablespoons)
About 5 carrots (1½ pounds), trimmed, peeled, and shredded (about 4 cups)
1 teaspoon freshly ground black pepper
¼ teaspoon salt (optional)
⅓ cup olive or vegetable oil
1 tablespoon red wine vinegar
2 pounds (about 20) small plum tomatoes

Cut the anchovy fillets into ¼-inch pieces. Place them in a bowl and mix in the parsley, garlic, carrots, pepper, salt, oil, and vinegar. Cover tightly (we store ours in a jar) and refrigerate until ready to use.

Cut the tomatoes in half lengthwise and carefully hollow them out with a spoon that has a sharp edge (reserve the insides for soup, if desired). When you are ready to serve the salad, arrange the tomato barquettes on a serving platter and fill with the salad mixture.

Note on anchovies: Anchovies are sold in 2-ounce cans, about 12 fillets to the can. Transfer remaining fillets to a nonmetal container to store in the refrigerator for up to 2 weeks.

ABOUT 40 HORS D'OEUVRE

TUNA TARTARE ON DAIKON RADISH

T he hotness of the daikon radish complements the tuna. If you like, you can make tiny "sandwiches" by placing spoonfuls of the tartare between slices of radish.

Use very fresh good-quality tuna (or salmon or black sea bass) for this recipe.

1 pound fresh tuna, skin and
  sinews removed
½ cup chopped red onion
3 tablespoons minced scallion
  (about 2 scallions)
1 teaspoon chopped garlic (2 to
  3 cloves)
3 tablespoons virgin olive oil
½ teaspoon freshly ground
  black pepper
1 teaspoon salt
½ teaspoon Tabasco sauce
2 teaspoons red wine vinegar
1 teaspoon chopped tarragon
1 teaspoon Worcestershire sauce
1 red daikon radish (about 8
  ounces), 1½ inches in
  diameter
White toast or black bread
  (optional)

Chop the tuna by hand or in a food processor. If you are using a processor, place 1-inch pieces of tuna in the container and pulse for about 10 seconds. Be careful you do not overprocess—the tuna should not be chopped too fine.

If the red onion has a strong odor after you have chopped it, rinse it in a sieve under cool water (this removes the sulfuric acid compound that tends to sting your eyes). Drain it well and pat dry.

In a bowl, combine the tuna, onion, scallion, garlic, olive oil, pepper, salt, Tabasco, vinegar, tarragon, and Worcestershire sauce. Mix well. Peel the daikon radish and slice it into thin rounds. Place 2 to 3 teaspoons of the tuna mixture on each radish slice. Arrange them on a platter, and serve with toast or black bread.

Note: This can also serve as an appetizer for four to five people. Cut the daikon radish into julienne strips instead of rounds. Mound some tartare in the center of each plate, sprinkle it with a little olive oil, and garnish with the radish strips. Serve with toast or black bread if you like.

ABOUT 40 HORS D'OEUVRE

GUACAMOLE PIQUANTE

T here are many recipes for guacamole—I like mine fairly well seasoned. The important factor is the ripeness of the avocados, of course: They should yield to the touch but not have turned brown. You can serve guacamole with packaged natural fried corn chips, or with store-bought corn or flour tortillas that you have fried yourself.

¾ cup diced red onion (¼-inch pieces)

4 avocados (about 2 pounds)

3 to 4 cloves garlic, chopped (1 tablespoon)

1 very ripe tomato (about 4 ounces), halved, seeded, and cut into ¼-inch dice (1 cup)

4 scallions, cleaned and minced fine (⅔ cup)

1½ teaspoons salt

1 teaspoon Tabasco sauce

2 tablespoons olive oil

3 tablespoons lime juice

1 small jalapeño pepper, seeded and chopped (optional)

3 tablespoons chopped cilantro (coriander or Chinese parsley)

Packaged corn chips; or fresh or frozen tortillas, prepared according to package instructions

Rinse the chopped red onion in a sieve under cold water, and drain.

Cut the avocados in half, remove the pits, and spoon the flesh into a mixing bowl. Mash it coarsely with a fork. Add the onion, garlic, tomato, scallions, salt, Tabasco, olive oil, lime juice, and jalapeño pepper. Stir well and imbed the avocado pits in the mixture. Cover tightly with plastic wrap so that it lies directly on the guacamole, and set aside until serving time.

At serving time, remove the pits and stir in some of the cilantro. Arrange the guacamole in an attractive serving dish, sprinkle the remaining cilantro on top, and serve with chips.

4 CUPS

YOU CAN MAKE GUACAMOLE AHEAD OF TIME. IT WON'T TURN BROWN IF YOU SUBMERGE THE AVOCADO PITS IN THE MIXTURE AND COVER IT TIGHTLY SO THE PLASTIC WRAP ACTUALLY SITS ON THE GUACAMOLE.

POTATOES AND RED CAVIAR

T his is delightful as an hors d'oeuvre for a special cocktail party or as a first course for a sit-down dinner. It is best while the potatoes are still lukewarm.

There are two types of red caviar: "natural" and "red," which has a deeper color than the natural. Good natural caviar has an eye (a darker spot inside the egg).

The eggs in both varieties should be separate, not part of a mushy mass. Each egg should "crunch" when bitten, yet still be tender enough to almost melt in your mouth. The caviar should have a lightly salted, nutty flavor with no bitter aftertaste. To ensure that the caviar is good quality, buy it at a reputable store that has a high turnover.

2¾ to 3 pounds small red potatoes (about 20) or larger red potatoes
1½ cups sour cream
8 ounces good natural or red salmon caviar

Wash the potatoes thoroughly in cool water, and place them in a saucepan. Cover with water and bring to a boil over high heat. Boil gently until just tender, 20 to 22 minutes for small potatoes, longer for larger ones. Drain and set aside to cool. (The heat in the potatoes will absorb any remaining moisture, producing a better-tasting potato than if cooled under cold water.) When they are cool enough to handle, trim the potatoes slightly on two sides (enabling the halves to stand), and cut them in half. Cut larger potatoes into slices ¾ to 1 inch thick.

Place 2 teaspoons of sour cream on each potato half or slice, and top each with 1 teaspoon caviar. Arrange on a tray and serve immediately.

40 HORS D'OEUVRE

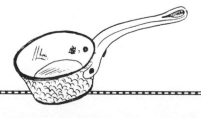

BLACK BEAN HUMMUS WITH SMOKED OYSTERS AND SOUR CREAM

This interesting combination is inspired by chick-pea hummus from the Middle East and the black bean purées found in Mexico. Served with sour cream and oysters, it makes an exciting dish.

I use canned black beans, but of course you can cook your own, which will tend to be darker than the canned. This is also good when made with red kidney or other types of beans. I suggest serving it as a first course, but it can also be served as a dip with corn chips, melba, or other toasts.

1 can (16 ounces) black beans
3 cloves garlic, peeled
⅓ cup oil, half vegetable oil and half olive or walnut oil
1 tablespoon red wine vinegar
1 teaspoon Tabasco sauce
½ teaspoon salt
2 tablespoons coarsely chopped cilantro (coriander or Chinese parsley)
1 cup sour cream
1 can (3¾ ounces) smoked oysters (about 14 oysters)
Whole cilantro leaves, for garnish
Toast triangles or melba toasts

Drain the black beans in a sieve to remove most of the liquid, and place them in a food processor with the garlic. Process until the garlic is finely chopped and the mixture is smooth. Add the oil, vinegar, Tabasco, and salt, and process for another 5 to 10 seconds to blend. Transfer to a serving bowl and stir in the chopped cilantro. Cover and refrigerate.

At serving time, spoon about ⅓ cup of the hummus on each plate, and spread it out in the middle of the plate. Place a generous spoonful of sour cream in the center, and top with 2 or 3 oysters. Sprinkle with the cilantro leaves. Serve the toasts alongside.

2 CUPS (6 SERVINGS)

TOMATO BASIL TOASTS

T his is a summertime special—to be made when the tomatoes are at their juiciest and the basil is tender and fresh. The contrast with the crisp toast is delightful. You can also use this tomato mixture for a sandwich filling, a cold pasta sauce, or a topping for poached or grilled fish.

2 pounds ripe beefsteak or plum tomatoes
1 cup diced red onion (⅛-inch pieces
6 scallions cleaned and diced (about 1 cup)
½ cup shredded basil leaves
⅓ cup virgin olive oil
2 tablespoons red wine vinegar
1 teaspoon salt
1 teaspoon freshly ground black pepper
¼ teaspoon Tabasco sauce
40 crisp toasts (see Note)

THE EASIEST WAY TO SHRED BASIL IS TO GATHER THE LEAVES INTO A PILE AND THEN CUT THEM INTO FINE STRIPS.

Plunge the tomatoes into boiling water for 15 to 30 seconds, drain, and when they are cool enough to handle, peel off the skins. Cut the tomatoes in half parallel to the stem, and press out the excess juice and seeds. Cut the tomato flesh into ¼-inch dice (you should have about 4½ cups).

Rinse the diced red onion in a sieve under cold water. Drain, and pat dry.

Combine the chopped tomatoes, onions, scallions, basil, oil, vinegar, salt, pepper, and Tabasco in a serving bowl and mix well. Allow the mixture to macerate for a few hours in the refrigerator to blend the flavors.

Place a serving spoon in the bowl and serve the tomato mixture in the center of a tray, surrounded by the toasts.

Note: You can use crackers, bagel chips or melba toasts, or grilled slices of bread or pita.

ABOUT 40 HORS D'OEUVRE

FONDUE AU FROMAGE

C heese fondue is a popular dish in the French part of Switzerland, not far from where I grew up in France. We ate it often in Bourg-en-Bresse, where I was born, calling it *ramequins*.

Requiring only a few ingredients and quickly assembled, this is a dish to be enjoyed with friends. The cheese is melted in white wine flavored with garlic and then placed over a burner on the table so it stays hot and melted. Although in Switzerland the ingredients are conventionally boiled together, thickened slightly with flour or cornstarch, and finished with kirschwasser, I don't thicken the mixture here. As a result, the cheese tends to stay in the bottom and the clearer liquid rises to the top, but this is the way it should be—you mix the ingredients together by stirring them with the bread as you dip it into the pot.

Unlike a meat fondue, which requires special forks, you can hold the bread easily with a regular table fork here. I use a crusty country-type French bread for dipping, cutting it into 2-inch squares. The bread pieces are impaled soft part first on a fork, so they don't fall off and drop into the fondue. (I am quite proficient at this because when I ate fondue in the cafés in France as a young man with my friends, anyone losing a bread chunk in the fondue had to buy a round of drinks for everyone in the party!) This dish is one of my daughter's favorites, high on her list of requests when she is home from college.

Fondue is great followed by a plate of cold cuts, a green salad, and a fruit dessert. The amounts listed here usually serve four as a first course. People unaccustomed to the taste may eat timidly at first, but the flavor grows on you—two people can consume this amount of fondue as a main course.

2 tablespoons unsalted butter
2 cloves garlic, peeled and
*   chopped (1 teaspoon)*
1½ cups dry white wine
¾ teaspoon salt
½ teaspoon freshly ground
*   black pepper*
3 cups (packed) shredded Swiss
*   cheese, preferably all or*
*   part Gruyère (about 12*
*   ounces)*
About 36 pieces of bread, each
*   about 2 inches square, from*
*   a crusty country-style loaf*

Heat the butter in a sturdy saucepan. When it is foaming, add the garlic and sauté for about 30 seconds, stirring. Add the wine, salt, and pepper and bring to a boil; then add the cheese. Mix gently with a wooden spoon or spatula over medium heat until the mixture returns to the boil. Remove the pan from the heat and place it on the table over a butane burner or Sterno.

Impale one piece of bread at a time, soft side first, on a fork and stir the mixture gently with it until the bread is coated with cheese.

When only about 1 cup of the cheese mixture remains, make the "soup": add eight to ten pieces of bread to the pot and mix them in well. Encourage your guests to enjoy the last pieces coated with the leftover liquid along with the crusty bits sticking to the bottom of the saucepan.

4 SERVINGS

CHEESE, APPLE, AND NUT BALLS

I use Camembert, Brie, and bleu cheeses for these flavorful hors d'oeuvre, but try other combinations with cheeses you have on hand—and if you don't have any pecans, other nuts can be substituted too. The little balls can be served on small toasts instead of carrot rounds.

MAKE THESE TASTY HORS D'OEUVRE WITH YOUR CHOICE OF CHEESES AND NUTS—OR OFFER A SELECTION OF DIFFERENT COMBINATIONS FOR VARIETY.

12 ounces cheese: a mixture of Camembert, Brie, and bleu
2 apples (12 ounces total), unpeeled
1 teaspoon finely ground black pepper
1 cup chopped pecans
1 large carrot, 1 to 1½ inches in diameter
2 tablespoons chopped chives, for garnish (optional)

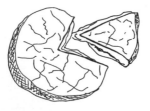

Cut the cheese into pieces and chop for 10 to 15 seconds in a food processor to combine the textures and tastes (or crush and mix the pieces of cheese with a fork). Place the cheese in a bowl.

Rinse, halve, and core the apples; then cut them into thin sticks about ½ inch long. Stir them into the cheese mixture. Sprinkle with the pepper.

Arrange the nuts in a single layer on a cookie sheet, and toast in a 400-degree oven until lightly browned, approximately 6 to 8 minutes. Add the nuts to the cheese-apple mixture, and stir together thoroughly. Refrigerate for at least 1 hour to firm the cheese. Meanwhile, peel the carrot and cut it into slices about ⅛ inch thick (about 40 rounds).

Form the cold cheese-apple-nut mixture into small balls, and place a ball on each carrot slice. Sprinkle with the chives, and serve.

40 TO 45 HORS D'OEUVRE

EGGS IN A SPINACH NEST

T his makes a terrific main dish for brunch or first course for dinner, which is the way eggs are often served in France.

If you prefer, you can cook the spinach ahead and reheat it in the oven before adding the eggs to finish the dish.

*1 pound prewashed packaged
   spinach*
*¼ teaspoon freshly ground
   black pepper*
¼ teaspoon salt
¼ cup extra-virgin olive oil
*4 large eggs, preferably from a
   health-food store*
¼ cup heavy cream

Pile the clean spinach into an oval gratin dish about 14 inches long and 8 inches wide. Place the dish on a foil-lined cookie sheet, and bake in a 400-degree oven for about 12 minutes. The spinach will have wilted considerably and be beginning to "melt" down into the dish. Remove the dish from the oven and press on the spinach with a fork to gather it together. Sprinkle with the pepper, salt, and oil, mix well, and press again into one layer in the dish.

If you are serving the dish immediately, break the eggs, one next to the other, on top of the hot spinach and return the dish to the oven for 7 to 10 minutes, until the egg whites are set but the yolks are still soft and runny. (Cook longer if you like your egg yolks hard.) Spoon the cream over the entire surface of the dish, and serve immediately.

If you will be serving it later, allow the spinach to cool. When you are ready to complete the recipe, return the dish to a 400-degree oven for 5 minutes to reheat the spinach before breaking the eggs on top. Complete the recipe as described above.

4 SERVINGS

USING PREWASHED PACKAGED SPINACH HERE IS A BIG TIME-SAVER; IT CAN GO DIRECTLY FROM THE BAG TO THE GRATIN DISH FOR COOKING. NOT ALL PACKAGED SPINACH IS PREWASHED, THOUGH—READ THE PACKAGE.

MOM'S CHEESE SOUFFLE

I have a very personal attachment to this soufflé. The recipe comes from my mother, who told me that when she was a young bride she wanted to make a soufflé for my father—who loved them—but she didn't know how. A friend told her that a cheese soufflé was composed of a *béchamel* sauce (white sauce), which she knew how to make, grated cheese, and eggs. So she proceeded to make one with these ingredients, not knowing that in a standard soufflé the eggs are separated—the yolks mixed in with the white sauce first and the beaten whites folded in later. She beat the whole eggs into the *béchamel* and was so happy with the result that she's made her soufflés in this manner ever since!

This kind of soufflé has many advantages, the most important being that you can prepare the mixture up to a day ahead, so there are no hectic last-minute preparations involved. Although it takes a little longer to cook than a standard soufflé and has a slightly less "airy" texture, it rises beautifully, browns well, and is quite delicious. My soufflé is made in a gratin dish so it cooks faster, is crustier, and is easier to divide into portions.

THIS IS THE IDEAL SOUFFLE TO ASSEMBLE AHEAD AND COOK AT THE LAST MOMENT.

2 tablespoons plus 1 teaspoon unsalted butter
3 tablespoons all-purpose flour
1¼ cups cold milk
¼ teaspoon salt
⅛ teaspoon freshly ground black pepper
⅛ teaspoon ground nutmeg
3 eggs
1½ cups grated Swiss cheese (about 4 ounces)
3 tablespoons coarsely chopped parsley or basil

Melt 2 tablespoons of the butter in a saucepan, add the flour, and stir with a whisk. When it is well mixed and sizzling, add the cold milk and bring to a boil, stirring and mixing with the whisk so it doesn't stick as it thickens. Boil for about 20 seconds, mixing continuously with the whisk. Add the salt, pepper, and nutmeg, and remove the pan from the heat.

Break the eggs into a bowl and beat them with a fork. Use the remaining teaspoon of butter to grease the bottom of a 3- to 4-cup oval gratin dish.

By now the white sauce should have cooled a little. Add the cheese to it and mix it in with the whisk. Then add the eggs and the par-sley and mix well. Pour the mixture into the prepared gratin dish.

When you are ready to cook the soufflé, place the dish on a foil-lined cookie sheet (for easy cleanup) and bake in a 400-degree oven for approximately 30 minutes, until well puffed and brown. Serve immediately.

4 SERVINGS

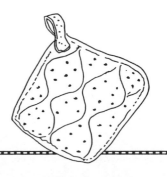

SOUPS

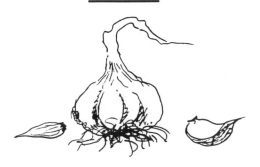

W e tend to assume that all soups take a long time to make, but in fact, of the twenty-one soups presented here, most can be made in 20 minutes or less, some in as little as 10 minutes. These recipes range from cold soups made with fruits or vegetables to earthy bean soups, a creamy mushroom soup, a squash soup, and a cheese soup. Many of them make use of fast thickening agents, such as Cream of Wheat, oatmeal flakes, cornmeal, or pasta, which lend texture, taste, and color.

I use a great deal of chicken stock in my soups, and although I sometimes resort to canned broth, I prefer to make my own stock and keep it on hand in the freezer. Sometimes it can go into the soup pot directly from the freezer—or it can be defrosted quickly in a microwave oven. Making homemade stock is time-consuming, but the actual work involved is minimal.

Chicken bouillon cubes are not listed among the ingredients here, but if my finished stock doesn't have enough flavor, I break a few of them into it to intensify the taste. These cubes and the dash of soy sauce I add for color provide the only salt in the stock; so you may want to add more salt to the soups you make with the homemade stock than to those made with canned broth, which contains salt.

BASIC CHICKEN STOCK

Very often I buy packages of chicken necks and backs at the supermarket and store them in the freezer. Then, when I find myself spending a day in the kitchen preparing other recipes, I take them out and make a stock. When the stock has finished cooking, I strain it, cool it, defat it completely, pour it into plastic containers with tight-fitting lids, and store it in the freezer. This way I always have it on hand for use in soups.

3 pounds chicken bones (necks, backs, and gizzards, skinless or with as little skin as possible)
6 quarts lukewarm tap water
1 tablespoon herbes de Provence (see Note)
1 large onion (about 8 ounces), peeled and cut into 4 pieces
12 whole cloves
1 teaspoon celery seed
1 tablespoon dark soy sauce

Place the bones and water in a large stockpot and bring to a boil over high heat. Reduce the heat and boil gently for 30 minutes. Most of the fat and impurities will rise to the surface during this time; skim off and discard as much of them as you can.

Add the remainder of the ingredients, return the liquid to the boil, and boil gently for 2 hours. Strain through a fine-mesh sieve or through a colander lined with a dampened kitchen towel or with dampened paper towels.

Allow the stock to cool. Then remove the surface fat and freeze the stock in plastic containers with tight-fitting lids. Use as needed.

Note on herbes de Provence: If you do not have herbes de Provence, substitute equal amounts of any of the following: dried marjoram, thyme, summer savory, sage, fennel, basil, rosemary, or lavender.

3¼ QUARTS (13 CUPS)

IF YOUR STOCK DOESN'T HAVE ENOUGH FLAVOR, ADD A FEW CHICKEN BOUILLON CUBES.

CONSOMME WITH TOMATO GARNISH

Consommé is an elegant soup that can be served either hot or cold. It is particularly suitable for the first course of a special dinner. Made with stock or a mixture of stocks —chicken, beef, and/or veal—egg whites are added to make it crystal clear. Vegetables and ground meat are added to intensify the flavor. The leaves of the vegetables develop flavor quickly while they steep, like tea leaves, in the hot mixture. Serve the consommé plain or garnished, as it is here, with little pieces of tomato.

8 cups fresh or frozen
    homemade chicken stock
    (see Basic Chicken Stock,
    page 48) or canned chicken
    broth
1 tablespoon soy sauce
1 cup (loose) celery leaves
1 carrot, peeled and coarsely
    chopped (about ½ cup)
1 cup chopped leek or scallion
    greens (½-inch pieces)
1 cup (loose) herb mixture
    (parsley leaves, parsley
    stems, chives, tarragon,
    and/or other herbs)
1 teaspoon dried tarragon
1 teaspoon herbes de Provence
    (see Note, page 48)
½ teaspoon freshly ground
    black pepper
1 teaspoon salt, or to taste
2 egg whites
2 or 3 plum tomatoes (8 ounces
    total), peeled (see Note),
seeded, (reserve skin and seeds), and cut into ¼-inch dice (1¼ cups)

Combine all the ingredients except the plum tomatoes, mixing thoroughly so that the egg whites are well combined with the vegetables and liquid. Stir in the skin and seeds from the plum tomatoes. Bring to a boil over high heat, scraping the bottom of the pot with a long-handled spoon from time to time to keep the mixture from sticking and burning. It should take about 15 minutes to come to a boil.

The mixture will become cloudy as the egg whites set. Continue stirring until it reaches a strong boil. Let it boil vigorously for a few seconds, and then set the pot aside and allow the mixture to rest for about 5 minutes.

(continued)

Consommé with Tomato Garnish (continued)

Strain the soup through a sieve lined with dampened paper towels or with a dampened kitchen towel. The consommé should be crystal clear and a beautiful golden color.

Place about 2 tablespoons of the diced tomatoes in the bottom of each soup plate. Pour the hot consommé over the tomatoes, and serve immediately.

Note on peeling tomatoes: There are three ways to remove the skin from fresh tomatoes: Peel them with a sharp knife; impale them on a kitchen fork and rotate them over the flame of a gas burner until blackened and then, when cool enough to handle, peel off the skin; or dip them in boiling water for 15 to 30 seconds and then peel off the shriveled skin.

Cold Consommé with Caviar Prepare the consommé as described, adding 2 envelopes (1½ tablespoons) unflavored gelatin to the strained mixture. Bring to a boil, boil vigorously for 5 to 10 seconds, and then set aside for 5 minutes. Strain, cool to room temperature, and then refrigerate 1 to 2 hours, until congealed.

Divide the consommé among six soup plates, and place 1 tablespoon crème fraîche in the center of each serving; it should sit firmly in the thick consommé. Spoon 1 teaspoon caviar (black Beluga or Sevruga, or good-quality red) on top of the crème fraîche, and serve immediately.

Note on crème fraîche: *Crème fraîche*, the thick, slightly sour-tasting cream that is a staple in French kitchens, is available in specialty food shops and some supermarkets. If you can't find crème fraîche at your local shop, make your own by mixing equal amounts of heavy cream and sour cream, or use just sour cream.

6 SERVINGS (6 CUPS)

BORSCHT

———

Many people love borscht but don't often make it because it takes so long to cook the beets, the main ingredient in this classic Russian soup. To hurry things along, I use canned sliced beets, which are already cooked. If you have some homemade chicken stock or canned broth on hand, it won't take much more than 10 minutes to prepare this recipe. I add shredded Savoy cabbage to the borscht, and especially like it served with sour cream mixed with a little grated horseradish.

You can, of course, use fresh beets if you prefer, but instead of cooking them whole and unpeeled—the standard way—peel and shred them first so they'll cook faster.

1 tablespoon unsalted butter
1 onion (4 ounces), peeled and
    sliced thin (about 1 cup)
4 cups shredded Savoy cabbage
    (6 ounces)
1 carrot, peeled and shredded
    (about 1 cup)
6 cups fresh or frozen
    homemade chicken stock
    (see Basic Chicken Stock,
    page 48) or canned chicken
    broth
1 can (16 ounces) sliced beets
1 cup sour cream, for garnish
2 tablespoons horseradish,
    freshly grated or bottled, for
    garnish
1 teaspoon salt, or to taste
½ teaspoon freshly ground
    black pepper
1½ tablespoons cider vinegar
2 tablespoons chopped dill, for
    garnish

Melt the butter in a large stainless steel saucepan and add the onion, cabbage, and carrot. Sauté over high heat for about 5 minutes, until the mixture has wilted but not browned. Add the chicken stock and bring to a boil.

Reduce the heat and boil gently for 4 to 5 minutes.

Meanwhile, drain the beets, reserving the juice. Arrange the beets in stacks on a piece of plastic wrap spread out over a cutting board. Slice into julienne strips about ¼ inch thick.

Stir together the sour cream and horseradish.

Add the beets to the stock along with the reserved beet juice, salt, pepper, and vinegar; return to the boil. Divide the soup among six bowls. Garnish each with 1 tablespoon of the sour cream mixture and 1 teaspoon of the dill. Serve.

Note: This can also be served cold, with the garnish.

6 SERVINGS (9 CUPS)

COVER YOUR CUTTING BOARD WITH PLASTIC WRAP TO PREVENT IT FROM BECOMING DISCOLORED WHEN YOU CUT UP THE BEETS.

BREAD AND CHEESE SOUP

T his is a family favorite at our house. If you have homemade chicken stock or canned broth, a little leftover bread, and some good Swiss cheese—preferably Gruyère—on hand, it can be prepared easily in a matter of minutes.

I toast the bread and shred the cheese ahead, then sprinkle some of each in the soup bowls while I heat the stock. Pour the boiling stock over the toast and cheese, and the soup is ready!

*6 cups fresh or frozen
    homemade chicken stock
    (see Basic Chicken Stock,
    page 48) or canned chicken
    broth*
Salt to taste
*½ teaspoon freshly ground
    black pepper*
*4 slices bread (4 ounces),
    toasted*
*4 ounces Gruyère cheese,
    shredded (1 cup)*

Bring the chicken stock to a strong boil and add the salt and pepper. Meanwhile, break the toast into pieces and place the equivalent of 1 slice in each of four soup bowls. Divide the cheese among the bowls, pour the boiling stock on top, and serve immediately.

4 SERVINGS (6 CUPS)

WITH THREE BASIC ITEMS IN YOUR LARDER—CHICKEN STOCK, BREAD, AND CHEESE—YOU CAN MAKE THIS DELICIOUS SOUP IN A FEW MINUTES.

BUTTERNUT SQUASH SOUP

I usually make this soup with fresh butternut squash, but frozen cubed squash from the supermarket works quite well if you are in a hurry. The soup is seasoned with apple cider, which gives it an appealingly sweet taste.

2 tablespoons unsalted butter
4 scallions, cleaned and minced
(⅔ cup)
1 onion, peeled and cut into ½-
inch dice (¾ cup)
1 carrot (4 ounces), peeled
and cut into ¼-inch dice
(¾ cup)
2 cups apple cider, preferably
unfiltered
3 cups fresh or frozen
homemade chicken stock
(see Basic Chicken Stock,
page 48) or canned chicken
broth
1 butternut squash (about 1½
pounds untrimmed), peeled,
seeded, and cut into ½-inch
dice (4 cups); or 1 pound
frozen diced squash
1 white turnip (about 4
ounces), peeled and cut into
½-inch dice (¾ cup)
1 teaspoon salt, or to taste

½ teaspoon freshly ground
black pepper
¼ teaspoon ground nutmeg

Melt the butter in a large saucepan, and add the scallions, onion, and carrot. Sauté over high heat for about 3 minutes; then add the cider, stock, fresh or frozen squash, and turnip. Bring the mixture to a boil. Cover, reduce the heat, and simmer gently for 25 minutes.

Mix in the salt, pepper, and nutmeg, and serve immediately.

6 SERVINGS (8 CUPS)

IF YOU'RE IN A HURRY, USE FROZEN CUBED SQUASH FROM THE SUPER-MARKET.

SOUPE AU VERMICELLE

This is my daughter's favorite soup, and she always asks her grandmother to make it when she visits us from France. It's an easy soup to prepare, especially if you have chicken stock on hand. It can be made with either leeks or scallions and that very fine pasta called "angel hair" that comes in nestlike bundles. After the stock has come to a boil, the pasta cooks very quickly—the whole soup can be prepared in a little more than 10 minutes.

(continued)

Soupe au Vermicelle (continued)

*4 cups fresh or frozen
  homemade chicken stock
  (see Basic Chicken Stock,
  page 48) or canned chicken
  broth*
1 cup water
*5 scallions, cleaned and minced
  fine (about ¾ cup)*
*4 ounces capelli d'angelo or
  vermicelli in bundles (about
  1 cup)*
*¼ teaspoon freshly ground
  black pepper*
Salt to taste

Pour the stock and water into a pot and bring to a boil over high heat. Add the scallions and cook for 1 minute. Break the pasta bun-dles into strings (so they don't form a block as they cook) and add to the boiling stock. Stir to separate the strands, and boil gently for 4 to 5 minutes. Add the pepper and salt, and serve immediately.

Note: This soup can be made ahead and reheated at serving time.

4 SERVINGS (5 CUPS)

MOST OF THE TIME REQUIRED TO MAKE THIS SOUP IS SPENT WAITING FOR THE CHICKEN STOCK TO COME TO A BOIL.

CHUNKY VEGETABLE SOUP

This vegetable soup is made with water, which retains the vegetables' flavors better than chicken stock does. I used onion, celery, scallions, carrots, zucchini, turnips, and cabbage because I had them on hand when I made the soup; you can use the same assortment or substitute other vegetables you have available in your refrigerator or freezer.

After being peeled, the vegetables are thinly sliced in a food processor. The herbs and garlic can be prepared in the processor as well, and there's no need to wash the bowl between these uses.

The herb/garlic garnish is added to the soup just at the end of the cooking period to give it a fresh flavor.

1 onion (about 4 ounces), peeled
1 rib celery (about 2 ounces), cleaned
4 scallions, cleaned
1 tablespoon corn oil
2 tablespoons unsalted butter
2 carrots (about 4 ounces), peeled
1 zucchini (about 7 ounces), trimmed and rinsed
1 white turnip (about 3 ounces), peeled
1 piece of white cabbage (about 4 ounces)
2 or 3 potatoes (8 ounces total), peeled
1½ teaspoons salt
7 cups water
3 cloves garlic
About ½ cup parsley or basil leaves, or a mixture of both
½ teaspoon freshly ground black pepper

Fit a food processor with the 1-millimeter slicing blade and process the onion, celery, and scallions.

Heat the oil and butter in a large stockpot, and when the mixture is hot, add the sliced vegetables. Sauté about 3 minutes.

Meanwhile, slice the carrots, zucchini, turnip, cabbage, and potatoes in the food processor. Add these vegetables to the stockpot, along with the salt and water, and bring to a boil. Cover, reduce the heat, and boil gently for 20 minutes.

Meanwhile, mince the garlic and herbs together in the food processor (fitted with the steel chopping blade). Add the herb mixture to the stockpot, mix well, season with the pepper, and serve.

6 TO 8 SERVINGS (10 CUPS)

ALL THE VEGETABLES AND THE HERB/GARLIC GARNISH ARE PREPARED IN THE FOOD PROCESSOR, AND THERE'S NO NEED TO WASH THE BOWL BETWEEN STEPS.

LIMA BEAN, SAUSAGE, AND BREAD SOUP

L ima beans are the basic ingredient in this soup, but it can be made with another variety of canned beans if limas are not to your liking. It is quite flavorful, hearty, and filling—and the ingredients are common enough that you might even have them available for quick assembly when unexpected guests appear. I keep kielbasa sausage in the freezer specifically for use in soups such as this, and I usually have stale leftover bread or rolls on hand that I can use as a thickening agent.

USE STALE, LEFTOVER BREAD OR ROLLS IN THIS SIMPLE, HEARTY SOUP.

1 tablespoon corn oil
5 ounces kielbasa sausage, cut into ½-inch pieces
1 onion (about 4 ounces), peeled and sliced thin (¾ cup)
1 can (16 ounces) green lima beans
3½ cups fresh or frozen homemade chicken stock (see Basic Chicken Stock, page 48) or canned chicken broth
Salt to taste
2 ounces dried bread or rolls, broken into pieces (about 1½ cups)
¼ teaspoon freshly ground black pepper

Heat the oil in a large saucepan or stockpot. When it is hot, add the sausage and the onion, and sauté over medium to high heat, covered (to prevent splatters), for about 3 minutes. Add the lima beans with their liquid, and the stock, salt, bread pieces, and pepper. Bring to a boil. Cover, reduce the heat, and boil gently for about 2 minutes. Mix well and serve.

4 SERVINGS (6 CUPS)

BEAN AND HAM SOUP

I f you have a can of beans on your shelf and a piece of ham in your freezer or refrigerator, you can make this earthy, satisfying soup in just a few minutes. I use white kidney beans, but another type can be substituted. The soup has a chicken stock base and is flavored with scallions. Add some croutons for a heartier version.

1 tablespoon virgin olive oil
2 scallions, cleaned and minced
    (⅓ cup)
½ cup chopped onion
½ teaspoon dried thyme leaves
2 cups fresh or frozen
    homemade chicken stock
    (see Basic Chicken Stock,
    page 48) or canned chicken
    broth
1 can (16 ounces) white kidney
    beans
2 thick slices cooked ham
    (about 3 ounces total), cut
    into ½-inch cubes
⅛ teaspoon freshly ground
    black pepper
Croutons, for garnish (optional;
    see page 104)

Heat the olive oil in a large saucepan. When it is hot, add the scallions, onion, and thyme and cook gently for about 2 minutes. Then add the stock and bring to a boil.

Meanwhile, place the kidney beans and their liquid in the bowl of a food processor and process for 5 to 10 seconds. (The mixture will not be completely smooth; little pieces of bean should still be visible throughout.)

Add the processed beans and the ham to the stock, and bring the mixture to a boil. Stir in the pepper, sprinkle with croutons if desired, and serve.

4 SERVINGS (5 CUPS)

IT ONLY TAKES A FEW MINUTES TO MAKE THIS SOUP IF YOU HAVE A CAN OF BEANS AND A LITTLE HAM ON HAND.

CORN, COD, AND POTATO CHOWDER

I use codfish in this earthy, wholesome fish chowder because I like its thick white fillets—but if you don't like cod or can't find it at your market, substitute fillets of scrod or some other type of fish.

Because this recipe involves a little work—dicing the pork, fish, and vegetables—I make enough to serve a large party at one sitting or a small group for two or three meals. If you use frozen hash-brown potatoes and frozen corn, you can eliminate much of the work and the soup can be prepared from start to finish in no more than 30 minutes. The chowder will keep, refrigerated, for 4 or 5 days.

3 ounces salt pork or unsliced
    bacon, cut into ½-inch cubes
1 cup diced onion (½-inch
    pieces)
1 small leek, cleaned and cut
    into ¼-inch pieces (about 1
    cup)
1 teaspoon dried thyme leaves
5 cups fresh or frozen
    homemade chicken stock
    (see Basic Chicken Stock,
    page 48) or canned chicken
    broth
1 cup water
12 ounces potatoes, peeled and
    cut into ½-inch dice; or 3
    cups packaged frozen hash-
    brown potatoes
1½ cups fresh or frozen corn
    kernels (about 6 ounces)
1 pound codfish fillets, cut into
    1-inch pieces

½ cup heavy cream
½ teaspoon freshly ground
    black pepper
½ teaspoon salt, or to taste

A VERY FILLING SOUP THAT MAKES A MEAL WITH THE ADDITION OF A SALAD

Place the salt pork or bacon pieces in a large pot and cook over high heat for 5 to 6 minutes, until they are crisp, nicely browned, and have rendered most of their fat. Add the onion and leek, and sauté for 2 minutes. Stir in the thyme leaves, chicken stock, water, and potatoes, and bring the mixture to a boil. Reduce the heat, cover, and boil gently for 10 minutes.

Add the fresh or frozen corn kernels and the fish and return to the boil. Cover, reduce the heat, and boil gently for about 1 minute. Then add the cream, pepper, and salt. Return to the boil and serve immediately.

8 TO 10 SERVINGS (ABOUT 10 CUPS)

MUSHROOM SOUP

Prepared in 10 minutes, this robust soup is made with packaged sliced fresh mushrooms from the supermarket. (You can substitute frozen slized mushrooms if you have a package of them in your freezer.) The soup is thickened with cornmeal, which cooks quickly.

2 tablespoons unsalted butter
8 ounces cleaned sliced
*   mushrooms*
1 small leek, cleaned and sliced
*   thin (about 1 cup); or 1 cup*
*   thinly sliced scallions*
4 cups fresh or frozen
*   homemade chicken stock*
*   (see Basic Chicken Stock,*
*   page 48) or canned chicken*
*   broth*
¼ cup yellow cornmeal
1 cup light cream
1 teaspoon salt, or to taste
¼ teaspoon freshly ground
*   black pepper*

Heat the butter in a large saucepan. When it is hot, add the mushrooms and leek, and cook over high heat for about 3 minutes. Then add the stock and bring to a boil. Using a whisk, mix in the cornmeal. Cover, reduce the heat, and simmer for about 5 minutes.

Add the cream, salt, and pepper and bring to a boil. Serve immediately.

4 SERVINGS (6 CUPS)

SAVE TIME BY USING CLEANED SLICED FRESH MUSHROOMS, AVAILABLE PACKAGED OR AT THE SALAD BAR, OR FROZEN SLICED MUSHROOMS.

CREAM OF PUMPKIN SOUP

T he main ingredient of this elegant soup is a can of pumpkin purée. With some chicken stock and cream at hand, it can be ready in a few minutes—with or without croutons, as you prefer.

1 can (16 ounces) unseasoned
    pumpkin purée
2½ cups fresh or frozen
    homemade chicken stock
    (see Basic Chicken Stock,
    page 48) or canned chicken
    broth
1 cup light cream
1 tablespoon honey
¼ teaspoon freshly ground
    black pepper
1 teaspoon salt, or to taste
¼ teaspoon curry powder
Croutons, for garnish (optional;
    see page 104)

COMBINE ALL THE INGREDIENTS FOR THIS QUICK, EASY, BUT ELEGANT SOUP DIRECTLY IN THE SAUCEPAN.

Place all the ingredients in a saucepan and mix well. Bring to a boil, divide among four soup bowls, sprinkle with croutons if desired, and serve immediately.

4 SERVINGS (6 CUPS)

PARMENTIER SOUP

M y favorite soup is made of potatoes and leeks, sometimes with the addition of onion. Now and then I make the coarse version, cutting the potato, leek, and onion into chunks, but in its classic form—Parmentier—the soup is puréed. It is traditionally made with a combination of stock and water, although it could be made exclusively with one or the other.

    Served cold the following day, the soup is transformed into the famous *vichyssoise* with the addition of cream and chives.

Conventionally, when preparing a cream soup like the Parmentier, the vegetables are cooked first and then puréed. In this easy version I use frozen hash-brown potatoes, which come already diced, and I liquify the vegetables before cooking.

2 leeks (about 6 ounces)
1 onion (about 4 ounces), peeled and cut into 4 to 6 pieces
2 cups water
2 cans (13¾ ounces each) chicken broth, or 3⅓ cups fresh or frozen homemade chicken stock (see Basic Chicken Stock, page 48)
1 tablespoon unsalted butter
1 tablespoon canola or corn oil
1 pound packaged frozen hash-brown (diced) potatoes (about 3 cups), defrosted
Salt to taste
½ teaspoon freshly ground black pepper
1½ cups broken pita toasts (see page 84)

Clean the leeks: Remove and discard any roots, but do not discard the entire green area. Instead, remove the first dark green layer of leaves, which is often damaged and usually fibrous and tough, and cut away any dark or damaged inner leaves. Do not remove leaves that are lighter in color (indicating tenderness). Since this enables you to use most of the inside of the leek, it eliminates waste.

Cut the leeks into pieces and rinse thoroughly in a sieve. Place in the bowl of a food processor with the onion and ½ cup of the water, and process for 15 to 20 seconds, until puréed. Transfer the purée to a soup pot and add the chicken broth, butter, and oil. Bring to a boil.

Meanwhile, combine the hash-brown potatoes with 1 cup of the remaining water in the bowl of the food processor, and process until smooth. Add this to the mixture in the pot along with the remaining ½ cup water and the salt and pepper. Bring the mixture back to the boil. Then cover the pot, lower the heat, and boil gently for about 25 minutes. The soup will be slightly grainy but creamy, and a lovely light green color.

Divide the soup among six bowls, and garnish with the pita toast.

6 SERVINGS (6½ CUPS)

> **DON'T WASTE EXPENSIVE LEEKS— USE THE TENDER PALE GREEN INNER LEAVES IN ADDITION TO THE WHITE PART.**

VICHYSSOISE

1 cup heavy cream
Salt to taste
3 tablespoons chopped chives
1 recipe Parmentier Soup
    (page 60), chilled

Stir the cream, salt, and half the chives into the cold Parmentier Soup. Divide the soup among 6 soup bowls, sprinkle the remaining chives on top, and serve.

6 SERVINGS (7½ CUPS)

CREAM OF LEEK SOUP

I make this delicious soup with the cooking liquid from Leeks Vinaigrette (page 216). Another vegetable stock or chicken stock can be substituted if the cooking liquid is not available. Each version will have its own distinctive flavor.

The soup is thickened here with Cream of Wheat—but you can also use tapioca, semolina, or even oat flakes. This easy, quick, comforting soup is also good reheated (you may want to dilute it with a little water or milk).

4 cups cooking liquid from
    Leeks Vinaigrette (page
    216) or if unavailable,
    vegetable or chicken stock
2 chicken bouillon cubes (omit
    if using chicken stock)
½ cup Instant Cream of Wheat
½ cup heavy cream
Salt and freshly ground black
    pepper to taste

1 tablespoon chopped chives, for
    garnish

QUICK AND EASY TO MAKE, THIS COMFORTING SOUP IS THICKENED WITH CREAM OF WHEAT.

Bring the leek cooking liquid to a boil in a saucepan, and crumble the bouillon cubes into it. When they have dissolved, add the Cream of Wheat, mixing it in with a whisk. Return to the boil and boil gently for about 3 minutes. Then stir in the cream and taste for seasonings. If the bouillon cubes have not added sufficient salt for your taste, add a dash of salt and, if you desire, pepper. Ladle into soup bowls and sprinkle with the chives. Serve immediately.

6 SERVINGS (5 CUPS)

TOMATO SOUP WITH CHIVES

As with most recipes that call for tomatoes, this soup is best made in a stainless steel pan; this prevents discoloration of the pan and ensures that the tomatoes retain their bright red color. Rather than purée the uncooked tomatoes in a food processor and then strain them through a sieve, I prefer to press the cooked soup through a food mill to remove the tomato seeds and skin. (The best food mills are plastic or stainless steel and have a removable bottom screen. They are inexpensive and very useful in the kitchen.)

If you eliminate the stock in this recipe, you have a good standard tomato sauce for serving with pasta and other dishes. You can substitute canned Italian plum tomatoes here for the fresh ones with good results.

The soup is enriched by the addition of 3 tablespoons of butter just before serving. You can substitute an equal amount of olive oil or a mixture of olive oil and vegetable oil, if you prefer, or eliminate this final addition altogether.

(continued)

Tomato Soup with Chives (continued)

2 tablespoons olive oil

2 tablespoons canola or
 safflower oil

3 onions (12 ounces total),
 peeled and cut into 1-inch
 pieces (about 2 cups)

1 teaspoon herbes de Provence
 (see Note, page 48)

3 large cloves garlic, peeled and
 crushed

1 rib celery, diced (about ¼ cup)

3 pounds fresh tomatoes, cut
 into 2-inch chunks; or 1½
 cans (28 ounces each)
 Italian plum tomatoes

1 can (13¾ ounces) chicken
 broth, or 1⅔ cups fresh or
 frozen homemade chicken
 stock (see Basic Chicken
 Stock, page 48)

½ teaspoon salt, or to taste

1 teaspoon sugar

½ teaspoon freshly ground
 black pepper

3 tablespoons unsalted butter

2 tablespoons chopped chives

2 cups croutons or bagel chips,
 whole or broken into pieces,
 for garnish

Heat the oils in a large stainless steel saucepan, and when the mixture is hot, add the onions, herbes de Provence, garlic, and celery. Cook over medium to high heat for about 5 minutes. Then stir in the fresh or canned tomatoes (with their liquid), chicken broth, salt, sugar, and pepper. Bring to a boil over high heat, cover, and cook over medium heat for about 10 minutes.

Push the whole mixture through a food mill fitted with a fine screen (this should yield about 7 cups). Whisk in the butter, garnish with the chives, and serve with whole bagel chips alongside or bagel chip pieces sprinkled on top.

6 SERVINGS (7 CUPS)

COLD RAW TOMATO SOUP

This is a favorite at our house. It also makes a great base for Bloody Marys and can be used as a sauce for a cold pasta salad.

For best results, use very ripe, fleshy, summer tomatoes. A food mill allows you to remove the skin and seeds from the purée more easily than is possible with a conventional sieve.

3 pounds very ripe tomatoes
1 teaspoon thyme leaves
  (optional)
½ teaspoon Tabasco sauce
½ teaspoon freshly ground
  black pepper
1½ teaspoons salt
¼ cup extra virgin olive oil
2 tablespoons red wine vinegar
¼ cup shredded basil leaves
1 cup sour cream
6 whole basil leaves

Cut the tomatoes into pieces, and purée them in a food processor. Strain the purée through a food mill fitted with the fine-mesh screen (this should yield about 5 cups). Stir in the thyme leaves, Tabasco, pepper, salt, oil, vinegar, and shredded basil. Set aside in a cool place or refrigerate.

At serving time, divide the soup among six bowls, and serve each with a dollop of sour cream in the center and a whole basil leaf on top.

Hot Cream of Tomato Soup
Purée and strain the tomatoes as described, and pour the purée into a saucepan. Add the thyme leaves, Tabasco, pepper, salt, oil, and vinegar, and bring to a boil. Boil for 30 seconds. Then stir in 1 cup heavy cream and heat through.
Divide the soup among six soup plates, sprinkle with ½ cup shredded basil, and serve.

6 SERVINGS (5 CUPS)

COLD PEACH SOUP WITH BLUEBERRIES

I used to make this soup at La Potagerie, a restaurant in New York, where it was a great success in summer. Although I've done it here with canned peaches, which we usually have on hand at our house, do replace them with unsweetened frozen peaches for a fresher taste if you are able to find them at your supermarket. (Combine ⅓ cup sugar and ½ cup water to replace the canned syrup.)

Leftover peach soup is excellent mixed with a plain hot or cold breakfast cereal.

(continued)

Cold Peach Soup with Blueberries (continued)

1 large can (28 ounces) sliced
    peaches in light syrup
1 cup water
½ teaspoon ground cinnamon
⅛ teaspoon ground nutmeg
⅛ teaspoon ground cloves
2 tablespoons sugar
1 tablespoon cornstarch
    dissolved in 3 tablespoons
    water
1 cup fruity white wine, such as
    Chenin Blanc
2 very ripe fresh peaches (12 to
    14 ounces total)
1 cup sour cream, for garnish
1 cup fresh blueberries, for
    garnish

Drain the peaches, reserving the syrup. In a saucepan combine the syrup and water with the cinnamon, nutmeg, cloves, and sugar. Bring to a boil and boil 1 minute.

Then add the dissolved cornstarch, and stir until the mixture boils (it will thicken). Stir in the wine and transfer to a bowl.

Purée the drained peaches in a food processor, and add them to the mixture in the bowl.

Peel the fresh peaches with either a vegetable peeler (if they are very firm) or a knife (if they are soft). If you don't object to the skin, leave them unpeeled. Cut the peaches into slices about ¼ inch thick (you should have about 2 cups). Add them to the soup, cover, and refrigerate.

At serving time, divide the soup among six bowls. Garnish each with a large dollop of sour cream and some blueberries and serve.

6 SERVINGS (ABOUT 6½ CUPS)

COLD YOGURT-CUCUMBER SOUP

This is a terrific soup to make in the summer—it is fragrant, spicy, and the fresh mint complements it well. There is no cooking involved and assembly is quick and easy; the hardest part of the job is peeling and dicing the cucumber.

I use regular yogurt for this recipe. If you want to make the soup richer, replace some or all of the yogurt with sour cream.

If you want to make it less rich, use a low-fat yogurt and decrease the amount of oil by half.

1 cucumber (about 1 pound),
    preferably the "seedless"
    English variety
1 container (16 ounces) plain
    yogurt
1 cup cold water
¼ cup olive oil
2 tablespoons cider vinegar
½ teaspoon Tabasco sauce
1 teaspoon salt
1 large clove garlic, peeled,
    crushed, and chopped fine
    (1 teaspoon)
About 18 mint leaves, piled
    together and cut into
    narrow strips (about 2
    tablespoons)

Peel the cucumber, cut it in half lengthwise, and remove the seeds. Cut the flesh into strips and then into ¼-inch dice (yielding about 2½ cups).

Put the yogurt in the soup tureen or bowl from which it will be served, add the cold water, and mix with a whisk until well combined. Then add the oil, vinegar, Tabasco, salt, and garlic, and mix well with the whisk. Stir in the cucumber and shredded mint and serve.

6 SERVINGS (5 CUPS)

THIS COLD SOUP IS MADE RIGHT IN THE SERVING BOWL.

BREADS, PIZZA, AND HOT SANDWICHES

T his is an exciting chapter. All the recipes use bread in one form or another, either bread that is made from scratch, bread that is bought as dough from the supermarket and finished at home, or commercial breads that are used in interesting and original ways (see Pan Bagna, Hot Bean Tortilla Pizza, and English Muffins Gloria, for example).

Although making your own bread can be time-consuming and somewhat messy, the satisfying aroma as it bakes in the oven makes the process worthwhile—the house seems cozier, the family more content, even the world beyond a friendlier place. Fortunately, these days there are many ways that bread can be made easily at home, even in the busiest of schedules.

A good bread dough is made with high-gluten (high-protein) flour, water, yeast, salt, and sometimes oil. You can find good-quality fresh or frozen packaged bread dough in most supermarkets. The fresh dough is ready to bake right away; the frozen dough has a substantially longer storage life and is ready to use with very little advance notice—it thaws overnight in the refrigerator or in an hour or so at room temperature. I often buy 1-pound frozen loaves in packages that contain one to five loaves. I wrap the loaves separately and keep them in the freezer to use as needed.

Fougasse, a specialty of the South of France, and Foccacia, an Italian flatbread, are great made with fresh or frozen store-bought dough. You'll have a delicious, attractive bread with a minimum of work, and your home will smell like a baker's paradise. Breakfast Rolls, Pizza Maison, and Calzone are also made with the same dough. Accompanied by a piece of cheese and a glass of wine, most of these breads make a good lunch. Big and hard-crusted, they look great on a buffet table and are terrific as sandwiches with fillings ranging from tomatoes to sardines.

Leftover bread is good reheated. Crisp individual slices by toasting them lightly. To reheat a whole loaf, dampen it lightly with water (to add crispness to the crust and moisture to the interior) and reheat it on a baking sheet in the oven.

PROCESSOR BAGUETTES
WITH BRAN

I love to make bread but sometimes don't have time to prepare it in the conventional way. This dough, made in a food processor, is easy and gives terrific results. The dough is not kneaded by hand and doesn't even touch the table, so there isn't much cleanup involved, which suits me fine. I have a large plastic bowl with a tight-fitting lid that I use for letting the dough rise, and I use this same bowl beforehand for measuring the flour. So, when I finish this recipe, all I have to wash are the food processor bowl and steel blade, my plastic bowl, and the cookie sheet on which I bake the baguettes. I oil the bowl, which makes cleanup easier, and since the dough retains a little of that oil, it doesn't stick to the baking sheet either.

The yeast and water is mixed right in the processor bowl, but be careful when you add the flour and begin "kneading" the dough: As more flour is added, the mixture stiffens and the machine tends to "walk" on the counter. The best solution is to hold the base of the machine while it "kneads" the dough.

If the room air is dry, the dough will tend to form an outer skin or crust while it is rising, especially during the second rise. To prevent this, either spray the baguettes a few times with water while rising (I use a standard plant sprayer for this), or slide the baking sheet with the baguettes into a large plastic bag, taking care to prevent them from coming into contact with the bag and sticking to it as they rise.

In professional bread-baking ovens, steam is automatically injected into the oven at the beginning of the baking time; this gives the bread a thick, strong crust. To imitate this situation, I throw about 2 tablespoons of water into the oven when I first put the bread in, and then repeat this a few minutes later.

If you like, you can cook the baguettes partially—creating "brown and serve" loaves—and then finish baking them later. Securely wrapped in plastic, the partially cooked loaves will keep in the refrigerator for 3 or 4 days or in the freezer for weeks.

(continued)

Processor Baguettes with Bran (continued)

When you are ready to eat them, all you have to do is moisten them lightly and bake them until they are brown and crusty.

I have added bran to this recipe to create a type of whole-wheat bread; if you prefer, you can add cracked wheat or nuts instead.

2 cups tepid water
2 envelopes dry yeast (½ ounce
  total)
1 teaspoon sugar
5 cups bread flour (1½ pounds)
1 cup wheat bran (2 ounces)
1 teaspoon salt
2 teaspoons corn oil
2 tablespoons cornmeal
¼ cup water (for throwing onto
  oven floor)

Place the tepid water in the bowl of a food processor, and sprinkle the yeast and sugar over it. Set aside for 5 minutes.

Measure the flour, bran, and salt into a large plastic bowl, and add the mixture to the processor bowl. Process for 1½ to 2 minutes, holding the base of the machine to prevent it from "walking" on the counter. The dough should be formed into a ball at this point.

Oil the same bowl with the corn oil, and transfer the ball of dough to the bowl. Cover and allow to rise at room temperature for about 1½ hours, or until the dough has doubled or tripled in bulk.

When the dough is ready, pull it from the sides of the bowl and push it down into the bowl, forming it into a ball. Place the ball of dough on a thick unrimmed aluminum cookie sheet that measures about 14 by 18 inches. Press on the dough until it is about 8 inches wide and about the length of the cookie sheet. Cut this rectangle into four lengthwise strips, and arrange them on the cookie sheet so that are equidistant. Sprinkle the loaves with half the cornmeal, then turn them over and sprinkle with the remainder of the cornmeal. Set aside for about 45 minutes. Spray (or sprinkle and brush) the dough with water if it begins to form a dry crust as it rises.

Using a razor blade, cut four or five gashes about ¼ to ½ inch deep on a slight diagonal across the top of each baguette, or cut one long gash down the center. Place the cookie sheet on the middle shelf of a 425-degree oven, and immediately throw 2 tablespoons of the ¼ cup water onto the floor of the oven before closing the door. After 3 or 4 minutes, repeat this procedure, throwing the remaining 2 tablespoons water onto the oven floor.

If you are baking the bread completely, continue cooking it for 25 to 30 minutes, until the loaves are brown and crusty. Remove and cool on racks. Serve warm or at room temperature.

If the bread is to be partially cooked, remove the loaves from the oven after 12 minutes, when they will have reached their ultimate size. (They will still be whitish at this point.) Cool completely, then wrap securely in plastic wrap and refrigerate for 3 or 4 days or freeze for up to 3 weeks. When you are ready to finish baking them, pass the frozen or refrigerated loaves under cool tap water to wet them lightly all over. Arrange the loaves on a cookie sheet, and bake in a 425-degree oven for 12 to 14 minutes, until nicely browned and crusty. Remove and cool on racks. Serve warm or at room temperature.

4 BAGUETTES

THIS DOUGH IS MADE AND "KNEADED" RIGHT IN THE FOOD PROCESSOR BOWL, SO CLEANUP IS MINIMAL.

FOUGASSE

The dough for this classic bread from Provence is shaped, as it is traditionally, to resemble a leaf.

1 teaspoon vegetable oil
1 pound packaged frozen bread dough
¼ cup pitted olives (either a spicy oil-cured variety, green Calamata, or even a mixture of olives, pimentos, and capers), cut into ¼- to ½-inch pieces
3 tablespoons virgin or extra-virgin olive oil
2 teaspoons herbes de Provence (see Note, page 48)
¼ teaspoon freshly ground black pepper

Grease a cookie sheet (preferably rimless to simplify cleanup) with the vegetable oil. Place the frozen dough on the cookie sheet, cover with plastic wrap, and allow to defrost overnight in the
(continued)

Fougasse (continued)

refrigerator or for about 1½ hours at room temperature.

When the dough has defrosted, dampen your hands with water and spread the dough out on the cookie sheet. The dough is elastic and will tend to shrink back and resist your efforts to extend it, but keep pressing and spreading until you have an oval approximately 14 inches long, 10 inches wide, and ¼ inch thick (with a slightly thicker edge).

Combine the olive pieces and the olive oil and spread the mixture evenly over the surface of the dough, pressing the olives into the dough. Sprinkle with the herbes de Provence and pepper.

Cut the dough to resemble a leaf: Leaving a 2-inch uncut strip down the center of the length of the oval, cut four slits (each 3 to 4 inches long) on either side of this strip at an angle to imitate the veins of a leaf. Do not extend the slits to the edges of the dough; they should stop about 1 inch from the edge. Cut through the dough firmly and open each slit wide, or it will tend to close up when the dough is rising and/or baking.

Allow the dough to rise at room temperature for 40 to 50 minutes. Then bake it in a 425-degree oven for 18 to 20 minutes, until the *fougasse* is nicely browned and very crusty.

Set the *fougasse* aside to cool briefly; then remove it from the cookie sheet with a large spatula, and place it on a wire rack until completely cool. Serve at room temperature. Leftovers can be frozen and reheated (after lightly dampening the crust).

1 LOAF

CALZONE

———

Calzone is a type of Italian peasant bread that is something like a turnover: The dough is folded over a filling. It is excellent eaten while still warm from the oven. Cut the *calzone* into four slices and serve them with a meal, or enjoy one whole for lunch, with a salad and a glass of wine.

I make two different versions of *calzone* here, one with Brie and one with mozzarella, although the bread can be stuffed with anything from my dried tomato mixture (see page 22) to fillings containing ground sausage meat, sliced cooked sausage or salami, mushrooms, or shrimp. Use your imagination and what you have on hand.

Defrost the bread dough overnight in the refrigerator or for about 1½ hours at room temperature.

BRIE CALZONE

1½ tablespoons olive oil
8 ounces packaged frozen bread
    dough, defrosted
4 ounces Brie cheese
2 or 3 pickled hot chile or
    cherry peppers, or to taste
About 3 scallions, sliced (¼
    cup)
1 tablespoon chopped cilantro
    (coriander or Chinese
    parsley)

Grease a 10-inch round baking sheet or pizza pan with 1 teaspoon of the oil. Place the bread dough on the baking sheet, and press to flatten it. Then wet your hands and spread the dough out. It will tend to shrink and slide back, especially since the tray is oiled, but keep pressing and spreading until the dough is extended to a diameter of 10 inches. It should be about ½ inch thick, a bit thicker around the perimeter.

Cut the Brie into seven or eight slices, and arrange them on half the dough, leaving uncovered a border of about 1 inch. Cut the peppers into pieces and arrange them on top of the Brie. Top them with the scallions and cilantro. Sprinkle with about 1 tablespoon of the remaining olive oil. Fold the unfilled half of the dough over to cover the filling, and press all around the edges to seal it well. Sprinkle the remaining ½ teaspoon oil on top, and spread it evenly over the surface of the dough. Let the dough rise at room temperature for 40 to 50 minutes (depending on the temperature and humidity), until it has doubled in size.

Bake the *calzone* in a 425-degree oven for 15 to 20 minutes. Sometimes a filling, especially one containing cheese, will seep out. When you remove the bread from the oven, allow it to cool and set

(continued)

Brie Calzone (continued)

for about 10 minutes; then push any filling that has spilled out back into the spot where it emerged. Transfer the *calzone* to a wire rack and let it cool to lukewarm before serving.

1 CALZONE (2 SERVINGS)

MOZZARELLA CALZONE

2 teaspoons olive oil
8 ounces packaged frozen bread
dough, defrosted
4 ounces mozzarella cheese
1 can (2 ounces) anchovy fillets
in oil, undrained
2 tablespoons flat parsley leaves

Grease a 10-inch round baking sheet or pizza pan with 1 teaspoon of the oil. Place the bread dough on the baking sheet, and press to flatten it. Then wet your hands and spread the dough out. It will tend to shrink and slide back, especially since the tray is oiled, but keep pressing and spreading until the dough is extended to a diameter of 10 inches. It should be about ½ inch thick, a bit thicker around the perimeter.

Shred the cheese or cut it into thin slices. Arrange it on half the dough, leaving a 1-inch border of dough uncovered. Arrange the anchovy fillets on top of the cheese, and pour the oil from the can over the anchovies. Sprinkle the parsley evenly over the anchovies.

Fold the unfilled half of the dough over to cover the filling, and seal by pressing firmly all around the edge. Sprinkle the remaining olive oil on top, and spread it evenly over the surface of the dough. Let the dough proof at room temperature for 40 to 50 minutes, or until doubled in size.

Bake the *calzone* in a 425-degree oven for 15 to 20 minutes. Sometimes a filling, especially one containing cheese, will seep out. When you remove the bread from the oven, allow it to cool and set for about 10 minutes; then push any filling that has spilled out back into the spot where it emerged. Transfer the *calzone* to a wire rack and let it cool to lukewarm before serving.

1 CALZONE (2 SERVINGS)

CREATE YOUR OWN TASTY FILLINGS FOR THESE MEAL-IN-ONE TURNOVERS.

FOCACCIA

I garnish my version of this Italian flatbread with onions and garlic. It's delicious as a snack or as an accompaniment to soups and salads.

1 teaspoon vegetable oil
1 teaspoon olive oil
1 pound packaged frozen bread
dough
1 onion, peeled and sliced very
thin (about 1 cup)
3 cloves garlic, peeled and
sliced thin (about 1
tablespoon)
2 teaspoons fresh or 1 teaspoon
dried oregano
3 tablespoons olive oil
2 tablespoons grated Romano or
Parmesan cheese
¼ teaspoon freshly ground
black pepper

Grease a cookie sheet (preferably rimless to simplify cleanup) with the vegetable oil. Place the frozen dough on the cookie sheet, cover with plastic wrap, and allow to defrost overnight in the refrigerator or for about 1½ hours at room temperature.

Focaccia is usually round, so use a pizza pan or round cookie sheet, preferably without sides. Oil the surface of the pan with the 1 teaspoon olive oil, and place the thawed dough in the center of the pan.

Wet your hands with cold water and press on the dough, extending it to form a circle 10 to 12 inches in diameter. The dough is elastic and will tend to shrink back, so press firmly until the circle holds its shape. Prick the dough about 10 times with a fork.

Combine the onion, garlic, oregano, and 3 tablespoons olive oil. Spread the mixture evenly over the dough. Sprinkle it with the cheese, and let it rise at room temperature for 40 to 50 minutes.

Bake in a 425-degree oven for approximately 25 minutes, until the dough is nicely browned and the onions are cooked. Let the *focaccia* cool on the pan for a few minutes, then transfer it to a wire rack and cool completely. Cut into wedges and serve.

1 LOAF

FRENCH BREAD STICKS GRATINEE

Look for brown-and-serve French bread sticks at the supermarket—these long, narrow rolls are handy to have in the freezer in case you run out of bread or have unexpected guests. Before browning them, coat the bread sticks with olive oil and sprinkle them with Parmesan cheese and pepper— the added flavor and color make them seem like homemade!

6 packaged brown-and-serve
French bread sticks (each
about 9 by 1½ inches)
6 tablespoons olive oil
2 tablespoons grated Parmesan
cheese
½ teaspoon freshly ground
black pepper

Split the bread sticks in half lengthwise. Pour the olive oil on a rimmed cookie sheet or a jelly roll pan, and press the bread sticks, cut side down, into the olive oil so they are well moistened.

Turn them over, and sprinkle the cut side with the Parmesan cheese and pepper. Bake in a 425° oven for 8 to 10 minutes, until crisp and brown.

6 SERVINGS

> ADDING OLIVE OIL, PARMESAN CHEESE, AND PEPPER TURNS THESE STORE - BOUGHT ROLLS INTO HOMEMADE.

CORNMEAL AND CHEDDAR BREAD

A great addition to a breadbasket and good with soup, this bread takes little preparation time. I combine the ingredients in a food processor, but you can whisk them together by hand if you prefer.

½ teaspoon vegetable oil
1 cup all-purpose flour
1 cup yellow cornmeal
2 teaspoons double-acting
    baking powder
1 egg
⅛ teaspoon cayenne pepper
½ teaspoon salt
1 tablespoon sugar
¼ cup corn oil
1½ cups grated Cheddar cheese
    (about 6 ounces)

Lightly grease a 6-cup loaf pan with the vegetable oil. Place the remaining ingredients in a food processor and process for a few seconds, or mix in a bowl with a

IF YOU USE PACKAGED GRATED CHEESE, THIS RECIPE CAN BE READY FOR THE OVEN IN A MATTER OF MINUTES.

whisk. Pour the batter into the loaf pan, set the pan on a cookie sheet, and bake in a 400-degree oven for about 45 minutes, until the loaf is well set and nicely browned. Cool on a rack for a few minutes. Then unmold, slice, and serve (preferably warm).

1 LOAF (4 TO 6 SERVINGS)

CHEESE STICKS

Like the Cinnamon Sticks (see page 268), these are made with packaged puff pastry. They are excellent served with soup or with cheese, and make an unusual addition to your breadbasket.

1 10-inch square sheet (8
    ounces) packaged frozen
    puff pastry
1 tablespoon unsalted butter
⅓ cup grated Parmesan cheese
1 teaspoon paprika
⅛ teaspoon cayenne pepper

Place the frozen pastry on a cookie sheet lined with aluminum foil, and let it sit at room temperature for 15 to 20 minutes. Then, while the pastry is still partially frozen, unfold the dough (even though it will tend to crack

(continued)

Cheese Sticks (continued)

at the seams) and rub half the butter over the surface.

Combine the Parmesan cheese, paprika, and cayenne. Sprinkle half of this mixture over the butter, spreading it with your fingers to distribute it evenly. Turn the pastry over and repeat, using the remaining butter and cheese mixture. Cut the pastry into ten 1-inch-wide strips, and then cut the strips into thirds to yield thirty sticks, each about 1 inch wide and 3 inches long. Work quickly because the pastry is eas-

ier to handle while it is still partially frozen.

Arrange the sticks evenly on the cookie sheet, and bake in a 375-degree oven for about 12 minutes, until they are dark brown. Transfer to a wire rack and cool completely before serving.

ABOUT 30

> RUBBING A LITTLE BUTTER ON PACKAGED PUFF PASTRY MAKES IT TASTE ALMOST HOMEMADE.

GARLIC AND HERB BREAD

This is especially good with a hearty soup. I use a long, thin French-style baguette, but you can use another type of unsliced bread if you prefer. Although the bread can be prepared ahead, it is best to cook it at the last moment and serve it while it is still warm.

1 French-style baguette bread loaf (8 ounces)
3 tablespoons safflower or corn oil
About 4 cloves garlic, chopped fine (2 teaspoons)
1 teaspoon Italian seasoning
¼ teaspoon freshly ground black pepper

Split the baguette in half horizontally. In a small bowl mix together the oil, garlic, Italian seasoning, and pepper. Spread this mixture on the cut side of each half.

Just before serving time, arrange the bread halves, cut side up, on a cookie sheet and bake in a 400-degree oven for about 12 minutes. Cut into pieces and serve while still warm.

1 LOAF (4 SERVINGS)

SEASON THE BREAD AHEAD, BUT BAKE IT AT THE LAST MINUTE AND SERVE IT WHILE IT'S STILL WARM.

BREAKFAST ROLLS

These small rolls are flavored with butter and rolled oats. They can be added to any luncheon or dinner breadbasket, and are especially welcome at breakfast. One pound of frozen bread dough makes from 12 to 16 breakfast rolls, depending on how large you make them. Allow the dough to defrost for 1 to 1½ hours at room temperature or overnight in the refrigerator.

*1 pound packaged frozen bread
    dough, defrosted
1 tablespoon unsalted butter
¾ cup rolled oats*

STORE THESE EASY-TO-MAKE ROLLS IN THE FREEZER FOR A QUICK BREAKFAST.

Cut the dough in half lengthwise; then slice each half crosswise to form a total of twelve equal pieces. Melt the butter and pour it onto a plate. Spread the rolled oats on another plate. Shape each piece of dough into a ball (they don't have to be perfectly round), and roll them first in the butter and then in the oats. Arrange them on a cookie sheet that has been buttered or lined with parchment paper. Let the dough rise at room temperature for 45 minutes. Then bake in a 425-oven for 25 minutes. Serve warm.

Note: These freeze well: Let them cool completely on a wire rack, then wrap them individually in plastic wrap and pack in a plastic bag. At serving time, moisten the frozen rolls lightly with water and place them in a 400-degree oven. Recrisp for about 10 minutes, and serve.

12 ROLLS

BANANA BREAD

T here is practically no work involved in this recipe—it can be combined in a food processor in three steps and will take less than a minute to assemble. Use very ripe bananas; those with dark, spotted skin have the intense flavor that makes this bread so special.

This is excellent for breakfast and makes a nice addition to a breadbasket. Well wrapped, it will keep for a few days at room temperature or for 2 to 3 weeks in the freezer.

1 tablespoon corn oil
2 cups all-purpose flour
1 tablespoon double-acting
baking powder
4 tablespoons (½ stick)
unsalted butter
½ cup sugar
2 very ripe bananas
2 eggs
¼ cup milk
½ cup sunflower seeds

Grease a 9 × 5 × 3-inch loaf pan with the oil.

Combine the flour, baking powder, butter, and sugar in the bowl of a food processor, and process for 10 to 15 seconds, until the ingredients are well combined.

Peel the bananas, break them into pieces, and add them to the mixture in the processor. Process for 5 to 10 seconds, until the bananas are incorporated.

Add the eggs, milk, and sunflower seeds, and process again for a few seconds, just until the ingredients are well combined. Pour the batter into the greased loaf pan, and place the pan on a cookie sheet lined with aluminum foil. Bake in a 350-degree oven for about 60 minutes, until well set inside and nicely browned. Cool for a few minutes on a rack before unmolding.

1 LOAF (6 SERVINGS)

THIS BREAD TAKES LESS THAN A MINUTE TO ASSEMBLE IN A FOOD PROCESSOR.

CHEESE TART

I hope you'll find this simple tart a life-saver when unexpected guests drop in. Although you can certainly use a homemade pie crust, a frozen pie shell works very well and saves time.

1 9-inch packaged frozen pie
    shell
1 cup ricotta cheese (8 ounces)
2 eggs, lightly beaten
¼ teaspoon freshly ground
    black pepper
½ teaspoon salt
4 ounces grated Cheddar cheese
    (1 cup)
⅛ teaspoon ground allspice
2 teaspoons Hot Red Salsa
    (page 23)

Remove the pie shell from its aluminum-foil pan and place it on a cookie sheet lined with foil. Set it aside to defrost for about 30 minutes.

Mix the remaining ingredients together in a bowl.

Flatten the softened pie shell against the cookie sheet creating a flat circle of dough. Seal any cracks that develop by pressing the dough together gently but firmly with your fingers.

Pour the filling mixture into the middle of the round of dough, and spread it out to within 1 to 2 inches of the edge. Fold the extending border of dough back over

> **TO GIVE THE PASTRY A HOMEMADE LOOK, FOLD THE EDGES OF THE FLATTENED STORE-BOUGHT PIE SHELL BACK OVER THE FILLING.**

the filling, lifting it with the help of the foil, pushing it against the cheese, and then peeling back the foil.

Bake in a 400-degree oven for 25 minutes, until set and nicely browned. Cut into wedges and serve.

4 SERVINGS

PITA AND CHEESE TOASTS

———

These toasts are wonderful for serving with soups, salads, and main courses. They can be broken into pieces and used as croutons and even made into sandwiches. I top them with Parmesan cheese here, but you can make them without cheese. It is best to eat these within 24 hours, as the bread tends to soften and the butter turns rancid if they are kept too long.

2 tablespoons unsalted butter
2 tablespoons peanut oil
4 pita breads (about 4 ounces
    each, 4 inches in diameter)
2 tablespoons grated Parmesan
    cheese

Melt the butter, and pour it and the oil into a jelly roll pan. Stir to mix. Open the pita breads and press the halves, interior side down, into the butter-oil mixture. Then turn them over and sprinkle with the Parmesan cheese.

Place the pan under the broiler, about 5 to 6 inches from the heat, and broil for about 3 minutes, until nicely browned.

4 SERVINGS

CRISP WONTON WAFERS

———

Wonton wrappers make terrific toast. Wafer-like, they are ideal with spreads or dips (see Red Pepper Dip, page 32) or can be served on their own as an hors d'oeuvre. They are an interesting addition to a breadbasket and go particularly well with soups. I often cook them a few at a time in the toaster oven to eat as a snack.

6 wonton wrappers, 3 inches
    square
1 teaspoon canola oil

Arrange the wonton wrappers on a foil-lined baking tray and brush them with the oil. (You don't need to defrost them if they're frozen.) Bake in a 400-degree oven for 7 to 8 minutes, until nicely browned and crusty.

6 WAFERS

FRESH WONTON WRAPPERS, INEXPENSIVE AND AVAILABLE IN VACUUM PACKS AT MOST SUPERMARKETS, CAN BE TRANSFORMED QUICKLY INTO THESE DELICIOUS TOASTS. LEFTOVER UNCOOKED WRAPPERS CAN BE FROZEN FOR UP TO 2 WEEKS.

PIZZA MAISON

Everyone loves pizza, but most people buy it ready-made because they think it's too hard to make themselves. Made with frozen bread dough, this pizza requires very little work and the result is spectacular and delicious.

I garnish my pizza with tomato, garlic, herbes de Provence, and mozzarella, but you can create your own variations—try Swiss or Fontina cheese, zucchini, or onions.

8 ounces packaged frozen bread dough (half a 1-pound loaf)
2 tablespoons extra-virgin olive oil
1 large ripe tomato (7 to 8 ounces)
2 large cloves garlic, peeled and sliced thin
1 teaspoon herbes de Provence (see Note, page 48)
¼ teaspoon salt
¼ teaspoon freshly ground black pepper

5 ounces mozzarella cheese, grated (about 1½ cups)
Red pepper flakes, for garnish (optional)
Olive oil, for garnish (optional)

About 1 hour before you plan to make the pizza, remove the dough from the freezer. After 35 to 40 minutes it will be defrosted enough to be divided. Cut it in half lengthwise. Wrap half and return to the freezer. Allow the

(continued)

Pizza Maison (continued)

remaining half to sit for another 15 to 20 minutes.

Dampen your hands and spread the dough out on a pizza pan or a cookie sheet about 11 inches wide. The dough will tend to shrink back. Press it firmly with the tips of your fingers to make it form an 11-inch round. (If you're adept at manipulating pizza dough, hold the dough on your closed fist and pull and extend it as pizza makers often demonstrate in the windows of pizza parlors.) The dough should be no more than ¼ inch thick, with slightly thicker edges.

Spread 1 tablespoon of the olive oil over the entire surface of the dough. Then lift the dough, turn it over, and spread it out again in the pan.

Arrange the tomato slices evenly over the dough to within 1 inch of the edge. Sprinkle with the garlic slices, herbes de Provence, salt, pepper, mozzarella, and finally the remaining 1 tablespoon olive oil. Let proof at room temperature for 15 to 20 minutes.

Bake in a 425-degree oven for 25 to 30 minutes, until nicely browned and crusty on top.

Cut the pizza into slices and serve with red pepper flakes and a little additional olive oil, if desired.

Note: Pizza crust doesn't get as crisp on the bottom in a conventional oven as it does in a professional pizza oven.

4 SERVINGS

> CREATE YOUR OWN PIZZA EASILY AND QUICKLY BY USING FROZEN BREAD DOUGH.

HOT BEAN TORTILLA PIZZA

This makes a fast lunch. All you need are large flour tortillas, a can of red kidney beans, scallions, hot salsa, and Cheddar cheese. One of these per person is sufficient—they go well with a crisp salad and beer or chilled white wine.

The tortillas are broiled about 10 inches from the heat source—the cheese will melt before the beans are heated through if the dish is placed any closer to the heat. Line your cookie sheet with aluminum foil to eliminate a cleanup chore.

4 large packaged flour tortillas, about 7 inches in diameter
4 teaspoons olive oil
2 cans (16 ounces each) red kidney beans, drained
About 5 scallions, minced (¾ cup)
¼ cup Hot Red Salsa (page 23)
1½ cups shredded sharp Cheddar cheese (about 6 ounces)

Line one or two cookie sheets with aluminum foil. Sprinkle the tortillas on one side with the oil, and place them, oiled side down, on the sheet.

In a bowl, combine the beans with the scallions and salsa. Stir well, and then spread this mixture on the tortillas, dividing it evenly among them. Top with the cheese.

Place the tortillas under a preheated broiler on the middle or lower oven rack, about 10 inches from the heat. Cook for about 10 minutes, until the beans are heated through and the cheese has melted.

Using two large spatulas, transfer the tortillas to four plates, and serve.

4 SERVINGS

> **TO CATCH CHEESE SPILLS, LINE YOUR COOKIE SHEET WITH ALUMINUM FOIL.**

HOT CHEESE AND TOMATO CORN TORTILLAS

I love corn tortillas. I always have a package in my freezer—they defrost in a few minutes. These pizza-like open-face sandwiches are quick and easy to prepare for lunch—and are a guaranteed crowd pleaser. You can vary the topping according to what you like and what you have on hand.

To make cleanup easier, line your cookie sheet with aluminum foil. If cooked two at a time, these can be baked in a toaster oven.

(continued)

Hot Cheese and Tomato Corn Tortillas (continued)

4 packaged corn tortillas, 5 to 6 inches in diameter

8 thin slices red onion (1½ ounces total)

3 plum tomatoes (6 ounces total), sliced thin (about 24 slices)

2 scallions, cleaned and minced fine (2 tablespoons)

8 slices Cheddar cheese (6 ounces)

1 teaspoon dried oregano

½ teaspoon freshly ground black pepper

KEEP A PACKAGE OF TORTILLAS IN THE FREEZER—THEY DEFROST IN MINUTES.

Line one large or two smaller cookie sheets with aluminum foil.

SERVED ONE PER PERSON, THESE OPEN-FACE SANDWICHES MAKE A GREAT LUNCH; CUT INTO SMALLER PIECES, THEY MAKE A DELICIOUS HORS D'OEUVRE.

Arrange the tortillas on the sheets, and place the onion slices, tomatoes, scallions, and cheese in that order on top of the tortillas. Sprinkle with the oregano and pepper, and bake in a 400-degree oven for 10 to 12 minutes. Transfer the tortillas to individual plates, and cut each into four wedges. Serve.

4 SERVINGS

HOT SAUSAGE AND MUSHROOM CORN TORTILLAS

I use garlicky Polish kielbasa sausage here, preferring it to pepperoni on this open-face tortilla sandwich. If you don't want to make your own salsa, good hot salsa is available fresh or bottled at most supermarkets.

I use Gruyère cheese, but you could try Fontina or mozzarella as well.

4 packaged corn tortillas, 5 to 6
  inches in diameter
6 ounces kielbasa sausage, sliced
  thin
1 cup thinly sliced mushrooms
  (4 ounces)
2 tablespoons Hot Red Salsa
  (page 23)
¾ cup grated Gruyère cheese
  (about 3 ounces)

Line one large or two smaller cookie sheets with foil. Arrange the tortillas in a single layer on the sheets, and top them with the kielbasa, mushrooms, salsa, and cheese in that order. Bake in a 400-degree oven (toaster or conventional) for 10 to 12 minutes, until the cheese is bubbly. Transfer to serving plates, cut each tortilla into four wedges, and serve.

2 SERVINGS

USING PACKAGED MUSHROOMS
THAT ARE ALREADY CLEANED AND
SLICED IS A REAL TIME-SAVER
HERE.

BRIE TORTILLA
CROQUE-MONSIEUR

The traditional *croque-monsieur* is a thin ham and cheese sandwich that is browned in butter in a skillet. For this adaptation, I use large flour tortillas instead of bread, filling them with Brie and ham. The sandwiches can be made in just a few minutes and are terrific with a salad for lunch. For best results, don't keep flour or corn tortillas for more than a couple of weeks in the freezer, or they will develop a "freezer taste."

8 packaged flour tortillas, about
  7 inches in diameter
6 ounces ripe Brie cheese, cut
  into 8 thin slices
4 slices cooked ham (about 3
  ounces total)

¼ teaspoon freshly ground
  black pepper
2 tablespoons unsalted butter

Arrange 4 tortillas on the counter, and place a slice of Brie

(continued)

Brie Tortilla Croque-Monsieur (continued)

on top of each, pressing on the cheese to extend it to the outer edge of the tortilla. Place a slice of ham on top of the cheese, and sprinkle with the pepper. Cover with the remaining cheese, again pressing to extend it to the edge, and then place the remaining tortillas on top and press on them gently to make them adhere well.

Heat 1½ teaspoons of the butter in each of two nonstick skillets. When it is hot, add a filled tortilla to each skillet, and cook over medium to low heat for 2 to 3 minutes on each side. Set aside

and let rest for 4 to 5 minutes before removing from the skillet, so the cheese can set up a little. Remove to a plate and keep warm. Repeat with the two remaining filled tortillas.

Cut each of the tortilla sandwiches into four wedges, and serve.

4 SERVINGS

FLOUR TORTILLAS REPLACE THE BREAD IN THIS VARIATION OF THE CLASSIC *CROQUE-MONSIEUR*.

ENGLISH MUFFINS GLORIA

My wife, Gloria, often prepares hot sandwiches for lunch. This family favorite is made with English muffins, mozzarella, garlic, and basil.

RUBBING THE SPLIT SIDE OF TOASTED MUFFIN HALVES WITH GARLIC CLOVES IMPARTS A WONDERFUL FLAVOR TO THESE SANDWICHES. THEY CAN BE GRILLED UNDER THE BROILER OR IN A TOASTER OVEN.

4 English muffins, split in half
2 large cloves garlic, peeled
4 teaspoons olive oil
About 24 basil leaves
8 ounces mozzarella cheese,
*   sliced (about 12 slices)*
¼ teaspoon freshly ground
*   black pepper*

Toast the muffin halves until nicely browned. Rub the split side of each muffin with the garlic, using about ¼ clove for each. Cover each muffin half with 1 teaspoon of the oil, and then arrange the basil leaves evenly over the surface. Place the mozzarella on top, and sprinkle with the pepper.

Arrange the muffins on an aluminum foil–lined cookie sheet (to catch cheese drips), and broil for 3 to 4 minutes, just until the cheese melts. Serve immediately.

4 SERVINGS

RED PEPPER AND CHEESE SANDWICH

A delicious open-face sandwich is created here with an unusual assortment of ingredients. The finishing touch, Muenster cheese, melts nicely in the oven and lends a delicate flavor.

1 French baguette-type bread
    loaf (about 10 ounces)
1 red bell pepper, seeded and
    sliced thin (about 2 cups)
¼ cup sunflower seeds or
    pignola nuts
7 to 8 cloves garlic, sliced thin
    (2–3 tablespoons)
½ teaspoon freshly ground
    black pepper
¼ cup virgin olive oil
8 ounces Muenster cheese, sliced
    thin
½ teaspoon herbes de Provence
    (see Note, page 48)

Cut the baguette in half horizontally. Line a cookie sheet with

foil and place the bread halves, cut side up, on the sheet. Lay the pepper slices on top of the bread, dividing them evenly between both halves. Sprinkle the seeds and the garlic on top, then season with the pepper and olive oil. Arrange the cheese slices on top of that, and sprinkle with the herbes de Provence.

Cook in a 400-degree oven for 10 to 12 minutes, until the bread is crisp, the cheese has melted, and the sandwich is heated through. Cut each half in half again and serve, one piece per person.

4 SERVINGS

HOT FRENCH BREAD AND STILTON SANDWICH

I love Stilton cheese and often make this sandwich with it, although I have made it with Gorgonzola—another favorite—and enjoyed it that way, too. I use a French-style baguette here, but the sandwiches can also be made on a large slice of country-type bread. A great luncheon dish, the sandwiches can be cooked quickly, a few at a time in a toaster oven or all together in a conventional oven. I always line the baking sheet with aluminum foil to catch the inevitable cheese spills.

Serve these with some cold white wine.

1 French-style baguette bread loaf (8 to 10 ounces), cut in half vertically and then horizontally to make 4 pieces
4 tablespoons virgin olive oil
1 onion (about 4 ounces), peeled and sliced thin (about 1 cup)
24 oil-cured olives, preferably pitted (see Note)
About 4 plum tomatoes (8 ounces total), sliced thin
¼ teaspoon freshly ground black pepper
⅛ teaspoon salt
4 ounces Stilton cheese, divided into 4 equal pieces

Place the 4 pieces of bread, cut side up, on a foil-lined baking sheet. Spread 1 tablespoon of the oil on each piece of bread, then cover with the onions, olives, to-matoes, pepper, salt, and cheese, in that order.

Bake in a 400-degree oven for about 12 minutes, until the cheese has melted and the bread is hot and crusty. Serve immediately.

Note: To pit the olives, press gently on them until they open up and the pits pop out.

4 SERVINGS

PAN BAGNA

T his sandwich is a specialty of Provence and tastes great with a cold rosé wine from that region. You can make individual *pan bagna* or one large one, as I've done here.

My filling consists of sliced tomato, cucumber, and cheese, but you can use a different assortment. With olive oil as the one standard ingredient, other popular additions include anchovy fillets or canned tuna along with olives, vinegar, and tomatoes.

The sandwich can be assembled the night before, wrapped carefully, and refrigerated with a 2- to 3-pound weight on top to make it hold together well when sliced.

1 small cucumber (7 to 8 ounces)
1 round or oval loaf of French- or Italian-style bread (1 pound)
2 tablespoons chopped basil, parsley, or chervil (optional)
6 tablespoons virgin olive oil
2 tablespoons red wine vinegar
2 ripe tomatoes (about 10 ounces total), cut into ¼-inch slices
½ teaspoon freshly ground black pepper
½ teaspoon salt
4 ounces Brie or Camembert cheese, sliced

PAN BAGNA TRANSLATES AS "BATHED BREAD." IT MAKES AN IDEAL SUMMER LUNCH.

Peel the cucumber, cut it in half lengthwise, and scoop out the seeds. Cut it into thin lengthwise slices (these won't slide off the bread as readily as crosswise-cut rounds).

Cut the loaf of bread in half horizontally, and sprinkle the cut side of each half with the herbs, oil, and vinegar. Arrange the tomato slices on the bottom half and sprinkle with half the pepper and salt. Cover with the cheese; then add the cucumber slices and the remaining salt and pepper. Position the top half of the bread loaf over the filling, wrap the sandwich tightly in plastic wrap or a plastic bag, and refrigerate for a few hours with a 2- to 3-pound weight on top.

At serving time, cut the sandwich into wedges.

4 SERVINGS

SALADS

A lthough in the classic French tradition salad is eaten at the end of the meal, it is often served first in French homes. My family prefers simple salads as a first course and larger, more complex salads as a main course for dinners at home. Some of both of these types of salads are included here, along with recipes for salads best suited for serving as a side dish accompaniment to a meal.

Dressed with a garlic-flavored vinaigrette, Salad à L'Aïl is a good first-course salad, as are Chicken-Avocado Salad and Greek Salad. Others, like the Hot Sausage Salad and the Salade Niçoise, are almost an entire meal in themselves, especially good with a soup or crusty bread.

For many of these salads, ingredients go far beyond simple greens, including such things as smoked fish, crabmeat, sausage, cheese, mushrooms, and red peppers. Any leftovers make good sandwich fillings.

At the last moment, when you don't know what to serve as a first course, try the Chick-pea Salad; when I made it for lunch, my wife and I enjoyed it so much we managed to eat the entire four-serving recipe between us. Many of the salads—Mushroom Salad Faro and the Red Pepper, Artichoke, and Olive Salad, for example—can be made ahead; they develop more taste if left to marinate for a while in their dressing.

WARM POTATO SALAD

T his salad makes use of cooked potatoes. If the potatoes are cold, slice them and then reheat them slightly—preferably in a microwave oven for 20 to 30 seconds. The flavor is much better if the salad is not ice cold.

1½ pounds cooked potatoes (see Basic Boiled Potatoes, page 224)
¼ cup mayonnaise
1½ tablespoons Dijon-style mustard (preferably "hot")
2 teaspoons white wine vinegar or rice vinegar
½ teaspoon salt
½ teaspoon freshly ground black pepper
½ teaspoon Worcestershire sauce
4 scallions, cleaned and minced (about ⅔ cup)

Scrape the skin from the potatoes and cut them into ¼-inch-thick slices. Rewarm them if necessary, and place in a serving bowl. Mix in the mayonnaise, mustard, vinegar, salt, pepper, Worcestershire, and scallions. Serve.

4 SERVINGS

USE LEFTOVER BOILED POTATOES IN THIS TANGY SALAD.

POTATO AND SMOKED BLUEFISH SALAD

M oist smoked bluefish is inexpensive and available at many markets. You could also use trimmings of smoked salmon or another smoked fish.

This salad is best when served at room temperature. If you prepare it ahead and refrigerate it, reheat it for 45 seconds or so in a microwave or for a few minutes in a conventional oven to take the chill off.

2 pounds small round red or
    new yellow potatoes
12 ounces smoked bluefish
4 or 5 scallions, cleaned and
    minced (¾ cup)
2 cloves garlic, peeled, crushed,
    and chopped fine (about 1
    teaspoon)
¼ cup flat parsley leaves
¼ cup olive oil
¼ cup peanut oil
1 tablespoon dark soy sauce
3 tablespoons red wine vinegar
1½ teaspoons freshly ground
    black pepper
1 teaspoon salt

Remove the eyes and any damaged parts of the potatoes. Wash the potatoes carefully under cold water, place them in a pot, and cover with fresh cold water. Bring to a boil and continue boiling gently until tender, 20 to 25 minutes. Drain them immediately, so that the moisture remaining on the potatoes evaporates because of their heat.

When the potatoes are cool enough to handle, cut them into ¼- to ½-inch slices, trying to keep the slices intact. As you slice, spread the potatoes out in a large gratin dish or on a tray. (They are less likely to break and are easier to toss when arranged like this in a single layer.)

Remove the skin from the bluefish, and peel off and discard some of the very dark flesh just under the skin. Flake the fish into ½-inch pieces (you should have about 2 cups). Add the fish to the potatoes along with the scallions, garlic, parsley, olive and peanut oils, soy sauce, vinegar, pepper, and salt. Toss lightly and cover with plastic wrap so that the wrap lies directly on the salad. Allow the salad to macerate for at least 45 minutes at room temperature or for 3 to 4 hours in the refrigerator before serving. Serve at room temperature.

6 SERVINGS

CRABMEAT SALAD

This is an easy recipe to make since cooked crabmeat is available now from most fishmongers (try to get the large lump crab from Virginia). Serve this rich first-course salad at room temperature in lettuce leaf cups.

(continued)

Crabmeat Salad (continued)

> BUY COOKED CRABMEAT FROM YOUR FISHMONGER FOR THIS SIMPLE BUT DELICIOUS SALAD.

8 ounces cooked crabmeat, drained
1 rib celery from the heart, as white as possible, cut into ¼-inch pieces (about ¼ cup)
1 clove garlic, peeled and chopped fine (about ½ teaspoon)
1 small onion, peeled and chopped (about ¼ cup)
¼ cup mayonnaise
¼ teaspoon Tabasco sauce
1 tablespoon white rice vinegar
⅛ teaspoon freshly ground black pepper

8 small lettuce leaves (preferably Boston), for use as receptacles

Combine all the ingredients except the lettuce in a bowl, and mix lightly. Arrange the lettuce leaves on four small plates, and divide the salad among the plates, piling it on top of the lettuce. Serve immediately.

4 SERVINGS

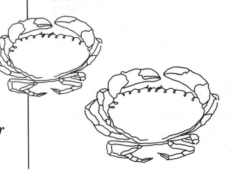

SALADE NIÇOISE

*S*alade niçoise makes an ideal lunch. A traditional dish from the South of France, specifically Provence, it is served everywhere there, from large bistros to fancy restaurants, and the variations are practically infinite. Our rendition includes canned tuna, anchovy fillets, olives, tomatoes, and basil. Make the salad according to your own taste—some versions include onions (red or yellow), cooked fava beans, artichokes, peppers, tiny string beans, or cucumbers—but always include tomatoes, garlic, olives, and greens.

This salad is excellent served with pita toasts (see page 84) broken into pieces on top, or with bagel chips. I especially like it with Fougasse (page 73), a classic bread from the South of France.

8 cups salad greens (Boston lettuce, red leaf lettuce, Romaine, or other)

½ cup Mustard Vinaigrette Dressing (page 26)

6 large cloves garlic, peeled and sliced thin (2 tablespoons)

6 scallions, cleaned and minced fine (1 cup)

¼ teaspoon salt

1 can (2 ounces) flat anchovy fillets in oil (about 12 fillets), drained (see Note, page 34)

1 small can (6½ ounces) tuna in water, drained and crumbled

About 3 ripe tomatoes (1 pound total), each cut into 6 wedges

3 hard-cooked eggs (see Note), coarsely chopped

About 12 basil leaves, coarsely shredded

About 6 ounces olives (see Note)

Wash the salad greens thoroughly in a sink full of cold water. Lift the greens from the water and dry completely in a salad spinner.

Place the dressing in a large bowl, and stir in the garlic and scallions. Add the salad greens and salt, and toss to mix well. Arrange on six plates. On top of each serving and around the edge of each plate, decoratively arrange 2 anchovy fillets, about 2 tablespoons of crumbled tuna, 2 to 3 tomato wedges, the equivalent of about half a hard-cooked egg, some shredded basil, some of the olives. Serve immediately.

Note: To cook the eggs, bring enough water to cover them to a boil in a small saucepan. Add the eggs and simmer gently for about 10 minutes. Place the eggs in ice-cold water until cool enough to handle, then shell immediately. Continue to cool the shelled eggs in the water until they are completely cold.

If you use the tiny Niçoise olives, serve 12 per person; if using Calamata, 6 per person.

6 SERVINGS

HOT SAUSAGE SALAD

I prepare this salad often at home, especially when I am pressed for time or when unexpected guests drop in. It makes a great lunch.

Frozen sausage can be thawed quickly by sealing it in a plastic bag and submerging the bag in hot water for 10 to 15 minutes, or by placing it in a microwave oven to defrost slightly. The sausage doesn't have to be completely defrosted before cooking.

*About 6 hot Italian-style
    sausages (1 pound)*
*1 large (or 2 smaller) very ripe
    tomatoes*
4 ounces mozzarella cheese
*4 cups salad greens, preferably
    curly endive, rinsed and
    thoroughly dried*
*¼ cup Mustard Vinaigrette
    Dressing (page 26)*
*½ teaspoon freshly ground
    black pepper*

Prick the sausages and place them on a hot barbecue grill, preferably one with a cover. Grill, covered, over medium heat for 10 to 12 minutes, turning occasionally to brown on all sides.

While the sausages are cooking, cut the tomato into slices about ⅜ inch thick. Cut the mozzarella into ¼-inch-thick slices; then stack the slices together and cut into sticks.

Mix the salad greens with the dressing, and arrange on individual plates. Garnish with the to-mato slices and mound the cheese sticks in the center. Sprinkle with the pepper. When the sausages are cooked, cut them in half lengthwise and arrange three pieces of sausage per person on top of the salad. Serve immediately.

Note: When serving this as a luncheon dish, 1½ sausages per person is sufficient. Serve 2 sausages per person if you are serving it as a main course, or ½ sausage per person for a first course.

4 SERVINGS

CHICK-PEA SALAD

Canned chick-peas—also called garbanzo beans—are an excellent substitute for the dry variety, which require a long cooking time. They do beg for seasoning, however, as in this highly flavored salad.

1 can (16 ounces) chick-peas, drained (2 cups)
3 tablespoons Hot Red Salsa (page 23; see Note)
3 tablespoons mayonnaise
3 scallions, cleaned and minced fine (about 3 tablespoons)
1 large clove garlic, peeled, crushed, and chopped (about 1 teaspoon)
¼ cup coarsely chopped cilantro (coriander or Chinese parsley) leaves
¼ teaspoon salt

Mix all the ingredients together and serve at room temperature.

Note: The salsa will liquify the mayonnaise and create a sauce. If fresh salsa is not available, replace it with about 1 teaspoon chopped hot pepper (such as jalapeño) and 2 to 3 tablespoons chopped fresh tomato or tomato juice.

4 SERVINGS

GREEK SALAD

I love the taste of Greek salads, with their distinctly flavored Calamata olives, feta cheese, and tomatoes. Happily, a reasonable facsimile of these wonderful concoctions can be made at home in a few minutes since the ingredients are readily available at your local market. The main difference between the salad you would find in Greece and this recipe is that I use much less oil in mine.

I like to make this salad a few hours ahead so the flavors have

(continued)

Greek Salad (continued)

time to blend and develop. Refrigerate it if making it ahead, but serve it at room temperature, taking the chill off by heating it momentarily in a microwave oven just before serving.

8 plum tomatoes (about 8 ounces total), each cut lengthwise into 4 wedges
About 20 Calamata olives (4 ounces)
6 ounces Feta cheese in brine, drained and broken into ½- to 1-inch pieces
1 red onion (about 5 ounces), peeled and sliced thin
1½ teaspoons dried oregano
½ teaspoon freshly ground black pepper
½ teaspoon salt
6 tablespoons virgin olive oil
4 teaspoons red wine vinegar
¼ cup flat parsley leaves

About 6 cloves garlic, peeled and sliced thin (1½ tablespoons)

Mix all the ingredients together in your salad bowl, and set aside until serving time. You can make the salad a few hours ahead and refrigerate it, but bring it back to room temperature before serving.

4 SERVINGS

MOZZARELLA AND CILANTRO SALAD

This salad can be made up to an hour ahead—and in fact the flavor improves if you do so, since it gives the dressing time to penetrate the other ingredients and season them well. Serve it as a first course with some crunchy bread.

I love the taste of fresh coriander, also called cilantro. If you find it too assertive, try this fresh-tasting salad with parsley, basil, chervil, or chives instead.

4 ounces mozzarella cheese, cut
  into ½-inch-thick slices and
  then into ½-inch-wide sticks
4 scallions, cleaned and cut into
  ½-inch pieces (¾ cup)
1 small onion, peeled and cut
  into ½-inch cubes
About 5 plum tomatoes (10
  ounces total), cored and cut
  into 1-inch pieces
1 cup cilantro (coriander or
  Chinese parsley) leaves
3 tablespoons virgin olive oil
1 tablespoon red wine vinegar
½ teaspoon freshly ground
  black pepper
½ teaspoon salt

Up to 1 hour before serving,
toss all the ingredients together
in a salad. Serve at cool room
temperature.

4 SERVINGS

FOR THE BEST FLAVOR, PREPARE
THIS SALAD UP TO AN HOUR AHEAD.
COMBINE THE INGREDIENTS RIGHT
IN YOUR SERVING BOWL.

MUSHROOM SALAD FARO

It takes only a few minutes to combine all the ingredients
for this salad, especially if you use the presliced, prewashed
mushrooms that are available in most supermarkets. Do
this ahead so the mushrooms can marinate in the dressing. A
terrific first course, it is also a great accompaniment for broiled
or sautéed fish or meat.

About 2½ cups sliced
  mushrooms (8 ounces)
1 teaspoon dry mustard
1 tablespoon white vinegar
½ teaspoon sugar
¼ teaspoon salt
¼ teaspoon freshly ground
  black pepper

2 teaspoons dark sesame oil
2 tablespoons safflower or
  corn oil
¼ teaspoon crumbled dried
  mint
2 tablespoons sunflower seeds
1 tablespoon light soy sauce

(continued)

Mushroom Salad Faro (continued)

Stir all the ingredients in a bowl together, and serve immediately or set aside until serving time. This can be made up to 1 day ahead and refrigerated, but should be served at room temperature.

4 SERVINGS

CAESAR SALAD

I had never had Caesar salad until I came to the United States. My wife, Gloria, made it for me when we first met, and we've used her recipe at home ever since.

*1 head Romaine lettuce, as
    white as possible*

CROUTONS
4 slices firm white bread
¼ cup canola oil

DRESSING
⅓ cup extra-virgin olive oil
*2 cloves garlic, crushed and
    coarsely chopped (about 1
    teaspoon)*
2 tablespoons lemon juice
*1 tablespoon Worcestershire
    sauce*
½ teaspoon salt
*¼ teaspoon freshly ground
    black pepper*
1 egg
*4 canned anchovy fillets (see
    Note, page 34)*

½ cup grated Parmesan cheese
*¼ cup crumbled bleu,
    Roquefort, or Stilton cheese*

Trim the lettuce and break it into 2-inch pieces (you should have about 8 cups). Rinse and dry thoroughly in a salad drier. Set aside.

Prepare the croutons: Cut the bread slices into ½-inch cubes. Heat the canola oil in a skillet, and when it is hot, sauté the bread cubes until brown on all sides. Set aside until serving time.

Prepare the dressing: Place the olive oil, garlic, lemon juice, Worcestershire sauce, salt, pepper, and egg in a bowl and beat with a fork until the mixture is well combined. Cut the anchovy fillets into pieces and add them to the dressing.

At serving time, toss the greens with the dressing. Add the cheeses and toss again. Scatter the croutons on top of the salad, and serve immediately.

6 SERVINGS

SALADS

TANGY RICE STICK SALAD

For a change in texture, look, and bite, try this Asian-influenced pasta salad. You can prepare it quickly and keep it in the refrigerator for several days.

1 pound rice stick noodles
2 cups Mushroom, Tomato, and
Nut Mix (page 22),
undrained
1 teaspoon salt
¾ teaspoon Tabasco sauce or
hot chile oil
½ cup shredded basil

Bring a pot containing 3 to 4 quarts of water to a boil. Drop the noodles into the water, and stir well to separate the strands. Return the water to the boil, and boil just 3½ to 4 minutes. Then immediately drain into a colander and sprinkle with cold water to stop the cooking. Allow the noodles to sit in the colander to dry out for at least 10 minutes.

Using a slotted spoon, remove the solids from the mushroom, tomato, and nut mix. Chop coarsely, by hand or in a food processor, into ¼-inch pieces, and place in a bowl. Add ⅓ cup oil from the mix, and stir in the salt, Tabasco, and basil. Add the rice noodles and toss until well coated. Serve immediately, or cover and set aside to serve later that day. The salad will keep for 2 to 3 days in the refrigerator. Bring back to room temperature for serving.

6 SERVINGS

RED PEPPER, ARTICHOKE, AND OLIVE SALAD

I often prepare this salad if I am pressed for time because, except for the cheese and parsley, the ingredients are all available in jars at the supermarket. Always a hit, it is better made ahead but can be assembled at the last moment. Leftovers will keep, refrigerated, for more than a week and are

(continued)

105

great stuffed into sandwiches with or without a meat filling. Bring the salad back to room temperature by heating it briefly in a microwave or conventional oven.

Serve this with crusty country bread and a cold red wine.

*1 jar (6 ounces) marinated
    artichoke hearts in oil*
*½ cup green olives (salad
    olives, sometimes stuffed
    with pimento, or in pieces)*
*½ cup bottled marinated
    eggplant, drained*
*1 cup (6 ounces) bottled peeled,
    sliced red peppers
    (sometimes called pimentos)*
*About 6 ounces spicy Cheddar
    cheese, cut into 1 x ½-inch
    sticks*
*½ teaspoon freshly ground
    black pepper*

3 tablespoons virgin olive oil
2 tablespoons parsley leaves
*1 teaspoon chopped hot pepper
    (jalapeño type), or ½
    teaspoon red pepper flakes*

Mix all the ingredients together in a bowl, and serve.

4 SERVINGS

MOST OF THE INGREDIENTS FOR THIS SALAD COME IN JARS FROM THE SUPERMARKET, SO IT COULDN'T BE EASIER TO ASSEMBLE.

SALADE A L'AIL

Thick-ribbed and nutty, escarole has a slightly bitter taste that goes very well with the garlic in the dressing for this winter salad. Unlike most lettuce salads, this one can be seasoned up to half an hour before serving—the escarole will soften slightly in the dressing.

1 head escarole (see Note)

GARLIC DRESSING
*2 cloves garlic, peeled and
    chopped fine (1 teaspoon)*

*1½ teaspoons Dijon-style
    mustard*
*⅛ teaspoon freshly ground
    black pepper*
⅛ teaspoon salt

1½ teaspoons red wine vinegar
3 tablespoons virgin olive oil

> UNLIKE MOST GREEN SALADS, THIS
> ONE TASTES BETTER IF DRESSED
> HALF AN HOUR BEFORE SERVING.

Remove and discard any wilted or damaged leaves from the escarole, and cut the remainder into 2-inch pieces (you should have 5 to 6 cups). Fill a sink with cold water and swirl the greens in it to remove any sand. Lift the greens from the water and dry in a salad spinner. (This can be done ahead; the greens will keep in a plastic bag in the refrigerator for 4 or 5 days.)

Up to 30 minutes before serving, whisk the dressing ingredients together in your salad bowl, add the greens, and toss.

Note: Select escarole with as white a center as you can find; this indicates tenderness and a nutty flavor.

4 SERVINGS

CHICKEN-AVOCADO SALAD

Of course you can poach or sauté chicken breasts especially for this delicious main-course salad—but I like it as a great way to use leftover chicken. (You can also use leftover turkey, roast pork, or veal.)

Shred the chicken (or other meat) rather than cutting it with a knife. It looks nicer, and the meat will absorb the dressing better.

1 tablespoon sherry vinegar
1 tablespoon dark soy sauce
½ teaspoon Tabasco sauce
3 tablespoons safflower or corn oil
1 teaspoon sugar
½ teaspoon salt
1 teaspoon Worcestershire sauce

3 scallions, cleaned and minced fine (about ½ cup)
2 cooked chicken breasts (8 ounces; see Note)
1 small ripe avocado (about 7 ounces)
12 leaves lettuce or other greens

(continued)

Chicken-Avocado Salad (continued)

Combine the vinegar, soy sauce, Tabasco, oil, sugar, salt, and Worcestershire in a large bowl, and blend thoroughly. Stir in the scallions.

Shred the chicken by pulling the meat apart along the grain, forming narrow strips. Add them to the dressing and toss well.

Make an incision around the widest portion of the avocado, cutting through to the pit, and twist the ends in opposite directions until the halves separate. Remove the pit. Using a sharp knife, slice through the flesh clear to the skin every ½ inch one way and then the other, creating a checkerboard pattern in both halves. Then, using a spoon, scoop out the precut cubes of avocado and add them to the bowl. Toss gently with the chicken and dressing.

Arrange the salad on the lettuce leaves and serve.

Note: If the chicken has been refrigerated, heat it in a microwave oven for 20 to 30 seconds to take the chill off.

4 SERVINGS

> TO SAVE ON TIME AND CLEANUP, CUT THE AVOCADO FLESH INTO CUBES WHILE IT'S STILL INSIDE THE SKIN.

TURKEY SALAD

Leftover turkey is never very satisfying when it's reheated in its own gravy or in a sauce. Try this flavorful salad instead. Or if you want sandwiches for lunch, omit the tomatoes, add some Hot Cucumber Relish (page 22), and fill pita breads with the mixture.

> IF COOKED MEAT IS SHREDDED RATHER THAN SLICED OR CUBED, IT WILL ABSORB THE SALAD DRESSING BETTER.

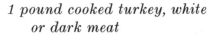

1 pound cooked turkey, white or dark meat
¾ cup diced red onion (¼-inch pieces)
3 scallions, cleaned and minced fine (½ cup)

2 cloves garlic, peeled, crushed,
    and chopped fine (1
    teaspoon)
¾ cup mayonnaise
2 tablespoons cider vinegar
1 tablespoon Dijon-style
    mustard (preferably "hot")
1 teaspoon salt
1 teaspoon freshly ground black
    pepper
1 teaspoon sugar
1 tablespoon Worcestershire
    sauce
2 large ripe tomatoes (1
    pound), sliced thin (about
    18 slices)
Watercress, for garnish

If the turkey meat is very cold, heat it in a microwave oven for 30 to 40 seconds to bring it to

THIS SPICY SALAD WILL USE UP THAT LEFTOVER TURKEY—AND IT MAKES GREAT SANDWICHES TOO.

room temperature. Then shred it into narrow strips (it will absorb the dressing better than if you cut it into cubes).

Place the shredded meat in a bowl, and stir in all the remaining ingredients except the tomatoes and watercress. Arrange the tomato slices on individual salad plates, and mound the turkey on top. Garnish with watercress and serve.

6 SERVINGS

PASTA AND RICE

I f we're wondering what to cook for dinner at my house, nine out of ten times we end up with pasta; there is always something in our refrigerator, in our freezer, or on our pantry shelves that we can use as the foundation for a delicious pasta sauce. The most important thing to remember when cooking pasta is to put a pot of water on to boil when you *begin* making the sauce; the most time-consuming part of these recipes is waiting for the pasta cooking water to come to a boil.

The Mushroom, Tomato, and Nut Mix from our Basics chapter (page 22) makes a delicious sauce with penne (see Penne with Mushroom, Tomato, and Nut Sauce), and fresh or canned clams can be used to create a sauce that goes beautifully with linguine (see Linguine with Clam Sauce Gloria). Pasta Primavera Ed, with a sauce consisting primarily of ripe tomatoes and basil from the garden, is a great favorite with us during the summer.

In each of the ravioli dishes here—Beef Pelminy in Chicken Broth, Shrimp Wonton Ravioli, and Ricotta Cheese Wonton Ravioli—the ravioli is made from wonton wrappers, available fresh and inexpensively at most supermarkets. A spoonful of filling is sealed between two 3-inch wrappers for each ravioli; and since the pastry is so delicate and delicious, I don't even trim the dough, although this can be done with a cookie cutter if you prefer a round shape.

Two rice recipes are included here: Brown Rice Ragout, featuring salt pork, and Rice with Mushrooms and Steamed Asparagus, a one-pot dish with the asparagus added when the rice is almost done so it can cook in the steam emerging from the rice.

PASTA PRIMAVERA ED

Pasta Primavera (*primavera* means "spring" in Italy) was conceived by my friend Ed Giobbi at New York's Le Cirque restaurant. Although a variety of vegetables has been used in the numerous adaptations that have evolved, at home Ed makes the dish with raw tomatoes only, flavoring them with olive oil, basil, onion, and garlic. The tomato-and-herb taste of this delightful first course does bring to mind a fresh spring day.

RAW TOMATO SAUCE
About 2 very ripe tomatoes (12 ounces total)
1 onion (about 3 ounces), peeled and chopped fine (about ⅔ cup)
2 cloves garlic, peeled, crushed, and chopped (1½ teaspoons)
½ teaspoon freshly ground black pepper
¼ cup extra-virgin olive oil
¼ cup shredded basil
½ teaspoon salt

1½ pounds spaghetti (#3 or #4)

2 tablespoons virgin olive oil
½ teaspoon freshly ground black pepper
¼ teaspoon salt
3 to 4 tablespoons grated Parmesan cheese

Prepare the Sauce: Cut the tomatoes in half parallel to the stem, press out the seeds, and cut the flesh into ¼-inch dice (you should have about 1½ cups).

Place the chopped onion in a sieve and rinse it under warm tap water (this removes the strong

FOR ADDED MOISTURE AND FLA-
VOR, RESERVE A CUP OF THE PASTA
COOKING LIQUID AND TOSS THE
DRAINED PASTA IN IT BEFORE ADD-
ING THE TOMATO SAUCE.

with a fork, stirring gently to
separate the strands. Bring the
water back to the boil and cook
for 6 to 8 minutes, until as tender
as you like.

Before the pasta has finished
cooking, remove about 1 cup of
the cooking liquid and pour it into
your serving bowl. To this liquid
add the 2 tablespoons olive oil, ½
teaspoon pepper, and ¼ teaspoon
salt. Drain the pasta, add it to
the bowl, and toss to mix well.

Divide the pasta among four
plates and sprinkle with the
grated cheese (or pass it at the
table). Spoon the room-temperature sauce over the pasta and
serve immediately.

4 SERVINGS

smell and acidic taste). Drain
well. Combine the tomatoes with
the onion, garlic, ½ teaspoon pepper, ¼ cup olive oil, basil, and ½
teaspoon salt. Toss well and set
aside.

Just before serving time, bring
6 quarts of water to a boil in a
large pot. Add the pasta and push
it below the surface of the water

LINGUINE WITH STEWED TOMATO SAUCE

There are many different types of pasta at the market and
their cooking time varies according to their thickness. The
linguine we use here (labeled #13) cooked in about 6
minutes. You can also use fresh Chinese egg noodles, which are
rounder, resembling spaghetti, and cook in just a few minutes.

The pasta here is seasoned with Stewed Tomato Sauce and
cheese. The French often serve Swiss cheese with pasta, and I
like it this way, but of course you can substitute the more familiar
Parmesan.

(continued)

Linguine with Stewed Tomato Sauce (continued)

Although most pasta manufacturers suggest otherwise, I cook pasta in unsalted water, to eliminate a little salt from my diet. It makes no difference in the taste of the final dish.

1 pound thin linguine (#13)
¼ cup virgin olive oil
1 teaspoon salt
¾ teaspoon freshly ground
*   black pepper*
¾ cup shredded good-quality
*   Swiss cheese, preferably*
*   Gruyère; or ¼ cup grated*
*   Parmesan cheese*
2 generous cups Stewed Tomato
*   Sauce (page 27)*
Crushed red pepper flakes to
*   taste (optional)*

Bring 3 to 4 quarts of water to a strong boil in a large pot (preferably stainless steel to prevent discoloration). Add the pasta and push it under the water with a spoon or fork to submerge it completely. While the water returns to the boil, stir gently to separate the strands of linguine.

Cook approximately 6 minutes after it has returned to the boil, until it is as tender as you like. Scoop ½ cup of the cooking liquid into a large stainless steel bowl, and drain the pasta.

To the reserved cooking liquid add the olive oil, salt, pepper, cheese, and the pasta. Toss until well combined. Divide among four plates and top each serving with ½ cup of the tomato sauce and, if desired, some red pepper flakes. Serve immediately.

4 SERVINGS

LEFTOVER UNSAUCED PASTA RE-HEATS PERFECTLY IN A MICRO-WAVE OVEN.

LINGUINE WITH CLAM SAUCE GLORIA

My wife, Gloria's linguine with clam sauce is a favorite —especially in the summer, when she often uses fresh clams and fresh clam juice. Sometimes, however, she doesn't have access to fresh clams, and she opts for the canned baby clams that are always stocked in the pantry. Although they may not produce exactly the same result, they still make a delicious dish.

CLAM SAUCE
8 cloves garlic, peeled
1 small jalapeño pepper, halved and seeded; or 1 teaspoon red pepper flakes
1 bottle (8 ounces) clam juice
1 cup (loosely packed) parsley leaves
½ cup virgin olive oil
1⅓ cups diced onion (¼-inch pieces)
1 cup dry fruity white wine
1 teaspoon Italian seasoning
2 cans (10 ounces each) whole baby clams

1½ pounds thin linguine (#13)
Salt to taste

Freshly ground black pepper to taste
Grated Parmesan cheese (optional)

Place a pot containing 3 to 4 quarts of water over high heat.

Meanwhile, prepare the sauce: If you have a mini-chop, place the garlic and jalapeño pepper halves in it and turn the machine on and off a few times to chop coarsely. Add enough of the clam juice to provide a little moisture, and then add the parsley, pushing it down on top of the other ingredients. Starting and stopping the machine a few more times, coarsely chop the parsley (the liquid will help it become incorporated). It can also be chopped in a food processor or by hand.

Heat the olive oil in a shallow saucepan. When it is hot, add the onion and sauté for 2 to 3 minutes. Add the garlic-parsley mixture and stir for 15 to 20 seconds. Then add the remainder of the clam juice. "Rinse" your mini-chop with the white wine, and add it to the saucepan with the Italian seasoning and the clams, juice and all. Bring to a boil and add salt if desired (depending on how salty the clams and clam juice are). Reduce the heat, cover, and simmer for 5 to 6 minutes.

Add the linguine to the boiling water in the pot. Stir well, return to the boil, and boil for about 10 minutes, until as tender as you like. Drain in a colander and return to the cooking pot. Add about ½ cup of liquid from the sauce, and mix it into the linguine to prevent it from sticking together. Add a dash each of salt and pepper. Divide the linguine among six plates, and pour some clam sauce over each serving.

Serve with Parmesan cheese if desired.

6 SERVINGS

PENNE WITH MUSHROOM, TOMATO, AND NUT SAUCE

I like to serve this delicious sauce over penne because the tube-shaped pasta absorbs the flavor so well. This will serve two as a main course.

8 ounces penne
¾ cup Mushroom, Tomato, and
    Nut Mix (page 22), with
    about ¼ cup oil from the
    mix (see Note)
¼ teaspoon salt
About 3 tablespoons grated
    Parmesan cheese, preferably
    Parmigiano-Reggiano

Bring 3 to 4 quarts of water to a strong boil in a large pot. Add the pasta, bring the water back to the boil, and cook for 10 to 12 minutes or until as tender as you like. Near the end of the cooking time, remove ½ cup of the cooking liquid and place it in a bowl. To this add the mushroom-tomato mix with its oil, and the salt, and mix well.

Drain the cooked pasta, add it to the bowl, and toss well. Divide among four plates, top with the grated cheese, and serve.

Note: If you like, cut the tomatoes into ½-inch pieces.

4 SERVINGS

RIGATONI WITH RED PEPPER SAUCE

Red Pepper Dip is delicious, can be made ahead, and, transformed into a sauce, goes particularly well with rigatoni, whose tube shape holds it so well. This recipe serves four as a first course but should be doubled for a main course.

8 ounces rigatoni (large tubes)
1 cup Red Pepper Dip
*   (page 32)*
2 tablespoons virgin olive oil
¼ teaspoon freshly ground
*   black pepper*
⅛ teaspoon salt
2 tablespoons grated Parmesan
*   cheese (optional)*

Bring about 3 quarts of water to a boil in a large pot. When it is boiling, add the pasta and stir well. Return the water to the boil,

and boil for about 10 to 12 minutes. Near the end of the cooking time, remove ½ cup of the cooking liquid from the pot and place it in your serving bowl.

Drain the pasta. Add the red pepper dip to the water in the bowl. Then stir in the oil, pepper, and salt. Mix well, and add the pasta. Toss to combine, and serve with Parmesan cheese if desired.

4 SERVINGS

BOW-TIE PASTA AND MUSHROOMS

This simple but delicious pasta sauce is composed of fresh mushrooms sautéed with garlic and scallions. Bow-tie pasta makes it a decorative first course.

2 cups farfalle *(butterfly, or*
*   bow-tie) pasta (8 ounces)*
¼ cup virgin olive oil
4 cloves garlic, peeled and
*   chopped fine (1 tablespoon)*
4 scallions, cleaned and
*   chopped fine (about ⅔ cup)*
4 ounces mushrooms, coarsely
*   chopped (1½ cups)*
½ teaspoon salt
¼ teaspoon freshly ground
*   black pepper*

3 tablespoons grated Parmesan,
*   Romano, or Swiss cheese, for*
*   garnish*

SAVE TIME BY USING THE PRE-SLICED, PREWASHED MUSHROOMS FOUND IN MOST SUPERMARKETS TODAY.

(continued)

Bow-Tie Pasta and Mushrooms (continued)

> ADDING A LITTLE OF THE PASTA COOKING LIQUID TO THIS DISH EXTENDS AND ENRICHES THE SAUCE.

Bring 3 to 4 quarts of water to a strong boil in a large pot. Add the pasta, bring the water back to the boil, and cook for 10 to 12 minutes. Near the end of the cooking time, remove ½ cup of the cooking liquid and set it aside.

Drain the cooked pasta in a colander, and return the pot to the stove. Add the oil, garlic, scallions, and mushrooms, and cook over high heat for about 2 minutes. Return the pasta and the reserved cooking liquid to the pot, season with the salt and pepper, and toss to mix well. Divide among four plates, and serve with the grated cheese sprinkled on top.

4 SERVINGS

MUSHROOMS AND RICE STICK NOODLES

Rice noodles have an absolutely wonderful texture when properly prepared. I prefer those that are at least ¼ inch wide—they're very easy to handle.

In this recipe the rice noodles are soaked in hot water and then drained. When the sauce is ready, the noodles are stir-fried at the last moment, just before serving.

1 pound rice stick noodles, about ¼ inch wide
12 ounces mushrooms
⅓ cup virgin olive oil
2 cups chopped onion
6 cloves garlic, peeled and chopped (about 1 tablespoon)
1 teaspoon salt

1 teaspoon freshly ground black pepper
⅓ cup coarsely chopped flat-leaf parsley
Grated Parmesan cheese (optional)

Fill a pot with hot tap water (about 140 degrees), and soak the rice noodles in it for about 15 minutes.

Meanwhile, cut the mushrooms into julienne strips, or slice them in a food processor using the 2-millimeter blade (you should have about 4 cups).

Heat the oil in a large nonstick saucepan. When it is hot, add the onion and cook over medium heat for about 3 minutes. Then add the garlic, mix well, and stir in the mushrooms. Cook about 5 minutes, until all the juice from the mushrooms has evaporated. Add the salt and pepper and set aside.

Drain the rice noodles, and let them sit in the colander until they are somewhat cool (to dry

them out a little). A few minutes before serving time, combine the noodles and the hot mushroom mixture in a wok or in two nonstick skillets, and sauté over high heat for 2 to 3 minutes, to warm the noodles and finish cooking them. Sprinkle with the parsley and serve immediately, with grated Parmesan cheese if desired.

6 SERVINGS

KEEP RICE NOODLES, AVAILABLE IN MOST SUPERMARKETS, ON HAND. THEY'RE QUICK AND EASY TO PREPARE.

SHRIMP WONTON RAVIOLI

Wonton wrappers are inexpensive and very useful, and are available now in most supermarkets. In most instances, the dough for the wrappers is rolled out in cornstarch—this is the white powder you see coating packaged wonton wrappers.

In this recipe the wontons are used to create ravioli, which are stuffed with a shrimp purée. You can buy shrimp in various forms—fresh or frozen, shelled or unshelled—at most supermarkets. If they are frozen, defrost them slowly in the refrigerator before processing in the food processor.

(continued)

Shrimp Wonton Ravioli (continued)

This recipe can be prepared quite quickly—a few seconds for processing the filling, and a few minutes for poaching the ravioli. It makes an elegant first course.

WONTON WRAPPERS, AVAILABLE AT MOST SUPERMARKETS, CAN BE USED FOR RAVIOLI AND DUMPLINGS AND CAN EVEN BE SHREDDED FOR USE AS A GARNISH IN SOUPS.

SHRIMP FILLING
1 slice white bread
8 ounces uncooked shrimp,
*   peeled*
1 scallion, cleaned and trimmed
1 clove garlic, peeled
¼ teaspoon dried tarragon
1 egg
¼ teaspoon salt
⅛ teaspoon freshly ground
*   black pepper*

24 wonton wrappers, 3 inches
*   square*

SAUCE
1 bottle (8 ounces) clam juice
½ cup heavy cream
¼ teaspoon salt
⅛ teaspoon freshly ground
*   black pepper*
½ teaspoon bottled chili paste
*   with garlic, or to taste (see*
*   Note)*
2 teaspoons potato starch
*   dissolved in ⅓ cup water*

Place the slice of bread in the bowl of a food processor and process for a few seconds (you should have ⅓ to ½ cup of bread crumbs). Transfer the crumbs to a dish and set aside.

Place the shrimp, scallion, garlic, tarragon, egg, salt, and pepper in the processor bowl and process for 10 to 15 seconds, just until the mixture is smooth and well combined. Transfer to a mixing bowl and lightly fold in the bread crumbs.

Lay 12 of the wonton wrappers out on a flat work surface, and wet them lightly around the edges by brushing with a little water. Divide the shrimp mixture among the wrappers, mounding approximately 1 tablespoon in the center of each. Cover with the remaining wrappers, aligning them with the squares beneath, and press gently around the edges to seal.

Bring 3 to 4 quarts of water to a strong boil in a large saucepan. Carefully place the filled wontons in the boiling water, moving them at first so they don't stick to the bottom of the pan. After a minute or so they will float to the top. Continue boiling gently for about 4 minutes.

Meanwhile, combine the clam juice, cream, salt, pepper, and chili paste in a saucepan. Bring to a boil, add the dissolved potato starch, and return to the boil, stirring.

Drain the ravioli and serve three per person, coating them with about ¼ to ⅓ cup of the sauce.

Note on chili paste: This chili paste has a very strong flavor. Omit it altogether if it doesn't appeal to you.

Note: The ravioli can be filled and cooked ahead of time; after draining them, submerge the ravioli in a bowl of cold water to stop the cooking. Then drain again, and set aside in a single layer. Reheat in a microwave oven, or very quickly in boiling water, just before serving with the hot sauce.

4 SERVINGS

RICOTTA CHEESE WONTON RAVIOLI

I follow the same procedure here as I did with the Shrimp Wonton Ravioli, but fill the ravioli with a ricotta cheese mixture and serve them with a light dressing-like sauce. These make an excellent first course.

CHEESE FILLING
1 cup ricotta cheese (8 ounces)
1 egg
2 tablespoons grated Parmesan cheese
¼ teaspoon salt
¼ teaspoon freshly ground black pepper
1 tablespoon chopped parsley

24 wonton wrappers, 3 inches square

SAUCE
2 tablespoons extra-virgin olive oil
2 teaspoons lemon juice
⅛ teaspoon freshly ground black pepper
⅛ teaspoon salt
2 tablespoons fresh or frozen homemade chicken stock (see Basic Chicken Stock, page 48) or canned chicken broth

(continued)

Ricotta Cheese Wonton Ravioli (continued)

Mix the ricotta, egg, Parmesan, salt, pepper, and parsley together in a bowl.

Lay 12 of the wonton wrappers out on a flat work surface, and wet them lightly around the edges by brushing with a little water. Divide the cheese mixture among the wrappers, mounding approximately 1 tablespoon in the center of each. Cover with the remaining wrappers, aligning them with the squares beneath, and press gently around the edges to seal.

Bring 3 to 4 quarts of water to a strong boil in a large saucepan. Carefully place the filled wontons in the boiling water, moving them gently at first so they don't stick to the bottom of the pan. After a minute or so they will float to the top. Continue boiling gently for about 5 minutes.

Meanwhile, combine the olive oil, lemon juice, pepper, salt, and chicken stock in a bowl, and stir well.

Drain the ravioli and serve three per person, with a little sauce drizzled on top.

Note: The ravioli can be filled and cooked ahead of time; after draining them, submerge in a bowl of cold water to stop the cooking. Then drain again, and set aside in a single layer. Reheat in a microwave oven, or very quickly in boiling water, just before serving with the sauce.

4 SERVINGS

IT ONLY TAKES A MINUTE TO PREPARE THE DELICIOUS DRESSING-LIKE SAUCE THAT IS SERVED WITH THESE RAVIOLI.

BEEF PELMINY IN CHICKEN BROTH

The beef-filled dumplings in this classic Russian dish are flavored with ground coriander, mint, and dill. Wonton wrappers make it easy. The dumplings can be poached ahead and reheated at serving time.

BEEF FILLING
8 ounces ground beef
¼ cup chopped onion
About 2 cloves garlic, chopped
    (1 teaspoon)
½ cup fresh bread crumbs
2 tablespoons chopped dill
½ teaspoon ground coriander
    seeds
1 teaspoon chopped mint, or ½
    teaspoon crumbled dried
    mint
½ teaspoon salt
¼ teaspoon freshly ground
    black pepper
¼ cup minced scallions

24 wonton wrappers, 3 inches
    square
6 cups fresh or frozen
    homemade chicken stock
    (see Basic Chicken Stock,
    page 48) or canned chicken
    broth
¼ teaspoon freshly ground
    black pepper
1 teaspoon salt, or to taste
2 chicken bouillon cubes
    (optional)

In a bowl mix together all the filling ingredients.

Lay 12 of the wonton wrappers out on a flat work surface, and wet them lightly around the edges by brushing with a little water. Divide the filling mixture among the wrappers, mounding approximately 1 tablespoon in the center of each. Cover with the re-maining wrappers, aligning them with the squares beneath, and press gently around the edges to seal.

Bring 3 to 4 quarts of water to a strong boil in a large saucepan. Carefully place the filled wontons in the boiling water, moving them gently at first so they don't stick to the bottom of the pan. After a minute or so they will float to the top. Continue boiling gently for about 6 minutes.

Lift the dumplings out of the water with a slotted spoon, and arrange them, three per person, in four soup bowls. Pour about 1½ cups of the hot chicken stock over the dumplings in each bowl. Serve immediately.

Note: The dumplings can be filled and cooked ahead of time: After draining them, submerge them in a bowl of cold water to stop the cooking. Then drain again, and set aside in a single layer. Reheat in a microwave oven, or very quickly in boiling water, just before serving with the hot stock.

4 SERVINGS

USE PACKAGED WONTON WRAP-PERS TO MAKE THE DUMPLINGS FOR THIS CLASSIC RUSSIAN DISH.

BROWN RICE RAGOUT

This dish is really a highly flavored, spicy rice. The pork gives it richness, and the ginger and jalapeño pepper give it zip. I use Wehani rice, available at most health-food stores, for this ragout. It is a dark, very-long-grain rice with a thick hull and a strong, nutty, delicious taste.

8 ounces salt pork, as lean as
    possible (see Note)
1 onion (about 3 ounces),
    coarsely chopped (1 cup)
6 scallions, cleaned and cut into
    ½-inch pieces (about 1 cup)
1 tablespoon chopped ginger
1 teaspoon chopped hot
    jalapeño or serrano pepper
About 2 cups brown rice (1
    pound), preferably Wehani
    (see Note)
5 cups water

Cut the salt pork into ½-inch-thick slices and then into ½-inch-thick sticks. Place them in one layer in a large saucepan, cover with cold water, and bring to a boil over medium to high heat. Boil 1 minute, drain, and rinse under cold running water. Pat dry with paper towels. Transfer to a clean saucepan, cover and cook over medium heat for 10 to 12 minutes, stirring occasionally. The fat should be rendered and the pork nicely browned.

Add the onion, scallion, ginger, and hot pepper. Mix well, and cook another 2 to 3 minutes. Then add the rice, stir well, and add the water. Bring to a boil, stirring occasionally. Reduce the heat to very low, cover tightly, and cook slowly for about 1 hour, testing it after about 30 minutes.

Note: Salt pork is unsmoked bacon. If you can't find salt pork, use slab bacon: Cover it with cold water, bring to a boil, and boil for 1 minute before using, to remove some of the smoked and salted flavor.

Note: Wehani rice, which comes from California, cooks in 1 hour and absorbs 2½ times its volume in liquid. Other brown rices will vary, taking from 30 minutes to an hour and using from 1½ to 3 cups of liquid per cup of rice.

6 SERVINGS

RICE WITH MUSHROOMS AND STEAMED ASPARAGUS

For this interesting recipe, brown rice is cooked until almost done, and then asparagus is laid on top of the rice and cooks in the steam emerging from it. Just remember to use a saucepan that is large enough to accommodate the asparagus.

1 tablespoon unsalted butter
2 tablespoons virgin olive oil
1¼ cups coarsely chopped onion (about 6 ounces)
2½ cups coarsely chopped mushrooms (about 6 ounces)
1 teaspoon herbes de Provence (see Note, page 48)
2 cups brown rice (about 12 ounces)
5 cups light chicken stock (2½ cups Basic Chicken Stock, page 48, or canned chicken broth mixed with 2½ cups water; or 2 chicken bouillon cubes dissolved in 5 cups water)
¼ teaspoon freshly ground black pepper
½ teaspoon salt
About 12 stalks asparagus with firm tips (1 pound)

Heat the butter and oil in a large saucepan, and sauté the onion for about 3 minutes, until it is almost transparent. Add the mushrooms and the herbes de Provence, and cook for another 2 minutes. Stir in the rice, light chicken stock, pepper, and salt. Bring to a boil, stirring occasionally. Then cover tightly, reduce the heat to very low, and cook for about 35 minutes, or until most of the liquid has been absorbed. (Some varieties of brown rice will need longer cooking and more liquid than others.)

While the rice is cooking, wash the asparagus thoroughly and either peel the lower third of the stalks or cut off and discard them.

After the rice has cooked for 20 to 25 minutes, lay the asparagus on top of it and continue cooking for another 12 to 15 minutes. As soon as the asparagus is cooked, serve it with the rice on individual plates.

6 SERVINGS

COOKING THE RICE AND VEGETABLE TOGETHER IN ONE POT IS A TIME- AND WORK-SAVER.

CORNMEAL MUSH WITH CHEESE

This is a type of *polenta*, which is the Italian word for a variety of yellow cornmeal, and is also used to describe the mush-like dishes made with this cornmeal.

I cook the cornmeal here in a light chicken stock and flavor it with Romano cheese. It is easy, takes only 20 minutes to make, and tastes great with roasted meat—especially if some of the meat juices are spooned over it. After cooling, leftovers can be sliced and sautéed in butter for a breakfast or lunch dish.

*3½ cups light chicken stock
    (1¾ cups Basic Chicken
    Stock, page 48, or canned
    chicken broth mixed with
    1¾ cups water; or 2 chicken
    bouillon cubes dissolved in
    3½ cups water)*
*¼ teaspoon freshly ground
    black pepper*
Salt to taste
1 cup yellow cornmeal
¼ cup grated Romano cheese
1½ tablespoons unsalted butter

Bring the stock and pepper to a boil in a large saucepan, and add salt to taste. Pour the cornmeal in a slow, steady stream into the boiling stock, whisking continuously as you pour. Bring the mixture back to the boil, reduce the heat to very low, and continue cooking for 20 minutes, stirring with your whisk (especially in the corners) every now and then to prevent it from sticking. Add the cheese and butter, mix well, and serve immediately.

4 SERVINGS

MAKE LIGHT CHICKEN STOCK BY COMBINING EQUAL AMOUNTS OF HOMEMADE STOCK OR CANNED BROTH AND WATER.

SHELLFISH AND FISH

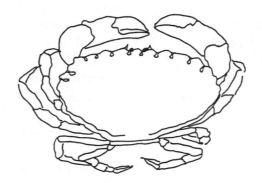

I still buy most of my fish in a fish store because of the variety and freshness. But seafood is getting better at the supermarket, and many of the recipes in this chapter can be made with supermarket shellfish and fish, either fresh or canned.

There is something here for every seafood taste—recipes for everything from oysters, shrimp, scallops, crabmeat, and lobster, to fillet of sole, tuna, scrod, striped bass, and salmon. Most of the following dishes can be used as a main course; start the meal with a salad and serve the fish with a complementing side dish from the chapter on vegetables (see page 201).

Remember that when you are pressed for time, fish cooks very quickly, and most of these recipes require only minimal effort.

SARDINES IN TOMATO SAUCE

We often enjoy this as a first course at our house—simple but flavorful, it is one of my daughter's favorites. Serve some crunchy French bread alongside.

About 2 cups salad greens (such as Boston, red leaf, or iceberg lettuce) thoroughly rinsed and dried
1 can (16 ounces) sardines in tomato sauce
1 onion (about 3 ounces), preferably red, peeled and sliced thin
1 tablespoon red wine vinegar
1 tablespoon olive oil
¼ cup parsley leaves, preferably flat-leaf
¼ teaspoon freshly ground black pepper
2 ripe tomatoes (about 10 ounces total)

Place the salad greens on a platter and arrange the sardines with tomato sauce on top. Distribute the onion slices over the sardines, and sprinkle with the vinegar, olive oil, parsley, and pepper.

Cut the tomatoes in half lengthwise, and then into ¼-inch-thick slices. Arrange them attractively around the edge of the platter and serve.

Note: This will serve two as a luncheon main dish.

4 SERVINGS

MUSSELS A LA BELGE

Belgians are great lovers of mussels and I have a dear friend who often prepares them Belgian-style, garnished with French fries. They are equally good, though, served with sautéed potatoes (see Potatoes Persillade, page 227, Potatoes with Walnuts and Croutons, page 229, and Parsley Potatoes with Butter, page 225).

Seasoned primarily with celery and onion, the mussels here are served country-style—shells and all—in large bowls. If you want to be a bit fancier, remove the mussels from the shells after cooking them, and then serve them on the half shell with the cooking juices spooned over them.

The mussels that are available now are raised commercially and so are much cleaner than they used to be. You don't need to scrape the shells; just wash them once in cold water before using. If a shell is open, touch the mussel inside with the point of a sharp knife. If the shell closes, you know the mussel is still alive and will be edible; if it doesn't close, discard the mussel.

I do not add liquid or salt to this recipe. The mussels create their own juice, which usually has a salty flavor. Add salt only if needed.

---

3 pounds mussels
2 onions (about 6 ounces total), peeled and diced (about 1¼ cups)
1¼ cups sliced celery
½ teaspoon Tabasco sauce
3 tablespoons olive oil

Place the mussels in a large bowl of cold water and rub them one against another to clean them. Remove the beards, if any. Check to make certain that all the mussels are alive (see above). Lift the mussels from the water and place them in a saucepan, preferably stainless steel. Add the onion, celery, Tabasco, and olive oil. Cover and bring to a boil. Stir with a large spoon and cook for 3 to 4

minutes, until all the mussels have opened.

Divide the mussels, vegetables, and broth among four bowls and serve immediately.

4 SERVINGS

MUSSELS RAVIGOTE

Ravigoter means "to invigorate," which aptly describes the effect this piquant dressing has on the mussels in this dish. There are many reasons to serve mussels: In addition to tasting good, they are inexpensive, usually come already cleaned, and cook in just a few minutes. I don't use the juice from the mussels here; it can be frozen for use in fish soup or fish sauces. Serve some crusty French bread with this dish.

About 36 mussels (2½ pounds)
1 tablespoon Dijon-style
  mustard
3 tablespoons virgin olive oil
¼ teaspoon Tabasco sauce
⅛ teaspoon salt
⅛ teaspoon freshly ground
  black pepper
2 scallions, tops discarded,
  cleaned, and minced fine
  (about 2 tablespoons)
1 clove garlic, peeled, crushed,
  and chopped fine (about ½
  teaspoon)
4 to 8 lettuce leaves, preferably
  Boston

Rinse the mussels in cool water. Don't worry if there is still some incrustation on the outside of the shells, because they will be discarded.

Place the mussels in a pot and set it over high heat. Cover and cook for about 5 minutes, shaking the pot occasionally, until all the mussels have opened and released their juice. Set aside, covered, to rest for about 5 minutes. Then pour into a roasting pan.

When the mussels are cool enough to handle, remove them from their shells and place them in a bowl. Discard the shells. Remove the beards, if any. Strain the juices into a plastic container with a tight-fitting lid (you should have about 1½ cups), and freeze for later use in soup or stock.

Add the remainder of the ingredients to the bowl and mix with the mussels while they are still lukewarm, so they will absorb the seasonings well. Serve at room temperature on the lettuce leaves.

4 SERVINGS

> **FOUR REASONS TO SERVE MUSSELS: THEY'RE GOOD, INEXPENSIVE, USUALLY COME CLEANED, AND COOK IN A FEW MINUTES.**

SMOKED HERRING LYONNAISE

W hen I was a child, one of the appetizers we would eat most often was smoked herring fillets prepared Lyonnaise-style—combined with carrots, onions, bay leaves, and thyme, and marinated in oil in a crock. It is especially good served with potato salad and crunchy French bread, and makes a particularly appetizing first course or buffet dish. It will keep for 2 to 3 weeks in the refrigerator.

Unfortunately, it is not easy to get plump, soft smoked herring fillets here, so I usually use kippers (smoked unboned herring) instead, filleting them myself.

4 whole kippers (2 packages)
   about 1¾ pounds
1 large onion (about 5 ounces),
   peeled and sliced thin (see
   Note)
2 carrots (4 ounces), peeled and
   sliced very thin
1 teaspoon dried thyme leaves
1 teaspoon coarsely ground
   black pepper
4 bay leaves
2 cups corn or canola oil

Prepare the kippers: Place the fish flat on a work surface, and cut along the central bone. Pull the fillets away from the bone, and cut off and discard the surface skin and dry edges. Cut each fillet lengthwise into two strips.

Arrange the herring strips with the remainder of the ingredients in a glass or ceramic crock. Cover with a piece of plastic wrap laid directly on the surface of the mixture. Let macerate in the refrigerator for at least 5 to 6 hours before serving. The herring will keep for 2 to 3 weeks in the refrigerator.

Note: For the best results, use the 1-millimeter blade on a food processor to slice the onion.

6 SERVINGS

THIS DISH WILL KEEP, REFRIGERATED, FOR 2 TO 3 WEEKS, SO KEEP SOME ON HAND FOR UNEXPECTED GUESTS.

SHRIMP SAUTE PIQUANTE

During crayfish season in Louisiana, those tiny lobsterlike crustaceans are brought piping hot to the table in a big bowl and everyone digs in with their hands, finally sucking on the shells to extract every last bit of flavor from them. This shrimp dish duplicates that experience and should be shared with family and close friends, since eating unshelled shrimp is a rather messy process.

The secret to preparing this dish well is to sauté the shrimp quickly over extremely high heat. This is best done in two skillets, or in two batches in one skillet, so there is only one layer of shrimp to absorb the intense heat. If too many shrimp are cooked at one time, they tend to boil and don't achieve the desired taste and texture.

*1 pound large, unshelled
    shrimp (26 to 30 per
    pound)*
4 tablespoons virgin olive oil
1 teaspoon thyme leaves
1 teaspoon oregano leaves
½ teaspoon cayenne pepper
½ teaspoon salt
4 tablespoons water

THIS DISH CAN BE PREPARED IN 10 MINUTES.

Rinse the shrimp well, and pat dry with paper towels.

Heat 2 tablespoons of the oil in a cast-iron or stainless steel skillet. Sprinkle the shrimp with the thyme, oregano, cayenne, and salt. Just when the oil begins to smoke, add half the shrimp in one layer and sauté for 1¾ to 2 minutes, tossing them in the skillet or turning them with tongs so they cook on both sides.

Transfer the shrimp to a bowl and deglaze the pan: Add 2 tablespoons of the water and swirl it around to melt any caramelized juices. Pour over the shrimp in the bowl.

Repeat this process with the remaining oil and seasoned shrimp, and add them to the bowl.

Serve immediately as a main dish, or cool slightly and serve lukewarm as an hors d'oeuvre.

4 SERVINGS

SHRIMP IN "HOT" BROTH

T his is one of my mother-in-law's favorite summer dishes. Since shrimp always taste best when cooked in their shells, we eat this family-style and peel them with our fingers at the table—messy and delicious. Don't forget to suck on the shells to extract the last bit of flavorful juice. Dip the shrimp in melted butter, and serve some bread alongside. And since you've already got your sleeves rolled up, serve some hot corn on the cob too!

3 tablespoons cider vinegar
¾ teaspoon salt
1 tablespoon herbes de Provence
    (see Note, page 48)
2 bay leaves
1 onion, peeled and sliced (1
    cup)
½ teaspoon red pepper flakes
12 sprigs cilantro (coriander or
    Chinese parsley)
2 cups water
1 pound large shrimp (26 to 30
    per pound), unshelled

Place all the ingredients except the shrimp in a saucepan and bring to a boil. Cover and boil for about 1 minute. Then add the shrimp, stirring to mix them well with the broth, and bring the mixture back to the boil. As soon as it comes to the boil, cover the pan, remove it from the heat, and set it aside; the shrimp will continue to cook in the hot broth.

Serve lukewarm, with melted butter, or serve cold.

Note: These make an excellent shrimp cocktail. Chill the shrimp in the broth, then drain, peel, and serve them with some Horseradish Sauce (page 24).

4 SERVINGS

MUSTARD BROILED SHRIMP

S helling the shrimp is the hardest part of this recipe, so buy shelled raw shrimp—often called rock shrimp—at the market if you can. This is a festive appetizer with a sweet-hot

(continued)

Mustard Broiled Shrimp (continued)

taste. (You can also cool the shrimp and serve them as hors d'oeuvre on slices of party rye.)

1 pound large shrimp (26 to 30 per pound), preferably shelled
3 tablespoons honey mustard (see Note)
2 tablespoons dark soy sauce
¼ teaspoon Tabasco sauce

If the shrimp are not already shelled, shell them and rinse thoroughly under cool water; pat dry with paper towels.

In a small bowl combine the honey mustard, soy sauce, and Tabasco. Stir the shrimp into the sauce to coat them well. Then remove them from the sauce (reserving what's left) and arrange in a single layer in a gratin dish or on a baking sheet lined with aluminum foil.

At serving time, place the shrimp under a preheated broiler, about 5 inches from the heat. Cook about 2 minutes on one side, turn with tongs, and cook on the other side for about 2 minutes.

Arrange them on a serving platter or individual plates, and serve with the reserved sauce.

Note: You can create your own honey mustard by mixing enough honey into whole-grain mustard to give it a sweet-hot taste.

4 SERVINGS

IF YOU BUY SHELLED SHRIMP, THIS DISH WILL TAKE ONLY 5 MINUTES TO PREPARE.

SHRIMP WITH CABBAGE AND CAVIAR

There is an interesting and unusual combination of flavors here: The crunchy cabbage is a terrific accompaniment for the just barely cooked shrimp, and the saltiness of the salmon caviar, which looks like small pink pearls around the shrimp, complements the dish.

16 extra-large unshelled shrimp
  (about 1 pound)
½ teaspoon salt
¼ teaspoon freshly ground
  black pepper
3 tablespoons unsalted butter
4½ cups shredded cabbage
1 cup heavy cream
½ cup water
2 tablespoons red salmon caviar

THIS WONDERFUL, DISTINCTLY FLAVORED DISH MAKES AN EASY BUT ELEGANT FIRST COURSE FOR A SPECIAL DINNER.

Peel and devein the shrimp, and sprinkle them with the salt and pepper. Melt the butter in one large or two smaller skillets. When it is hot, add the shrimp and sauté over high heat for 50 to 60 seconds. Using a slotted spoon, transfer the shrimp to a plate and set aside in a warm place.

Add the cabbage to the juices in the pan and sauté for about 20 seconds. Then add the cream and water, stir, and bring to a boil. Reduce the cabbage-cream mixture over high heat for 2 to 3 minutes. Taste and correct the seasonings, if necessary.

With a large slotted spoon, transfer the cabbage to a large serving dish or divide it among six individual plates. Arrange the shrimp on top of the cabbage and sprinkle with the caviar. Serve immediately.

6 SERVINGS

CRABMEAT CROQUETTES

I like to cook these flavorful croquettes at the last moment, but if you have a larger party and want to prepare them ahead, you can; just reheat them under the oven broiler for a few minutes before serving. You will notice that the crabmeat mixture is soft; it will stiffen as it cooks, and the result will be quite delicate. These can be served on their own but are also good with Horseradish Sauce (page 24) or Mustard Vinaigrette Dressing (page 26).

(continued)

Crabmeat Croquettes (continued)

1½ slices bread
8 ounces cooked crabmeat pieces
2 scallions, cleaned and minced
    fine (⅓ cup)
1 teaspoon chopped ginger
¼ teaspoon Tabasco sauce
1 egg
2 tablespoons safflower or
    corn oil

Process the bread in a food processor (you should have about ¾ cup crumbs).

Place the crabmeat, scallions, ginger, Tabasco, and egg in a bowl. Mix lightly with a fork to combine. Add the bread crumbs and toss just until incorporated. Using a spoon, divide the mixture into 8 parts and press them together lightly in your hands to form 8 patties, each about 1½ inches thick.

Heat 1 tablespoon of the oil in a nonstick skillet. When it is hot, sauté 4 of the patties over medium heat for about 2 minutes on each side until nicely browned. Transfer them to a plate, and cook the 4 remaining patties. Serve immediately, or cool and reheat under an oven broiler for a few minutes just before serving.

4 SERVINGS

> THESE CAN BE COOKED AHEAD AND THEN REHEATED UNDER THE BROILER JUST BEFORE SERVING.

SCALLOP BREAD WITH CILANTRO AND GINGER

This stuffed roll, which can be made ahead, becomes a favorite with everyone who tries it. Although you can use a single large bread loaf and cut it into wedges for serving, I prefer to use hard rolls, and serve one per person. Be sure to select rolls that don't have holes on the sides or bottom, as the butter has a tendency to seep out.

If you are not fond of the herbs I have selected here—cilantro and ginger—use parsley with either garlic or shallots instead. Since I live in Connecticut, whenever possible I use Niantic Bay scallops, which are medium-size, very sweet bay scallops. I recommend either these or small sea scallops, although any fresh scallops will work well.

---

8 small round or oval hard rolls
    (about 1¼ ounces each)
1 tablespoon virgin olive oil
1 pound scallops (about 40),
    preferably Niantic Bay
    variety
8 tablespoons (1 stick, 4
    ounces) unsalted butter
2 cloves garlic, chopped fine
    (1 teaspoon)
3 tablespoons chopped cilantro
    (coriander or Chinese
    parsley)
1 teaspoon chopped ginger
½ teaspoon freshly ground
    black pepper
¼ teaspoon salt

Cut off the top of each roll about a third of the way down, and with your fingers, twist out the soft insides; they should come out in one piece. Place these insides and the roll "lids" in a food processor and process until crumbed. Mix 1 cup of the crumbs (reserving the remainder for another use) with the olive oil and set aside.

Rinse the scallops to remove any sand, and drain thoroughly. Combine the butter, garlic, cilantro, ginger, pepper, and salt in a bowl and mix well. Place about ½ tablespoon of the mixture in the bottom of each hollowed-out roll. Arrange the scallops, about 5 per roll, over the butter mixture and cover with the remaining butter. Lightly press the reserved bread crumbs on top, mounding them in the center.

Arrange the rolls on a foil-lined baking sheet and bake in a 375-degree oven for 25 minutes, until cooked through and nicely browned on top. Serve immediately.

6 SERVINGS

THESE STUFFED ROLLS CAN BE PREPARED AHEAD AND COOKED WHEN NEEDED.

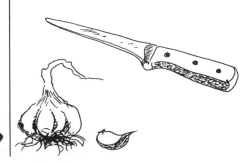

SCALLOPS IN A SKILLET

———

Cook these scallops quickly in a very hot cast-iron or aluminum skillet, just until their surface is light brown. The sauce is also very good with other types of shellfish.

1 pound scallops, preferably
    medium-size sea scallops

MAYONNAISE AND LEMON SAUCE
1 tablespoon mayonnaise
2 teaspoons lemon juice
1 teaspoon Worcestershire sauce
1 tablespoon safflower or corn
    oil
1 tablespoon chopped scallions
    (¼-inch pieces)
¼ teaspoon Tabasco sauce

3 tablespoons virgin olive oil
½ teaspoon salt
½ teaspoon freshly ground
    black pepper

Rinse the scallops well to remove any sand, and dry them thoroughly on paper towels.
Mix all the sauce ingredients

SCALLOPS ARE BEST WHEN THEY ARE COOKED FAST IN A VERY HOT HEAVY SKILLET.

together in a serving bowl, and set aside.

Place a heavy skillet over high heat. When it is very hot, add the olive oil, and heat until the oil begins to smoke. Sprinkle the scallops with the salt and pepper, and place them in the hot skillet. Cook for about 1½ minutes, turning to brown on all sides. Transfer the scallops to individual plates and serve immediately, with the sauce.

4 SERVINGS

SCALLOPS VINAIGRETTE

———

I love scallops cooked just until lukewarm, tossed with a vinaigrette, and served as a first course. It is an impressive dish, quite quickly prepared, and delicious if the scallops are not overcooked. I like to use medium- or small-size sea scallops; if you use larger ones, cut them into 1-inch pieces.

This dish takes only a few minutes to prepare and is best done at the last moment.

1 pound scallops, rinsed under
    cool water to remove sand, if
    necessary
2 tablespoons water

DRESSING
2 teaspoons Dijon-style mustard
    (preferably "hot")
1 tablespoon red wine vinegar
¼ cup extra-virgin olive oil
¼ teaspoon freshly ground
    black pepper
¼ teaspoon salt
2 scallions, cleaned and minced
    fine (about ⅓ cup)

10 to 12 Boston lettuce leaves

If the scallops are large, cut them into 1-inch pieces.

Place the scallops and water in a stainless steel skillet and bring to a boil. Cook over medium to high heat, shaking the pan occasionally, until they are opaque, about 2 to 3 minutes. Drain, cover, and set aside.

Combine the dressing ingredients, adding to them any moisture that has collected around the scallops. Arrange the lettuce leaves on individual plates, place the scallops on top, and spoon the dressing over them. Serve immediately.

4 SERVINGS

THIS IMPRESSIVE FIRST-COURSE DISH TAKES ONLY A FEW MINUTES TO PREPARE.

RED LOBSTER STEW

Lobster is a favorite at our house, for family meals as well as company fare. This particular dish is better eaten with family and close friends, since the shells are broken open and the meat extracted with your fingers at the table. Serve it with pasta and corn on the cob.

(continued)

Red Lobster Stew (continued)

Conventionally raw lobster is cut into equal-size pieces, but it's a difficult job to perform, so in this recipe I divide it into pieces by breaking off the claws and twisting the tail out of the body. (A fishmonger can do this for you if you find it distasteful.) I calculate approximately 1 lobster per person for a main-course serving, so you will need a very large (12-quart) pot or two slightly smaller ones. If you use two pans, combine the drippings from both and finish the recipe in one of the pans.

Be sure the lobsters you buy are alive and freshly caught. The fresher the lobster, the fuller and firmer the meat will be.

6 live lobsters (1¼ pounds each)
½ cup extra-virgin or virgin olive oil
2 cups coarsely chopped onion
About 6 cloves garlic, peeled and chopped (2 tablespoons)
1 can (28 ounces) Italian plum tomatoes, undrained
2 tablespoons herbes de Provence (see Note, page 48)
1½ teaspoons crushed red pepper flakes
½ cup chopped parsley, basil, and chives (a mixture or one of the three)

Protecting your hands with a kitchen towel, grab hold of and break off the claws from each of the lobsters. Then twist off the tails, separating them from the bodies.

To make it easier to extract the meat from the claws after cooking, crack the shells: Place each claw on the counter and cover with a towel to prevent splattering. Using a meat pounder or the bottom of a heavy saucepan, pound on the claw until the shell cracks. Place the tails and cracked claws in a large bowl to preserve any juices that may be released.

Heat the oil in one very large or two slightly smaller saucepans. When it is hot, add the claws, tail pieces, and bodies, and any juices that have accumulated around them. Shaking the pan(s) and stirring occasionally, sauté the lobster pieces, covered, over medium-high heat for about 10 minutes, until the shells are bright red and the meat almost cooked through.

Transfer the tail and claw pieces to a bowl, and return the pan to the heat. (If you used two pans, combine the drippings in one of them.) Add the onion, garlic, plum tomatoes with their juice, and herbes de Provence to the drippings. Bring to a boil, stirring, and boil until the mixture thickens slightly and the taste is concentrated. Remove the lobster bodies and discard them.

Return the lobster pieces to the sauce, and stir in the pepper flakes and fresh herbs. Heat gently for about 5 minutes, until the lobster is heated through. Arrange on a large platter, and serve.

Note: You can prepare the sauce and the lobster ahead of time, and then warm the lobster —unpeeled, if you like—in the sauce just before serving.

6 SERVINGS

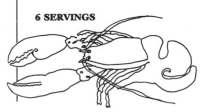

LOBSTER IN PAPRIKA SAUCE ON TOAST

This is a rich, impressive dish, ideal as a first course for a fancy dinner party. Lobster meat is expensive, of course, but in the summer it is more reasonably priced, of the best quality, and usually available cooked from most fishmongers. All that is involved here is cutting up the lobster meat, combining it with the sauce ingredients, and serving it over toast rounds.

4 slices firm-textured bread
1 pound cooked lobster meat,
    cut into 1-inch pieces
1 teaspoon paprika
½ teaspoon salt
¼ teaspoon freshly ground
    black pepper
2 tablespoons unsalted butter
1 tablespoon cognac
⅔ cup heavy cream
1 tablespoon chopped chives

> **THIS COULDN'T BE EASIER: ALL YOU HAVE TO DO IS CUT UP COOKED LOBSTER MEAT AND COMBINE IT WITH THE QUICKLY MADE SAUCE.**

Toast the bread slices in a toaster and trim them to create squares or rounds. Place a piece on each of four plates.

(continued)

Lobster in Paprika Sauce on Toast (continued)

Sprinkle the lobster pieces with the paprika, salt, and pepper. Melt the butter in a skillet, and when it is foaming, add the lobster and sauté for about 1 minute, just long enough to heat through. Add the cognac and the cream, bring to a boil, and simmer gently, uncovered, for about 1 minute to reduce slightly.

Spoon the lobster and sauce over the toast pieces, sprinkle with the chives, and serve.

4 SERVINGS

SAUTE OF LOBSTER WITH BASMATI RICE

This dish is made with fresh cooked lobster meat, available from most fishmongers. Served with the Basmati rice, which has a distinctive nutty taste, it is perfect as the first course for an elegant dinner or as the main course for a light brunch.

RICE
2 tablespoons unsalted butter
½ cup chopped onion
1 teaspoon herbes de Provence (see Note, page 48)
1¼ cups Basmati rice, or another variety of white rice
¼ teaspoon freshly ground black pepper
2¼ cups fresh or frozen homemade chicken stock (see Basic Chicken Stock, page 48) or canned chicken broth
½ teaspoon salt (optional)

LOBSTER
About 3 plum tomatoes (8 ounces)

2 tablespoons unsalted butter
2 tablespoons virgin olive oil
1 cup diced red onion (½-inch pieces)
3 shallots, peeled and cut into ¼-inch dice (about ¼ cup)
3 cloves garlic, crushed and coarsely chopped (1 tablespoon)
1 teaspoon herbes de Provence (see Note, page 48)
½ cup dry white wine
½ teaspoon salt
½ teaspoon freshly ground black pepper
½ pound cooked lobster meat, cut into 1-inch pieces
¼ cup minced parsley

Prepare the Rice: Heat the butter in a saucepan with a tight-fitting lid. When it is hot, add the onion and sauté for about 1½ minutes over medium-high heat. Mix in the herbes de Provence, rice, and pepper. Then add the chicken stock, and salt, if desired. Bring to a boil, stirring, over high heat. Cover, reduce the heat to very low, and continue cooking for 20 minutes.

Prepare the Lobster: While the rice is cooking, cut the tomatoes into ½-inch dice, and set them aside along with their seeds and juice (you should have about 2 cups).

Heat the butter and oil in a saucepan. When the mixture is hot, add the onion and shallots, and sauté over high heat for 3 minutes. Then stir in the garlic and cook for about 10 seconds. Add the tomatoes with their juice and seeds, herbes de Provence, wine, salt, pepper, and lobster pieces. Bring to a boil, cover, reduce the heat to low, and simmer gently for 5 minutes.

Mound the rice in the center of each plate, and spoon the lobster and sauce over it. Sprinkle with the parsley, and serve immediately.

4 SERVINGS

FRESH COOKED LOBSTER MEAT FROM YOUR FISHMONGER MAKES THIS DISH EASY.

INSTANT GRAVLAX WITH OLIVES

Gravlax is cured, herb-seasoned fish. Traditional Scandinavian gravlax consists of large pieces of salmon cured with a lot of sugar, a little salt, and a great amount of dill. It is generally served with a sweet mustard mayonnaise.

In modern cooking, the gravlax treatment is applied to different types of fish, among them tuna and blackfish. Often the fish are cut very thin, and they are cured in different ways, sometimes with citric acid in the form of lemon or lime juice.

This salmon gravlax could also be called "carpaccio," a name which used to be applied only to meat but now refers to uncooked

(continued)

meat or fish that is pounded very thin and served with a garnish ranging from mayonnaise to plain olive oil.

Most fish markets now carry fresh salmon, generally the "raised" Norwegian variety, which I recommend. It is flavorful and fatty enough for this dish, and since it is raised in a controlled environment, the quality is reliable.

---

*4 pieces (2 ounces each)
  salmon, completely cleaned
  of sinews, skin, and bones
1½ teaspoons salt
1½ teaspoons freshly ground
  black pepper
2 tablespoons finely chopped
  shallots
2 tablespoons chopped oil-cured
  black olives (¼-inch pieces)
2 tablespoons extra-virgin olive
  oil
1 tablespoon coarsely chopped
  flat-leaf parsley
2 teaspoons lemon juice
6 pieces of toast, trimmed,
  halved, and buttered*

Place the salmon pieces in a single layer, with space between them, on a large square of plastic wrap, and cover it with another square of plastic wrap. Using a meat pounder or the base of a glass or small saucepan, pound the salmon to flatten it, forming pieces about 7 inches in diameter. The pieces should be so thin that they are almost transparent. Remove the top layer of plastic wrap.

Sprinkle half the salt and pepper on four serving plates. In-

vert a salmon piece onto each plate, peeling off the plastic wrap as you go. Sprinkle the top of the salmon with the remaining salt and pepper. Cover the plates tightly with plastic wrap, and refrigerate for at least 4 hours.

Just before serving, place the shallots in a sieve and rinse them under cold water; drain thoroughly (this removes their harsh, acidic taste). Sprinkle the shallots over the salmon, followed by the olives, olive oil, and parsley. Sprinkle with the lemon juice, surround with the toast, and serve immediately.

> **THIS IS A GREAT DO-AHEAD (AND RELATIVELY INEXPENSIVE) RECIPE FOR A DINNER PARTY.**

Note: You can keep the salmon up to 24 hours in the refrigerator after pounding, coating with the salt and pepper, and wrapping it well. Add the shallots, olives, oil, and parsley up to 30 minutes before serving, but don't sprinkle the lemon juice over the salmon until the last moment. If the lemon juice is added ahead of time, it will "cook" the salmon, setting the protein and turning it an opaque white.

4 SERVINGS

MINUTE SALMON STEAKS

Fresh salmon, one of the most delicious varieties of fish, is usually available year-round from fishmongers. (The "raised" Norwegian species is excellent.)

This is an elegant dish to serve as the main course for a special dinner or lunch. Most steamed and buttered vegetables, from potatoes to broccoli, go well with it.

4 salmon steaks (5 to 6 ounces each), completely cleaned of bones and skin (about 1 pound total)
1 teaspoon salt
½ teaspoon freshly ground black pepper
1 tablespoon corn, canola, or peanut oil
1 teaspoon chopped tarragon
1 tablespoon chopped parsley
1 clove garlic, peeled, crushed, and chopped fine (½ teaspoon)
¼ cup olive oil
4 teaspoons lemon juice

Sprinkle the salmon steaks with the salt, pepper, and corn oil. Arrange them on an aluminum foil-lined baking sheet and set aside.

Mix the tarragon, parsley, garlic, and olive oil together in a bowl.

Place the steaks under the broiler, about 4 to 5 inches from the heat. Cook about 2 minutes on one side, then turn and cook 2 minutes on the other side.

Add the lemon juice to the sauce. Transfer the salmon steaks to warmed dinner plates, spoon the sauce over them, and serve immediately.

4 SERVINGS

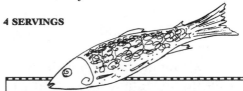

THESE STEAKS COOK IN ONLY A FEW MINUTES, AND THE SAUCE CAN BE MADE AHEAD.

SALMON CROQUETTES WITH CUCUMBER SALSA

T his dish can be prepared at the last minute and makes an excellent lunch or first course. The croquettes will brown nicely, but use a nonstick pan and turn them gently, as they are very delicate.

2 to 3 slices bread
1 can (7½ ounces) red salmon
  in water
3 or 4 scallions, cleaned and
  minced (½ cup)
1 teaspoon chopped tarragon,
  or ½ teaspoon dried
  tarragon
1 tablespoon Hot Red Salsa
  (page 23)
3 tablespoons mayonnaise
About 2 tablespoons corn or
  canola oil
½ cup cucumbers from Hot
  Cucumber Relish (page 22)
  coarsely chopped
½ cup liquid from Hot
  Cucumber Relish

Place the bread in a food processor and process until crumbled (you should have 1 cup crumbs).

Crumble the red salmon, with its liquid, into a bowl. Add the scallions, tarragon, bread crumbs, salsa, and mayonnaise. Mix lightly but thoroughly, and form into 8 patties.

Heat the corn oil in a nonstick skillet. When it is hot, add 4 croquettes and cook them over medium to high heat until nicely browned on both sides, about 2½ minutes on each side. Since the croquettes are delicate, turn them carefully with a large flat spatula.

Combine the chopped cucumbers and cucumber liquid, and divide among four plates. Arrange two croquettes on each plate and serve immediately.

4 SERVINGS

KEEP A CAN OF SALMON ON HAND FOR THIS QUICK, EASY LUNCHEON OR FIRST-COURSE DISH.

POTTED SMOKED SALMON

T his interesting dish is impressive to look at, delicious, and can be prepared up to a day ahead. It is especially elegant accompanied by asparagus in a vinaigrette dressing, but it is very good without any garnish if you prefer.

2 teaspoons chopped chives
1 small container (4 ounces)
   soft cream cheese (about 6
   tablespoons)
About 4 large slices smoked
   salmon (4 ounces)
1 red onion, sliced very thin
   (about ¼ cup)
1 tablespoon capers, preferably
   small, drained
¼ teaspoon freshly ground
   black pepper

ASPARAGUS VINAIGRETTE
8 medium to large asparagus
   (about 6 ounces total)
1 tablespoon peanut oil
1 teaspoon red wine vinegar
⅛ teaspoon salt
⅛ teaspoon freshly ground
   black pepper

6 slices black bread

Line each of four ½-cup soufflé molds with a 7-inch square of plastic wrap. Place about ¼ teaspoon of the chives in the bottom of each mold, and cover with 1 tablespoon of the cream cheese. Then press ½ slice of the salmon into the cream cheese to form a flat layer. Sprinkle with half the pepper. Divide half the onion among the four molds, and then layer on the remaining cream cheese, using about ½ tablespoon in each. Add the capers, distributing them evenly, then the remaining salmon and pepper. Press on the salmon slightly to make the mixture more compact. Sprinkle the remainder of the onion and chives on top, cover with plastic wrap, and refrigerate for at least 3 hours or up to a day ahead.

Prepare the Asparagus Vinaigrette: Peel or discard the lower third of the asparagus spears. Cut each trimmed spear into three pieces, about 2½ inches long.

To prepare the asparagus in a microwave oven, seal it in a plastic bag with 2 tablespoons water, and heat for about 3 minutes. Drain and combine with the oil, vinegar, salt, and pepper.

To prepare the asparagus on top of the stove, arrange the pieces in one layer in a stainless steel

(continued)

Potted Smoked Salmon (continued)

skillet. Add ½ cup water, bring to a boil, and cook for 2 to 3 minutes. Drain, and combine with the oil, vinegar, salt, and pepper.

Cover and refrigerate for at least 2 to 3 hours or up to a day ahead.

At serving time, unmold the potted salmon, lifting it out of the molds with its plastic-wrap liner. Invert onto individual plates, peel off the plastic wrap, and serve

ELEGANT AND DELICIOUS, THIS CAN BE MADE UP TO A DAY AHEAD.

with the asparagus arranged around it and black bread on the side.

4 SERVINGS

FISH ON WATERCRESS AU GRATIN

This attractive, fresh-tasting fish dish makes a perfect first course for an elegant dinner but could also be served as a main course for a special lunch or a simple dinner.

To save yourself some work, buy your fish already filleted, selecting either blackfish, tilefish, red snapper, or codfish, whatever is freshest. Remove (and reserve for stock) at least the bottom 2 inches of the watercress stems, approximately where they are usually bound together with elastic.

4 tablespoons virgin olive oil
2 cloves garlic, peeled and chopped fine (about 1 teaspoon)
2 bunches of watercress, trimmed (remove bottom 2 inches of stems), and washed (about 4 cups)

½ teaspoon salt
½ teaspoon freshly ground black pepper
4 fillets (about 6 ounces each) of blackfish, tilefish, red snapper, or codfish
2 slices bread

Heat 2 tablespoons of the olive oil in a large skillet. When it is hot, add the garlic and sauté for 5 seconds. Then add the watercress, still wet from washing, with ¼ teaspoon each of the salt and pepper. Sauté for about 1 minute, until the watercress has wilted.

Arrange the watercress, creating a bed, in a gratin dish large enough to accommodate the four fish fillets in a single layer. Let the watercress cool to room temperature, and then arrange the fish fillets on top. Sprinkle with the remaining ¼ teaspoon each of salt and pepper.

Place the bread in a food processor and process until crumbed (you should have about 1 cup crumbs). Mix the crumbs lightly with the remaining 2 tablespoons olive oil, and sprinkle on top of the fish. (The dish can be pre-pared to this point a few hours ahead, covered with plastic wrap, and refrigerated.)

When you are ready to cook the fish, place the dish under the broiler, about 10 inches from the heat, and cook for 10 to 12 minutes, until the fish is just cooked through and the bread crumbs are lightly browned. If you want the crumbs browner yet, move the dish closer to the heat source at this point and cook for another 2 to 3 minutes. Serve immediately.

Note: You can substitute an equal amount of spinach for the watercress.

4 SERVINGS

> BUY YOUR FISH ALREADY FILLETED
> TO SAVE YOURSELF SOME TIME AND
> EFFORT.

FILLETS OF SOLE IN RED PEPPER SAUCE

This is an attractive and delicious dish. Several varieties of sole—grey sole, lemon sole, flounder, authentic Dover sole—can be used, and if sole is not available, another type of white fish fillet (scrod or haddock, for example) will be very good prepared this way.

(continued)

Fillets of Sole in Red Pepper Sauce (continued)

The red pepper sauce can be made ahead and is also good on pasta or gnocchi.

RED PEPPER SAUCE
1 large or 2 medium-size red
*   bell peppers (about 12*
*   ounces)*
⅓ cup unseasoned tomato juice
½ teaspoon salt
½ teaspoon freshly ground
*   black pepper*
¼ cup extra-virgin olive oil
1 tablespoon unsalted butter

4 large fresh fillets of sole
*   (about 1¼ pounds total)*
¼ teaspoon salt
2 tablespoons water
About 12 basil leaves, coarsely
*   shredded, for garnish*

TRY THE RED PEPPER SAUCE ON PASTA OR GNOCCHI.

Prepare the Sauce: Cut the pepper(s) in half, remove the seeds, and cut into ½-inch pieces. Place the pieces in the bowl of a food processor along with the tomato juice, and process until liquified. Then push the mixture through a food mill fitted with the fine screen to remove the pepper skin. You should have approximately 1⅓ cups of the pepper-tomato mixture. Place it in a saucepan (preferably stain-less steel), add the ½ teaspoon salt, the pepper, olive oil, and butter, and bring to a strong boil, mixing with a whisk. Set aside and keep warm.

Cook the Fillets: Sprinkle the fillets with the ¼ teaspoon salt. If they are thin, fold them in half. Arrange in one layer in a nonstick pan, and add the water. Bring to a boil, cover, and cook 1½ to 2 minutes, depending on the thickness of the fillets. Remove them from the juice and arrange on individual plates.

Spoon some pepper sauce over each fillet, garnish with the basil, and serve immediately.

4 SERVINGS

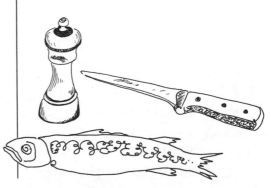

150

GRILLED PAPILLOTES OF STRIPED BASS

I n the summer, I like to cook fish outside on the grill (see Grilled Red Snapper with Herbs, page 153). One good way of grilling fish—especially when you have fillets—is to cook it *en papillote*, using aluminum foil instead of the standard parchment paper.

This is an easy recipe, and the fish will be moist and delicious. I use striped bass here, but other types of fish—from sole to trout to cod—would also be good. And you can vary the vegetables too, as long as whatever you select will cook in the 5 minutes allowed.

Rice, steamed potatoes, or pasta makes a good accompaniment.

4 fillets striped bass (about 6 ounces each), cleaned
4 tablespoons virgin olive oil
1 teaspoon salt
1½ cups diced ripe tomato (½-inch pieces)
1 teaspoon freshly ground black pepper
1 teaspoon dried thyme or 1 tablespoon fresh thyme leaves
2 tablespoons unsalted butter (optional)

Place each fillet in the center of a 12-inch square of aluminum foil. Sprinkle with the olive oil and salt, and distribute the diced tomatoes evenly over and a-round the fillets. Sprinkle with the pepper and thyme. Fold the foil so that the seam is on top and the fish and garnish are securely sealed in each package.

Place the packages on the rack of a very hot barbecue grill, and cook for approximately 5 minutes.

To serve, unwrap the foil packages and transfer the fillets and tomatoes to individual dinner plates; dot them with the butter, and serve. Or place an unopened package on each plate, and have your guests open their own packages.

4 SERVINGS

BROILED STRIPED BASS ORIENTAL

O nce a sport fish, striped bass is now raised commercially and has white, tender flesh. I do not remove the skin since it is flavorful and attractive. The fish should be macerated at least 30 minutes or as long as overnight (refrigerated) to absorb the flavors of the marinade.

Serve the fish with Potatoes with Walnuts and Croutons (page 229), Parsley Potatoes with Butter (page 225), or hash-brown potatoes.

4 fillets striped bass (about 6 ounces each), with skin
4 cloves garlic, peeled, crushed, and chopped (about 1 tablespoon)
1 piece of ginger (about 1 inch), peeled and chopped (about 1 tablespoon)
4 scallions, cleaned and minced fine (about ⅔ cup)
2 tablespoons dark soy sauce
2 teaspoons sugar
2 tablespoons vegetable oil

Place the fillets skin side up on a work surface, and using a sharp knife, cut two diagonal slits about ¼ inch deep through the skin of each one. (This helps the fish to absorb the marinade more readily and cook more evenly.)

Place the fillets in a plastic bag along with the garlic, ginger, scallions, soy sauce, sugar, and vegetable oil. Seal the bag and toss to mix the ingredients well. Refrigerate for up to 10 hours.

At cooking time, arrange the fillets skin side up in a single layer on a baking sheet lined with aluminum foil, or in a gratin dish from which they can be served. Place under a preheated broiler, 4 to 5 inches from the heat, and broil for 5 to 6 minutes. The skin will brown and bubble, and the heat will penetrate through the slits and cook the flesh.

Note: This preparation also works well with sea bass or black bass, as well as red snapper and other fish fillets.

4 SERVINGS

POACHED SCROD WITH BLACK BUTTER AND CAPERS

I like white, fleshy fillets—as thick as possible—for this dish so they remain moist in the center. Fresh scrod, haddock, and cod are all excellent.

4 *thick fillets of fresh scrod (each about 6 ounces, 1½ inches thick)*
4 *tablespoons (½ stick) unsalted butter*
1 *tablespoon olive oil*
2 *tablespoons capers, drained*
¼ *teaspoon freshly ground black pepper*
⅛ *teaspoon salt*
1 *tablespoon white wine vinegar*
⅓ *cup shredded basil leaves, for garnish*

Bring about 2 cups of water to a boil in a saucepan. Add the fish and bring the water back to the boil (this should take about 3 minutes). Boil gently for about 2 minutes, until the fillets are tender but still slightly resilient in the center.

While the fish is cooking, place the butter and oil in a skillet and cook over medium to high heat until the mixture turns brown. Drain the fish and arrange the fillets on four plates. Sprinkle each with capers, pepper, salt, and a few drops of vinegar. Pour the brown butter mixture over the fish, garnish with the basil, and serve.

4 SERVINGS

IT ONLY TAKES A FEW MINUTES TO POACH THE FILLETS AND PREPARE THE SAUCE FOR THIS DISH.

GRILLED RED SNAPPER WITH HERBS

When grilling fish at home, I use a folding metal wire grill and "sandwich" the fish between the two racks so that I can manipulate it easily. Before placing the fish inside, heat the wire grill on the hot barbecue for 15 to 20 minutes

(continued)

Grilled Red Snapper with Herbs (continued)

so the wires are very hot. Try to get the fish as close to the heat as possible. The fish will be less likely to stick if the grill is very hot, and the intense heat will give it a nice crusty exterior.

Whole fish is good for a casual family meal. Use your fingers to separate the flesh from the bones, and suck on the bones to remove every possible bit of flavor.

---

2 red snappers (about 1½ pounds each), scaled and gutted, heads left on
2 tablespoons corn or canola oil
½ teaspoon salt
8 bay leaves
4 sprigs thyme
2 sprigs mint
2 small jalapeño peppers
¼ cup olive oil

Place a hand-held wire grill on the barbecue to heat for 15 to 20 minutes.

Meanwhile, clean the fish well under cold water, removing the gills and any trace of blood from the inside. Dry thoroughly with paper towels. Cut two diagonal slits approximately ¼ inch deep and 2 inches apart on each side of both fish. Sprinkle the fish inside and out with the corn oil and the salt. Place the bay leaves in the cuts to partially anchor them, and press a sprig of thyme onto the side of each fish. Place a sprig of mint and a hot pepper inside each fish.

When the wire grill is extremely hot, place the fish inside, between the two racks. Cook as close to the heat as possible for 5 to 6 minutes on one side. Then, using pot holders, turn the grill and cook the fish on the other side for another 5 to 6 minutes.

Remove the fish from the grill and place them on a large platter (or divide the fish in half and place a half on each plate). Sprinkle with the olive oil and serve immediately.

4 SERVINGS

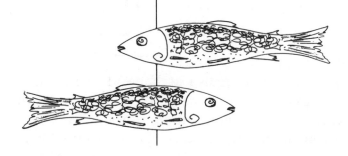

BROILED RED SNAPPER WITH LEMON VINAIGRETTE

Do not remove the skin when you broil fish—it browns beautifully and protects the flesh. If snapper is not available, substitute striped bass, black bass, or another variety of very fresh fish fillets.

Serve these with Parsley Potatoes with Butter (page 225) or Potatoes with Walnuts and Croutons (page 229).

4 fillets of red snapper (1¼ pounds total), with skin
½ teaspoon salt
¼ teaspoon freshly ground black pepper
2 teaspoons corn or canola oil

LEMON VINAIGRETTE
2 tablespoons virgin olive oil
2 teaspoons lemon juice
¼ teaspoon salt
¼ teaspoon freshly ground black pepper

1 tablespoon chopped chives

Place the fillets skin side up on a work surface, and cut two diagonal slits about ¼ inch deep through the skin of each one. (This helps the fish absorb the marinade more readily and cook more evenly.)

Place the fillets in a plastic bag along with the ½ teaspoon salt, ¼ teaspoon pepper, and the corn oil. Seal the bag and toss to mix the ingredients well. Refrigerate for at least 1 hour before cooking.

Arrange the fillets skin side up in a single layer on a baking sheet lined with aluminum foil or in a gratin dish from which they can be served. Place under a preheated broiler, no more than 4 inches from the heat, and broil for 5 minutes.

Meanwhile, make the vinaigrette: Combine the olive oil, lemon juice, ¼ teaspoon salt, and ¼ teaspoon pepper in a bowl, and blend well.

Remove the fish from the broiler (the skin should be bubbly, brown, and crusty). Spoon the vinaigrette over the fish, sprinkle with the chives, and serve immediately.

4 SERVINGS

CARPACCIO OF TUNA

A classic carpaccio is a paper-thin piece of raw beef covered with a flavorful mayonnaise. In this recipe I use tuna instead of beef, and a dressing of oil and vinegar with a garnish of diced vegetables.

This is particularly good as a first course for an elegant dinner party because it can be prepared a few hours ahead—all you have to do at serving time is to add the garnish.

Be sure to buy your fish from a reliable fishmonger. If you are not absolutely certain about its freshness, purchase it in advance and freeze it for at least 24 hours to kill any parasites. Then defrost it slowly in the refrigerator.

Serve this with black bread or crunchy French bread.

1 pound tuna, completely cleaned (see Note)
½ cup peeled, seeded, diced (¼-inch) red bell pepper (about ½ pepper)
½ cup peeled, seeded, diced (¼-inch) cucumber (about ¼ cucumber)
¼ cup finely chopped shallots (about 2 large shallots)
½ cup diced (¼-inch) mushrooms (about 3 medium mushrooms)
½ teaspoon lemon juice
1 teaspoon freshly ground black pepper
1 teaspoon salt
2 tablespoons coarsely minced parsley, preferably flat-leaf
1 tablespoon good-quality white wine vinegar
4 tablespoons virgin olive oil

Cut the tuna into six equal pieces. Place a piece of tuna on a sheet of plastic wrap, and lay another piece of plastic wrap on top. Pound the tuna with a meat pounder or a small heavy saucepan until it has flattened out to form a thin piece 5 to 6 inches in diameter. (The tuna should be very thin.) Remove the top layer of plastic wrap, and using the bottom layer, invert the tuna onto a serving plate. Leave the fish covered with the plastic wrap. Repeat this procedure with the remaining pieces of tuna, and refrigerate while you prepare the garnishes or for up to 24 hours.

About 1 hour before serving, prepare the red pepper, cucumber, shallot, and mushroom garnishes as instructed. Place the diced red pepper and cucumber in separate bowls.

Place the shallots in a sieve and rinse under cool water. (Rinsing removes the sulfuric acid, which tends to make chopped shallots and onions discolor and stings the eyes.) Drain, press in a towel to remove the moisture, and place in a bowl.

Mix the diced mushrooms with the lemon juice in a bowl to prevent them from discoloring.

At serving time, remove the plastic wrap from the plates con-

taining the tuna. Mix the pepper and salt together and sprinkle over the tuna. Spread the shallots, red pepper, cucumber, mushrooms, and parsley on top, and then sprinkle each portion with approximately ½ teaspoon vinegar and 2 teaspoons oil. Serve immediately.

Note: Buy about 1¼ pounds of tuna if you must remove skin, sinew, or bone.

6 SERVINGS

TUNA STEAK AU POIVRE WITH CUCUMBER SAUCE

Steak *au poivre*, a classic French dish, is traditionally made with beef steak. Tuna steaks, however, are an excellent variation; they are meaty, lean, filling, and juicy. It is an easy and fast dish to make, and the sauce can be made ahead and stored in the refrigerator.

CUCUMBER SAUCE
1 cucumber (about 10 ounces)
¾ teaspoon salt
2 teaspoons sugar
½ teaspoon red pepper flakes, or to taste
3 tablespoons cider vinegar
⅓ cup canola or safflower oil
2 teaspoons soy sauce

½ cup water
1 tablespoon black peppercorns (see Note)
2 teaspoons herbes de Provence (see Note, page 48)
6 tuna steaks (each about 6 ounces, 1 inch thick)
½ teaspoon salt
3 tablespoons olive oil

(continued)

Tuna Steak au Poivre with Cucumber Sauce (continued)

Prepare the Sauce: Peel the cucumber, cut it in half lengthwise, and remove the seeds by scraping them out with a spoon. Cut the cucumber halves into pieces and place them in the bowl of a food processor. Add the remaining sauce ingredients and process for a few seconds, until the mixture is chopped fine without being completely liquified. Transfer the sauce to a serving dish and set aside.

Prepare the Tuna: Spread the peppercorns on a work surface, and using a rolling pin or the bottom of a heavy saucepan, crush them. Stir the herbes de Provence into the crushed peppercorns on the work surface, and dip each tuna steak into the mixture, coating them on both sides. Sprinkle the steaks with the salt.

Heat 1 large or 2 medium-size skillets until very hot. Add the oil, spreading it quickly to coat the bottom, and add the steaks. Cook 1 minute on each side. Turn off the heat and allow the skillet(s) to remain on the stove, covered, to steam for 5 to 6 minutes (the interior of the steaks should be medium-rare). Serve immediately, with the cucumber sauce on the side.

Note: Instead of all black peppercorns, try a mixture of black, white, pink, green, and, if you like, Szechuan peppercorns and allspice berries.

6 SERVINGS

THIS PREPARATION ALSO WORKS WELL WITH SWORDFISH STEAK. THE SAUCE CAN BE USED WITH OTHER FISH DISHES, COLD MEAT, AND GRILLED MEAT OR POULTRY.

LEMON SOLE WITH HORSERADISH AND SOUR CREAM SAUCE

The sole is poached here in a little water, which takes only a few minutes since these fillets are so thin. The sauce, also made very quickly, is an unusual combination of flavors. Because there is a lot of horseradish in it, it tends to be a bit grainy; this doesn't detract from its taste, however.

> **THE THIN SOLE FILLETS COOK VERY QUICKLY AND THE SAUCE IS READY IN A MINUTE, SO THIS DISH IS IDEAL WHEN YOU DON'T HAVE MUCH TIME.**

1 cup sour cream
¾ cup water
3 tablespoons freshly grated or 5 tablespoons bottled horseradish
1 tablespoon capers, preferably small, drained
¼ teaspoon freshly ground black pepper
½ teaspoon salt
1½ pounds lemon sole fillets
1 tablespoon chopped cilantro (coriander or Chinese parsley), for garnish

Mix the sour cream, ¼ cup of the water, horseradish, capers, pepper, and salt together in a saucepan. Bring to a boil, and set aside.

Place the fish fillets in a large stainless steel or nonstick skillet and add the remaining ½ cup water. Bring to a boil, and immediately turn the fillets over with a spatula and cook on the other side for about 1 minute. Remove from the heat.

Lift the fish fillets from the skillet and arrange them on individual plates. Coat with the warm sour cream–horseradish sauce, and garnish with the cilantro. Serve immediately.

6 SERVINGS

POULTRY
AND MEAT

Y ou'll find a great variety of poultry, sausage, and meat
dishes here—some elegant, like the Chicken Niçoise in
Puff Pastry, made with packaged puff pastry, and some
exotic, like the Broiled Quail with Coriander Sauce, which takes
only a few minutes to make because the quail come already boned
and ready to broil.

The classic Roast Turkey with Garlic is always warm and
satisfying, especially when served with Cornbread and Ham
Dressing. No one will believe you've used turkey in the Scaloppini
of Turkey with Scallions because it takes on the moistness and
delicacy of veal when prepared this way.

I cook the short ribs for the Braised Short Ribs in Red Wine
Sauce in a pressure cooker; the ribs are wonderfully moist and
the dish is ready in half the time that it would take if the meat
were cooked in the conventional way. The more esoteric Tripe
Ragout also emerges wonderfully from the pressure cooker.

There are soul-satisfying dishes, like the Sausage Stew with
Mustard Greens and Beans and the Choucroute Garni, a specialty

of the Alsace region in France, which is made easily here and a terrific dish to serve at a big party.

Delicious and simple to prepare, the Poulet Cuisses Maison and the Suprêmes of Chicken with Herbes de Provence will never disappoint your guests. For an elegant summer meal, try the Grilled Thyme Veal Chops, which smell of the season and go well with most of the vegetable dishes in the book.

SUPREMES OF CHICKEN WITH HERBES DE PROVENCE

A *suprême* of chicken is a boneless, skinless chicken breast —fortunately available today at almost any supermarket. Virtually fat-free, a *suprême* cooks in a few minutes. The trick is to avoid overcooking it. The best way I've found to do this is to sauté the breasts until they are about three-quarters done, and then set them aside to finish cooking in their own heat. The result is a very tender *suprême,* flavorful and quick to make.

The chicken can be served with a salad, the White Bean Purée (page 206), sautéed potatoes, peas, or almost any vegetable dish in this book.

4 tablespoons (½ stick)
    unsalted butter
4 *skinless, boneless chicken*
    breasts (about 6 ounces
    each)
2 *teaspoons herbes de Provence*
    (see Note, page 48)
½ *teaspoon salt*
½ *teaspoon freshly ground*
    black pepper
2 *teaspoons lime juice*

AVAILABLE ALREADY SKINNED AND BONED AT THE SUPERMARKET, CHICKEN BREASTS MAKE A QUICK AND NUTRITIOUS MEAL.

Melt the butter in a large skillet. Sprinkle the chicken breasts with the herbes de Provence, salt, and pepper. Place them in the foaming butter and cook for approximately 2½ minutes on each side. Then cover the pan and set it aside for 8 to 10 minutes.

Arrange the chicken breasts, whole or sliced, on individual plates. Add the lime juice to the drippings in the pan, bring the mixture to boil, and pour over the chicken. Serve immediately.

4 SERVINGS

CHICKEN AND SPINACH SALAD

This salad is particularly good when made with young spinach—before it develops the very large, fibrous stems that characterize the end-of-season specimens.

1 recipe Suprêmes of Chicken
with Herbes de Provence
(page 162)
4 cups fresh spinach, well
rinsed
¼ cup Mustard Vinaigrette
Dressing (page 26)

Allow the chicken to cool to room temperature in the covered skillet. At serving time, toss the spinach with the dressing and divide it among four plates. Slice the chicken breasts, arrange them in the center of the salad, and sprinkle with the chicken cooking juices. Serve immediately.

4 SERVINGS

POULET CUISSES MAISON

I do this sauté at home and prefer it made with chicken legs rather than breasts—the legs stay more moist in this type of dish. Notice that the chicken is cooked skin side down only, for quite a long time: 20 to 25 minutes. This constitutes a

(continued)

recipe in itself; you can serve the chicken as is right out of the skillet, with a salad alongside. Or if you want to make it a little fancier, discard some of the fat from the skillet, add a little water to melt the solidified juices, and pour this mixture over the chicken.

Here I take the basic recipe a step further, creating a sauce with the chicken drippings (after first removing the chicken so its skin stays crisp).

A good sturdy skillet, preferably heavy aluminum, is important here to ensure that the chicken becomes crusty and brown but doesn't burn.

---

4 chicken legs (2 to 2½ pounds total)
¾ teaspoon salt
½ teaspoon freshly ground black pepper
1 tablespoon corn oil
1 onion, peeled and chopped fine (about ¾ cup)
2 cloves garlic, chopped fine (1 teaspoon)
1 tablespoon red wine vinegar
1 tablespoon balsamic vinegar
2 teaspoons steak sauce
½ cup water
Salt and freshly ground black pepper to taste
1 tablespoon finely chopped parsley, for garnish

With a sharp heavy knife cut off the tips of the chicken drumsticks and discard them. Sprinkle the legs with the salt and pepper.

Heat the oil in a large heavy skillet, and when it is hot, add the chicken legs, skin side down, in one layer. Cook over medium to high heat for about 5 minutes, until the meat has begun to brown. Then cover, reduce the heat to medium-low, and cook for 15 to 20 minutes, until the chicken is well browned and cooked through. Remove the chicken legs from the skillet, arrange them skin side up on an ovenproof plate, and place in a warm oven.

Discard all but 1 to 2 tablespoons of the fat in the skillet. Add the onion and garlic, and cook for about 1 minute. Then stir in both vinegars and the steak sauce. Cook, stirring, for about 1 minute longer, until most of the liquid has evaporated. Add the water and salt and pepper to taste. Cook, stirring to melt and mix in the solidified juices, for 1½ to 2 minutes. Pour the sauce over the chicken, garnish with the parsley, and serve immediately.

4 SERVINGS

GRILLED CHICKEN BREAST WITH SUNFLOWER AND CORIANDER SAUCE

T his dish is quick and easy to prepare. If you cannot cook the chicken on a grill (which gives it a distinctive taste), cook the breasts in a cast-iron skillet over very high heat for approximately the same length of time.

The recipe yields about 2 cups of the Sunflower Coriander Sauce. This can be made ahead and stored in the refrigerator for up to 1 week. It is spicy and invigorating and goes well not only with the chicken breasts, but also with leftover beef, veal, pork, or lamb roasts, fish (poached, steamed, or grilled), and grilled scallops or shrimp.

6 skinless, boneless chicken breasts (about 6 ounces each)
¾ teaspoon salt
¾ teaspoon freshly ground black pepper
1 teaspoon dried thyme, or 2 teaspoons fresh thyme leaves
1 tablespoon virgin olive oil

SUNFLOWER CORIANDER SAUCE
½ to 1 whole jalapeño pepper, or to taste
1 cup lightly packed parsley leaves
1 cup lightly packed cilantro (coriander or Chinese parsley) leaves
6 cloves garlic, peeled (about 1½ tablespoons)
⅓ cup sunflower seeds
1 teaspoon salt

¼ cup virgin olive oil
1 cup water

3 ripe tomatoes (about 1 pound total), thinly sliced

Sprinkle the chicken breasts with the salt, pepper, and thyme; then coat with the oil. Arrange in a single layer on a plate, cover with plastic wrap, and refrigerate for at least 1 hour and as long as 8 hours.

Meanwhile, prepare the sauce: Remove the seeds from the jalapeño pepper and cut the pepper into a few pieces. Place approximately half of all the sauce ingredients in the bowl of a mini-chop: jalapeño pieces, parsley, cilantro, garlic, sunflower seeds, salt, olive oil, and water.

(continued)

Grilled Chicken Breast with Sunflower and Coriander Sauce (continued)

Process until puréed to a smooth green liquid. Transfer the purée to a bowl, and process the remainder of the sauce ingredients. Add the rest of the purée to the bowl. (If you do not have a mini-chop, use a blender; it will do a better job than a food processor.)

At serving time, remove the chicken breasts from the refrigerator and place them on a very hot barbecue grill. Cover, and cook 2½ to 3 minutes on each side, until the chicken is well marked. Move it to a cooler place on the grill, or transfer it to a pan and place in a 250-degree oven. Cover

and let it cook for about 5 minutes in its own heat.

Arrange a few spoonfuls of the sauce (at room temperature) on each of six plates, and top with a grilled chicken breast. Garnish with tomato slices arranged attractively around the border, and serve.

6 SERVINGS

BOTH THE SAUCE AND THE CHICKEN CAN BE PREPARED AHEAD OF TIME, WITH THE GRILLING DONE AT THE LAST MINUTE.

CHICKEN NIÇOISE IN PUFF PASTRY

Packaged pastry shells are very handy. They go directly from the freezer to the oven, and can accommodate a variety of fillings, including shrimp, scallops, vegetables, and scrambled eggs. In this recipe I fill them with chicken in a delicious sauce containing diced black olives—definitely "dressy" enough for company. These oil-cured olives can be used unpitted (warn your guests) or, if you have time, pit them.

To make the pastry shells taste more like a buttery homemade puff paste, rub them with butter before cooking, and cook them longer than suggested on the package, at least 30 minutes in a 400-degree oven. After the shells are cooked, remove the lids with the point of a sharp knife. Inside you will find a soft dough that is cooked but not crisp; remove some of this dough from the center before spooning in the filling.

4 packaged frozen puff pastry
    shells
1 tablespoon unsalted butter, at
    room temperature

FILLING
2 tablespoons unsalted butter
2 tablespoons vegetable oil
4 boneless, skinless chicken
    breasts (about 6 ounces
    each), cut into ½-inch-thick
    strips
¾ teaspoon salt
½ teaspoon freshly ground
    black pepper
2 large shallots, peeled and
    chopped (about ¼ cup)
2 cloves garlic, peeled, crushed,
    and chopped very fine
    (about 1 teaspoon)
2 tablespoons good-quality red
    wine vinegar
1 teaspoon bottled steak sauce
¼ cup water
2 large ripe tomatoes (about 12
    ounces total), halved,
    seeded, drained, and cut
    into ½-inch dice
½ cup (about 20) black oil-
    cured olives, pitted or
    unpitted
1 teaspoon chopped tarragon,
    for garnish

Rub the top and bottom of the frozen puff pastry shells with the room-temperature butter. Place them on a cookie sheet, preferably aluminum, lined with parchment paper. Bake in a 400-degree oven for 30 minutes, until well puffed and quite brown. Turn the oven off, prop the door slightly open, and allow the shells to cool in the warm oven (this enables them to cool slowly and helps keep them from collapsing). When they have cooled enough to handle, remove them from the oven, lift off the lids with the point of a sharp knife, remove some of the soft interior, and then return the shells to the warm oven until serving time.

Meanwhile, prepare the filling: Heat the butter and oil in a large skillet. Sprinkle the chicken strips with the salt and pepper, and place them in the hot skillet. Sauté over high heat for about 1½ minutes, stirring to separate the pieces. Using a slotted spoon, transfer the chicken to a plate. Add the shallots and garlic to the drippings in the skillet, and cook for about 30 seconds. Then add the vinegar, and cook until the mixture begins to sizzle again. Add the steak sauce, water, and the tomatoes, and bring the mixture to a boil. Boil for about 1

(continued)

minute, and then add the olives. Return the chicken to the pan, heat through, and sprinkle the tarragon on top.

Place a pastry shell on each plate, and spoon the chicken mixture into them. Serve immediately.

Note: To prepare this dish ahead, sauté the chicken and prepare the sauce, but do not combine them until just before serving. If you don't have frozen pastry shells on hand, you can serve this plain or on toast.

4 SERVINGS

BAKED CHICKEN WITH MUSTARD CRUMBS

I like the dark meat of chicken and find the legs remain nicely moist when prepared this way. The initial cooking can be done ahead; then the legs are returned to the oven just before serving to finish cooking.

4 chicken legs (about 12 ounces each)
½ teaspoon salt
½ teaspoon freshly ground black pepper
2 or 3 slices of bread
1 tablespoon safflower or corn oil
2 tablespoons Dijon-style mustard

Grasping the skin with a cloth kitchen towel, pull it off the chicken legs. Cut halfway through the joint between the drumstick and thigh. Cut off and discard the tips of the drumsticks. Sprinkle the meat with the salt and pepper, and arrange the legs on an aluminum foil–lined tray. Bake in a 425-degree oven for 12 minutes.

Meanwhile, process the bread in a food processor to form 1¼ cups of crumbs. Lightly mix the bread crumbs with the oil to moisten them.

Remove the chicken from the oven, brush the surface with the mustard, and then pile the bread crumbs on top, pressing lightly to make them adhere. (You can prepare the chicken ahead to this point.)

Return the chicken to the 425-degree oven and continue cooking for 20 to 25 minutes, until the bread crumbs are brown and the meat is tender. Transfer the legs to individual plates and serve immediately, spooning any spilled crumbs alongside the meat.

4 SERVINGS

THESE CHICKEN LEGS CAN BE PREPARED THROUGH THE INITIAL COOKING, THEN FINISHED JUST BEFORE SERVING.

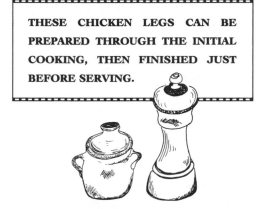

CHICKEN LIVERS PERSILLADE

This quick, easy dish should be prepared at the last moment and served immediately. It makes a nice appetizer for dinner, and can also be served with a salad as the main course for a brunch or light lunch.

Chicken livers are readily available and inexpensive. For best results, cook them over very high heat to seal in their juices, and cook them only briefly—they should still be slightly pink inside. For this recipe, the livers are simply sautéed, mixed with garlic and parsley (a mixture called *persillade*), and served on freshly toasted bread.

4 slices (each ½ inch thick and about 5 inches in diameter) bread from a large French-style country loaf
12 ounces chicken livers (about 14), preferably plump and pale in color
¼ teaspoon salt

¼ teaspoon freshly ground black pepper
3 tablespoons unsalted butter
1 tablespoon safflower or corn oil
4 cloves garlic, chopped fine (2 teaspoons)
1 tablespoon coarsely chopped parsley

(continued)

Chicken Livers Persillade (continued)

Toast the bread and keep it warm.

Separate the livers into two pieces, discarding any connecting sinew, and sprinkle with the salt and pepper. Heat the butter and oil in a nonstick pan at least 9 inches in diameter. When the mixture is a hazelnut color, add the livers in one layer and cook over high heat for 1 minute. Then turn and cook on the other side for 1 minute, taking care to avoid splatters. Add the garlic and par-

> FOR BEST RESULTS, SELECT PALE, PLUMP CHICKEN LIVERS AND COOK THEM FOR ONLY A COUPLE OF MINUTES.

sley, immediately remove the pan from the heat, and mix well.

Place a slice of toast on each plate, top with the livers, and serve immediately.

4 SERVINGS

BROILED QUAIL WITH CORIANDER SAUCE

This recipe will work well with either fresh whole quail (my preference) or frozen boned quail, which is what is usually available at the market. Defrost frozen birds slowly in the refrigerator.

Serve this with Cornmeal Mush with Cheese (page 126), rice, or pasta and a vegetable.

MARINADE
1 tablespoon Worcestershire
*   sauce*
1 tablespoon ketchup
1 tablespoon honey
½ teaspoon Tabasco sauce
½ teaspoon ground coriander

4 quail (each about 6 ounces
*   whole, 4½ to 5 ounces boned)*

2 tablespoons water

> COMBINE THE MARINADE INGREDIENTS DIRECTLY IN THE PLASTIC BAG SO YOU WON'T HAVE TO WASH A MIXING BOWL.

Combine the marinade ingredients in a large plastic bag and shake to mix well. Add the quail, and toss to coat with the marinade. Seal the bag and set it aside, rotating it occasionally, for at least 2 hours.

When you are ready to cook them, remove the quail from the marinade and arrange them in a foil-lined baking pan. Broil about 5 inches from the heat for 4 to 5 minutes. Turn, and broil for 4 to 5 minutes on the other side. Remove and set aside on individual plates in a warm place.

Place the water in the baking pan and stir to dissolve any solidified juices sticking to the foil. Pour the juices over the quail, and serve.

4 SERVINGS

ROAST TURKEY WITH GARLIC

I enjoy turkey at all times of the year, but especially over holiday periods, when it is available fresh in most markets, and when my brother, Roland, visits from France.

I like small turkeys—about 12 pounds—because they cook quickly and remain moist. I cook the turkey mostly upside down. I start it breast side up to brown the skin, but then turn it over; the juices naturally flow through the breast if the bird is cooked in this position, and the turkey comes out moist without basting.

I cook the dressing separate from the turkey; the turkey cooks faster because the heat can circulate through the cavity.

1 small turkey (12 pounds)
2 cups water
1 medium-size head garlic
½ teaspoon salt
½ teaspoon freshly ground
  black pepper
3 onions (about 12 ounces
  total), peeled and cut into
  1-inch dice

3 carrots (8 ounces total),
  peeled and cut into ½-inch
  dice
1 teaspoon potato starch
  dissolved in 1 tablespoon
  water
1 tablespoon soy sauce

(continued)

Roast Turkey with Garlic (continued)

Remove the neck, gizzard, heart, and liver from the turkey and place them in a saucepan. Add the water and bring to a boil. Cover, reduce the heat, and cook over low heat for about 1 hour. Drain, reserving the liquid and the solids separately (you should have about 1½ cups of liquid). Set aside.

Meanwhile, rinse the turkey thoroughly under cool water and pat it dry with paper towels. Peel 3 large cloves of garlic and cut them into slivers (about 12 total). Making small incisions here and there around the breast and leg, insert the garlic slivers under the skin of the turkey and even into the flesh. Sprinkle the salt and pepper on the turkey, inside and out.

Place the turkey, breast side up, in a large roasting pan and bake in a 425-degree oven for about 20 minutes, until nicely browned on top.

Using pot holders, turn the turkey so it is breast side down. Arrange the onions, carrots, and the remainder of the garlic cloves (unpeeled) around it. Reduce the oven temperature to 325 degrees. Cook for 1 hour.

Add the 1½ cups reserved cooking liquid, and bake for another 30 minutes. Turn the oven off, and let the turkey rest in the warm oven while you complete the rest of the preparations.

Pull the meat from the reserved turkey neck, and cut the liver, neck, and heart into ¼-inch dice. Set aside.

Transfer the turkey to an ovenproof platter, and return it to the warm oven. Strain the vegetables and cooking juices from the roasting pan through a sieve into a saucepan. (If you want to include the puréed vegetables in your gravy, strain them through a food mill.) Let the sauce rest for 4 to 5 minutes, until most of the fat has risen to the top, and then skim off as much fat as possible (at least 1 to 1½ cups). You should have approximately 2 cups of defatted juices remaining. Add the chopped neck meat and giblets, and simmer the mixture for 10 minutes to reduce it slightly. Stir in the dissolved potato starch and the soy sauce.

Carve the turkey, and serve it with the gravy, Cornbread and Ham Dressing (page 173), and a salad.

Note: Use leftover turkey meat instead of chicken in salads (see page 107), and add the bones when you are making chicken stock (page 48).

8 TO 10 SERVINGS

CORNBREAD AND HAM DRESSING

This is good with goose and pork and excellent, of course, with turkey (see page 171); spoon it onto individual plates, place slices of dark and white turkey meat over it, and ladle on some gravy.

You can make your own cornbread for this recipe, but I often use packaged cornbread from the supermarket. If you can't find cornbread, buy corn muffins, selecting those with the least amount of sugar. I like to add some ham and scallions to the crumbled cornbread, with just enough stock to moisten the mixture; it should be crumbly, not gooey. The dressing can be prepared ahead.

4 tablespoons (½ stick) unsalted butter
1 onion, peeled and coarsely chopped (1 cup)
2 ribs celery, cleaned and cut into ¼-inch dice (¾ cup)
5 scallions, cleaned and minced (about ¾ cup)
12 ounces cornbread or corn muffins, crumbled
1 cup fresh or frozen corn kernels
2 teaspoons herbes de Provence (see Note, page 48)
½ teaspoon freshly ground black pepper
3 slices ham (3 ounces total), cut into ½-inch pieces
¼ cup fresh or frozen homemade chicken stock (see Basic Chicken Stock, page 48) or canned chicken broth

Heat the butter in a skillet. When it is hot, add the onion, celery, and scallions, and sauté over medium-high heat for about 3 minutes. Transfer the vegetables to a bowl and add the crumbled cornbread or muffins, corn kernels, herbes de Provence, pepper, ham, and chicken stock. Toss lightly and place in a 6-cup loaf pan. Bake in a 350-degree oven for about 20 minutes, until nicely browned on top and hot inside.

6 TO 8 SERVINGS

YOU CAN MAKE YOUR OWN CORN-BREAD FOR THIS RECIPE, BUT PACKAGED CORNBREAD OR CORN MUFFINS FROM THE SUPERMARKET WORK VERY WELL TOO.

SCALOPPINI OF TURKEY
WITH SCALLIONS

Veal scaloppini are very expensive so I often substitute turkey, either cutting a whole fresh turkey breast into thin slices or buying it already cut and packaged, as it is available now at the supermarket. These take only a few minutes to sauté; in fact, the most common mistake you can make when preparing scaloppini—both veal and turkey—is to overcook them. These thin pieces of meat will remain moist, tender, and delicious if cooked only 1½ to 2 minutes per side.

The dish can be made 15 to 30 minutes ahead and kept warm in a 170- to 180-degree oven. If you are preparing it more than 30 minutes ahead, reduce the cooking time so the turkey doesn't overcook when you reheat it later. Veal scaloppini can be prepared in exactly the same manner.

1 tablespoon virgin olive oil
1 tablespoon unsalted butter
¾ teaspoon freshly ground
    black pepper
¾ teaspoon salt
1 pound (about 4) turkey
    scaloppini, ½ inch thick
6 scallions, tops removed,
    cleaned and minced (about
    1 cup)
2 cloves garlic, peeled and
    chopped fine (about 1
    teaspoon)

¼ cup fresh or frozen
    homemade chicken stock
    (see Basic Chicken Stock,
    page 48), canned chicken
    broth, or water

Heat the oil and butter in a large skillet (about 12 inches in diameter and preferably non-stick). Meanwhile, sprinkle half the pepper and salt on the scaloppini. When the mixture is hot, add the scaloppini and sauté over medium to high heat for no more than 2 minutes on each side. Remove the scaloppini from the pan, arrange them on a serving platter, and set aside in a warm place.

Add the scallions and garlic to the drippings in the pan, and

THIS DISH CAN BE MADE AHEAD, BUT UNDERCOOK THE SCALOPPINI A LITTLE SO THEY DON'T DRY OUT WHEN REHEATED LATER.

sauté about 10 seconds. Then add the chicken stock and the remainder of the salt and pepper. Cook, stirring to loosen and dissolve any solidified juices, for about 45 seconds, until some of the moisture has evaporated. Pour the mixture over the scaloppini and serve immediately.

4 SERVINGS

CASSOULET OF SAUSAGES

assoulet is a famous dish from southwestern France. It always contains white beans and usually some type of poultry—either duck or goose—as well as roast pork, veal, or lamb and sausages.

This satisfying simplified version is easily made with sausages and canned white kidney beans (cannellini) from the supermarket. I serve it in large individual soup bowls, but you could also prepare it in a large soup tureen and spoon it into individual bowls at the table. The ingredients can be assembled in the bowls and refrigerated, ready to cook, the night before serving; the cassoulet will then take slightly longer to cook since the ingredients will be cold.

1 tablespoon olive oil
¼ cup water
4 sweet Italian-style sausages
    (12 ounces)
1 onion, peeled and sliced thin
    (about 1 cup)
5 scallions, cleaned and cut into
    ½-inch pieces (about ¾
    cup)
2 cloves garlic, peeled and
    sliced (about 2 teaspoons)
2 cans (1 pound each) white
    kidney beans

1 teaspoon herbes de Provence
    (see Note, page 48)
½ teaspoon Tabasco sauce
8 ounces kielbasa sausage,
    peeled if the skin is tough,
    and cut into 4 pieces
8 ounces Canadian bacon, cut
    into 4 pieces
3 slices bread
2 tablespoons safflower or corn
    oil

(continued)

Cassoulet of Sausages (continued)

> **TO AVOID LAST-MINUTE WORK, PLACE INGREDIENTS IN BOWLS THE NIGHT BEFORE AND REFRIGERATE UNTIL READY TO COOK.**

Place the olive oil and the water in a large saucepan and add the Italian sausages. Cook over medium to high heat for about 10 minutes, shaking the pan occasionally so the sausages roll over and cook on all sides.

When most of the moisture has evaporated and the sausages are browning, add the onion, scallions, and garlic. Sauté for about 30 seconds. Then add the beans with their liquid, and the herbes de Provence, Tabasco, kielbasa, and Canadian bacon. Cover, bring to a boil, and cook for 15 minutes. Set aside off the heat.

Meanwhile, process the bread in a food processor to produce 1½ cups of crumbs.

Lightly toss the bread crumbs with the corn oil. Spoon the Ital-ian sausage, kielbasa, and Canadian bacon into four large (2½-cup) ovenproof soup bowls, and cover with the beans and juice, filling the bowls to within ¾ inch of the top. (Make sure the beans are submerged in liquid; add water or chicken stock if necessary to make the mixture slightly "soupy," because it will tend to dry out in the oven.) Sprinkle the bread crumbs over the beans, and arrange the bowls on a foil-lined baking sheet. Bake in a 400-degree oven for 30 minutes, until the mixture is bubbling and very hot. If you want the crumbs a little more brown, set the oven control to "broil" and place the bowls under the broiler.

Note: The cassoulet can be made ahead and refrigerated. Bake it for approximately 40 minutes, and then finish under the broiler if desired. Leftover roast pork, veal, or lamb can also be used in place of the sausages.

4 SERVINGS

LENTIL AND SAUSAGE STEW

 great deal can be done with sausage from the supermarket, whether it be cooked Polish-style kielbasa, link sausage, freshly ground seasoned pork patties, or Italian-style sausages made with seasoned ground pork. I especially like the taste of hot Italian sausage and eat it often at home, sometimes grilled, sometimes cooked in a stew, used in soup, or added to salads.

This recipe makes enough for 8 to 10 servings. Any leftover stew will keep up to a week in the refrigerator and weeks in the freezer. The best way to reheat the stew is in a microwave oven, although it can be reheated over low heat on a conventional stove—just add a little water to keep it from sticking.

Serve this stew with some Dijon mustard on the side. A green salad is all you need as an accompaniment.

1½ pounds hot Italian sausages
5½ cups water
1 pound dried lentils
3 large cloves garlic, peeled and chopped
1 large onion (6 ounces), peeled and cut into 8 pieces
2 carrots (about 6 ounces total), peeled and cut into ½-inch pieces
1 teaspoon Italian seasoning
1 jalapeño pepper, minced (optional)
½ cup dry white wine
1 chicken bouillon cube

Cut the sausages into 1½-inch pieces, and place them in a large deep saucepan or Dutch oven. Add ½ cup of the water and bring to a boil over high heat. Cover, and cook for 5 minutes, by which time the sausages will have released some fat. Uncover the pan and continue cooking until all the moisture has evaporated and the sausages are frying in their own fat. Fry for about 2 minutes.

Meanwhile, rinse the lentils under cold water. Add them to the pan with the remaining 5 cups water and all the other ingredients. Mix well and bring to a boil. Then cover the pan, reduce the heat to very low, and boil very gently for 40 to 45 minutes, until most of the liquid has been absorbed and the lentils are cooked.

8 TO 10 SERVINGS

Cream of Lentil Soup Purée leftover Lentil and Sausage Stew in a food processor, adding chicken stock or water to thin it to the consistency of a soup. Season with salt and pepper to taste, ladle into soup bowls, sprinkle with grated Swiss cheese, and serve with crusty French bread.

SAUSAGE STEW WITH MUSTARD GREENS AND BEANS

T his one-dish meal is a familiar feature at our house. It is easy to make, using canned beans, frozen mustard greens, and hot Italian sausage meat from the supermarket. You could substitute spinach or another green vegetable for the mustard greens if you prefer.

This dish can be frozen and is good reheated—most easily done in a microwave oven.

Serve this with a salad and crunchy French bread.

1¼ pounds hot Italian sausage meat
2 onions (about 8 ounces total), peeled and quartered
2 cans (1 pound each) red kidney beans
1 small jalapeño pepper, minced (optional)
1 teaspoon ground cumin
1 package (10 ounces) frozen chopped mustard greens

Divide the sausage meat into pieces. Dampen your hands, and form the pieces into balls, each about 1½ ounces. Heat a large cast-iron Dutch oven or saucepan over medium to low heat, and place the meatballs in the pan. Cook for about 20 minutes, covered, turning them over every 5 minutes. The sausage will release its juices during the first 10 minutes of cooking. After another 10, the meatballs will begin to brown.

At this point add the onions, and cook for 10 minutes. Then add the beans with their liquid, the jalapeño pepper, and the cumin. Bring to a boil, cover, and boil gently for 10 minutes. Add the mustard greens, allowing them to thaw for a few minutes in the hot liquid before breaking them apart. Cover and cook for 10 minutes longer, or for a total of 50 minutes.

6 SERVINGS

LOIN OF PORK WITH PORT AND PRUNES

Boneless pork loin steaks can be sautéed quickly for a delightful entrée. Pork is rich and so is complemented quite well by the prunes and sweet port wine in this sauce.

1 cup (4 ounces) pitted prunes
½ cup water
1½ tablespoons unsalted butter
4 boneless pork loin steaks (about 4 ounces each), ¾ inch thick
⅓ cup port wine
1 tablespoon bottled steak sauce
½ teaspoon freshly ground black pepper
¼ teaspoon salt

Combine the prunes and water in a bowl and heat in a microwave oven for about 2½ minutes (or combine the ingredients in a saucepan and boil, covered, for 4 to 5 minutes). Set aside.

Heat the butter in a skillet, and when it is hot, sauté the pork over medium to high heat for about 3 minutes on each side. Remove to a platter and set aside.

Add the port wine to the drippings in the pan, and boil for about 1 minute. Then add the steak sauce and the prunes with their cooking liquid. Bring to a boil, add the pepper and salt, and simmer for about 2 minutes.

Arrange a tenderloin on each plate, coat with the sauce, and serve.

4 SERVINGS

THIS ELEGANT BUT EASY ENTREE CAN BE PREPARED IN HALF AN HOUR.

CHOUCROUTE GARNIE

Choucroute (sauerkraut) with a sausage garnish is a popular specialty of Alsace, in northeastern France. Unlike the very crunchy sauerkraut that is served almost like a

(continued)

Choucroute Garnie (continued)

pickle in sandwiches in the U.S., this sauerkraut is cooked a long time, which gives it a mild, nutty taste. Flavored with juniper berries, it is served with different sausages, ham, and potatoes. It is usually cooked ahead and the garnishes added near the end of the cooking period, making it an ideal dish for a large party. It is particularly good served with hot mustard, black or rye bread, and a cold white wine from Alsace, such as a Pinot Blanc, Traminer, or Sylvaner.

---

3 slices bacon (about 2 ounces)
1 onion (about 6 ounces), peeled and sliced thin (½ cup)
1 bag (2 pounds) sauerkraut in brine (without sugar)
1 can (13¾ ounces) chicken broth
12 juniper berries
3 bay leaves
¼ teaspoon freshly ground black pepper
½ cup dry white wine, preferably from Alsace
4 potatoes (3 to 4 ounces each), peeled and set aside in water to cover
1 pound cooked ham, cut into 4 or 5 pieces
4 bratwurst
4 knockwurst

Cut the bacon into ¼-inch pieces, and place in a Dutch oven or pot large enough to hold the sauerkraut, potatoes, and meat. Cook over medium to high heat for 2 to 3 minutes, until the bacon is lightly browned and has ren-

dered some of its fat. Add the onion and sauté for 7 or 8 minutes.

Meanwhile, drain the sauerkraut in a sieve and rinse it briefly under cool tap water. Press it lightly between your palms to extract more liquid. Then add it to the pot along with the chicken broth, juniper berries, bay leaves, pepper, and wine. Bring to a boil, cover, reduce the heat to very low, and boil gently for 45 minutes. (The recipe can be prepared to this point up to a couple of days ahead; cool, cover, and refrigerate.)

Add the drained potatoes and the ham, and cook over medium heat, covered, for 20 minutes. Then add the bratwurst and knockwurst and cook for 10 minutes longer. Serve from the pot.

4 SERVINGS

SINCE THIS CAN BE PARTIALLY PREPARED AHEAD, IT IS AN IDEAL PARTY DISH.

GRILLED ROSEMARY PORK CHOPS

I like to grill food outside on the barbecue, especially in the summer when it's hot inside the house. Most often, I use a large gas grill with a domed lid.

Pork chops are as good grilled as they are sautéed, providing they are not overcooked. Buy thick loin chops and cook them over medium-high heat just until they are nicely crusted and brown on both sides. Then let them continue to cook in their own heat —this way, the meat will relax and become more tender. The center should be slightly pink and the meat juicy.

4 pork chops (about 8 ounces each), 1 to 1¼ inches thick
2 teaspoons chopped rosemary leaves, or ½ teaspoon chopped or broken dried rosemary
½ teaspoon freshly ground black pepper
¼ teaspoon salt
4 teaspoons corn or canola oil

Sprinkle the pork chops with the rosemary, pepper, and salt. Pour the oil onto a plate and dip the chops into the oil, just moistening them on both sides. If you will not be cooking immediately, cover with plastic wrap and set aside for up to 2 hours.

Heat your grill and arrange the rack so that it is 6 to 8 inches from the heat (the rack should be very clean). Place the chops on the rack, cover with the grill lid, and cook for 6 minutes. Then turn the chops and cook them, covered, for 6 minutes on the other side. Transfer them to the far side of the grill if possible, or to a platter, and place in a 180-degree oven. Keep warm for 10 to 15 minutes. Then serve.

4 SERVINGS

FOR TENDER, JUICY PORK CHOPS, AFTER GRILLING SET THEM ASIDE IN A WARM PLACE TO CONTINUE COOKING IN THEIR OWN HEAT.

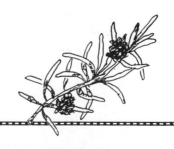

PORK STEW A LA SAIGON

S easoned with five-spice powder, available now in most supermarkets, this stew has a pronounced Oriental taste. (You
can make your own five-spice powder by combining star
anise, cinnamon, cloves, Szechuan peppercorns, and anise seed.)
Honey adds sweetness to the dish.

To ensure a good transfer of heat, the stew should be cooked
in a big heavy pot. The ideal choice would be an attractive cast-
iron pot, so the stew can go directly from the stove to the table.

Serve rice, potatoes, or pasta alongside.

---

3 pounds boneless pork
    shoulder or butt
2 tablespoons vegetable oil
2 onions (about 8 ounces total),
    coarsely chopped (about 2
    cups)
3 large cloves garlic, peeled,
    crushed, and chopped
    (about 1 tablespoon)
2 teaspoons all-purpose flour
2 teaspoons five-spice powder
2 tablespoons dark soy sauce
2 tablespoons honey
1 tablespoon Worcestershire
    sauce
1 cup water
½ teaspoon freshly ground
    black pepper
½ teaspoon salt
1 can (8 ounces) baby corn
    (about 24 small ears),
    drained
1 cup canned sliced bamboo
    shoots

1 can (16 ounces) straw
    mushrooms, drained (about
    1½ cups)
1 tablespoon chopped chives

Cut the pork into 2-inch cubes.
(Remove large layers of fat from
the exterior, but do not cut away
interior fat. It adds moistness and
flavor.) You should have approximately 18 cubes.

Heat the oil in a large sturdy
saucepan or Dutch oven. When it
is hot, add the pork cubes in one
layer. Cover, and brown over high
heat, turning the meat occasionally, for about 15 minutes. (The
meat will not brown immediately; it will release moisture and
steam for 7 to 8 minutes, at which
point the moisture will have
evaporated and the meat will begin to brown.)

Add the onions, garlic, flour,
and five-spice powder. Stir well.

Then mix in the soy sauce, honey, Worcestershire sauce, water, pepper, and salt. Bring to a boil, lower the heat, and cook over very low heat, covered, for 1 hour.

Stir in the corn, bamboo shoots, and straw mushrooms, and simmer for 5 minutes. Sprinkle with the chopped chives, and serve.

Note: This stew freezes well, so consider doubling or tripling the recipe and freezing the excess. Hold out the baby corn, bamboo shoots, and straw mushrooms, however; add them just before serving. The best way to reheat is portion by portion in a microwave oven.

6 SERVINGS

FILLET OF PORK CHARCUTIERE

T hese pork fillets are served with a spicy sauce that contains *cornichons*, sour French gherkins. You'll notice that the pork is not cooked for very long; the amount of fat in the meat is minimal—only about as much as in chicken meat—so it cooks quickly and can be eaten while still slightly pink inside.

2 pork fillets, cleaned of any
    surrounding fat or filament
    (about 1½ pounds total,
    cleaned)
¼ teaspoon salt
¼ teaspoon freshly ground
    black pepper
2 tablespoons unsalted butter
1 onion (6 ounces), chopped
    (1 cup)
4 cloves garlic, chopped (2
    teaspoons)
3 tablespoons red wine vinegar
1 medium-size tomato, cut into
    ¼-inch pieces (about 1 cup)

¼ cup ketchup
2 tablespoons bottled steak
    sauce
½ cup water
2 teaspoons thinly sliced
    French sour gherkins
    (cornichons)
½ teaspoon Tabasco sauce

> **THERE'S NOT MUCH FAT IN THESE
> PORK FILLETS, SO THEY COOK
> QUICKLY AND CAN BE EATEN WHILE
> STILL SLIGHTLY PINK INSIDE.**

(continued)

Fillet of Pork Charcutière (continued)

Sprinkle the pork fillets with the salt and pepper. Heat the butter in a skillet, and when it is hot, add the fillets. Cover and sauté over medium heat, turning occasionally, until nicely browned on all sides. Transfer the meat to a plate and keep warm in a 180-degree oven while you make the sauce.

Add the onion to the drippings in the skillet and cook for 30 seconds. Then add the garlic and cook for 10 seconds. Add the vinegar and boil until it has

evaporated. Stir in the tomato, ketchup, steak sauce, and water, and bring to a boil. Add the *cornichons* and the Tabasco sauce, and remove from the heat. Cut each fillet into three pieces and serve, one per person, with the sauce.

Note: You can cook the meat and sauce ahead of time. Reheat the pork briefly in the sauce before serving.

6 SERVINGS

BROILED HAM STEAKS

I often buy ham shoulders, the precooked boneless hams that are available at the supermarket. They are good in sandwiches or cooked with peas or lentils (see pages 202 and 221), and they can also be sliced into steaks. These cook in a few minutes under the broiler and are quite flavorful. They are especially good served with Steamed Cauliflower with Lemon Butter (page 208) or Zucchini Flan (page 238), as well as with potato dishes.

4 small ham steaks (about 1 pound total), ½ inch thick, from a ready-to-eat boneless cooked ham
2 tablespoons ketchup
4 teaspoons brown sugar
¼ teaspoon Tabasco sauce

1 teaspoon dry mustard

THESE FLAVORFUL HAM STEAKS COOK IN A FEW MINUTES UNDER THE BROILER.

Arrange the ham steaks on a foil-lined baking sheet. Mix together the ketchup, brown sugar, Tabasco sauce, and mustard, and spread this evenly over the steaks.

Place under a preheated broiler, about 5 inches from the heat, and cook, for about 10 minutes, until nicely browned.

4 SERVINGS

ROAST LEG OF LAMB WITH GARLIC

Now and then my supermarket has small boned and tied roasts of lamb from the leg, and that is what I use in this recipe. Weighing about 2½ pounds—more than enough for six people—the roast should be well trimmed, with only a thin layer of fat on top.

Try to get a roast that is plump and round so it will yield equal-size slices. The one I used here was about 6 inches long and 5 inches in diameter, and the roasting time produced a medium-rare meat. If your roast is of slightly different dimensions, or if you prefer your lamb cooked more or less than suggested here, adjust the cooking time accordingly—keeping in mind that the amount of time you let the meat rest after cooking is important, too. A roast like this one needs to rest for at least 15 minutes to be appealingly pink throughout. If need be, it can be kept for as long as 45 minutes to 1 hour in a 170-degree oven.

This dish is particularly good with Mashed Potatoes and Garlic (page 226), roasted potatoes, or noodles.

1 boned roast of lamb from the leg, trimmed and tied (2½ pounds)
2 to 3 large cloves garlic, peeled and cut diagonally into wedges (about 12 total)
½ teaspoon salt

½ teaspoon freshly ground black pepper
1 tablespoon olive oil
⅓ cup water
1½ teaspoons bottled steak sauce
1 tablespoon ketchup

(continued)

Roast Leg of Lamb with Garlic (continued)

Place the roast in a heavy ovenproof pan. With the point of a knife, puncture it all around in about twelve places, and push the garlic slivers into the holes. Sprinkle with the salt, pepper, and olive oil. Cook in a 425-degree oven for 30 minutes, then turn the meat and cook another 30 minutes. (At this point the internal temperature of the meat will be about 120 degrees.)

Meanwhile, stir together the water, steak sauce, and ketchup.

Pour out most of the fat from around the meat, leaving about 1 tablespoon in the bottom of the pan. Stir the ketchup mixture into the remaining fat and drippings in the pan, and return the meat to the oven for 5 minutes to cook the sauce. Remove the pan from the oven and allow the meat to rest for 15 to 20 minutes.

If you are not going to serve the meat right away, arrange a piece of aluminum foil loosely over the top and set the roast aside in a warm place. At serving time, slice the meat and serve it with some of the sauce.

6 SERVINGS

AFTER COOKING, THIS ROAST WILL REMAIN MOIST AND FLAVORFUL FOR UP TO AN HOUR IN A 170-DEGREE OVEN.

BROILED MARINATED LAMB CHOPS

Large shoulder lamb chops, which are very flavorful and much less expensive than the small center-cut chops from the loin, are very good prepared this way. If you'd rather use the smaller chops, however, substitute two of them for one of the larger chops.

Although the chops can be coated with the marinade at the last minute and broiled directly, the result is better if you marinate the meat for at least a couple of hours.

MIX THE MARINADE INGREDIENTS RIGHT IN THE PLASTIC BAG IN WHICH YOU WILL MARINATE THE CHOPS.

MARINADE
6 scallions, cleaned and chopped fine (1 cup)
4 cloves garlic, peeled, crushed and chopped fine (2 teaspoons)
3 or 4 strips of lemon peel (removed with a vegetable peeler), sliced into fine julienne
2 tablespoons Hot Red Salsa (page 23)
2 tablespoons safflower or corn oil
2 tablespoons soy sauce
4 shoulder lamb chops (7 to 8 ounces each), or 8 center-cut loin chops

Place all the marinade ingredients in a plastic bag and shake the bag to combine them. Add the lamb chops, and allow them to marinate for 2 to 3 hours at room temperature.

When you are ready to cook the chops, line a cookie sheet with aluminum foil. Remove the chops from the marinade (reserve the marinade), and place them on the foil-lined sheet. Broil about 5 inches from the heat for 5 minutes, then turn and cook on the other side for 5 minutes. Transfer the chops to individual plates, pour the reserved marinade over them, and serve immediately.

4 SERVINGS

LAMB SHANKS AND SPLIT PEA PUREE

This hearty stew can be prepared in a little over an hour in a pressure cooker.

Lamb shanks are readily available in supermarkets; they are at least 50 percent bone and are sometimes fatty. Be sure

(continued)

Lamb Shanks and Split Pea Purée (continued)

to remove most of the fat, but leave the silver skin on the meat. The shanks are browned in the pressure cooker until crusty on all sides, which imparts a lot of flavor to the dish.

---

4 lamb shanks (about 1 pound each)
1 package (16 ounces) dry split peas
About 2 onions (8 ounces total), peeled and cut into 2-inch pieces (about 1½ cups)
2 carrots (4 ounces total), peeled and cut into ½-inch pieces (about ¾ cup)
4 cloves garlic, peeled and sliced thin (about 2 tablespoons)
2 teaspoons herbes de Provence (see Note, page 48)
½ cup dry white wine
3 cups water
½ teaspoon freshly ground black pepper
1½ teaspoons salt

Trim the shanks to remove most of the surrounding fat, and place them in a pressure cooker. Cook covered (but not under pressure) over low to medium heat for 30 minutes, turning every 5 ·or 10 minutes, until brown on all sides.

Place the split peas in a sieve and rinse them under cool water. Drain the fat from the pressure cooker, and add the peas and the remainder of the ingredients.

Bring the mixture to a boil, stir, and cover. Bring the cooker to the appropriate pressure, following the manufacturer's guidelines. Cook for about 45 minutes.

Depressurize the cooker (again, according to the manufacturer's instructions), and serve directly from the pot.

Note: Leftovers reheat well in a microwave oven, or they can be transformed into soup.

4 SERVINGS

Split Pea Soup with Croutons
To make the soup, break the leftover meat into smaller pieces and discard any bones. Add enough water or chicken stock to thin the mixture to the desired consistency, and bring to a boil. Season with additional salt, pepper, and a dash of Tabasco sauce if desired, and serve with croutons.

COVER THE PAN WHEN YOU BROWN THE SHANKS TO PREVENT SPLATTERS.

SAUTEED LAMB CHOPS WITH SPINACH

I use shoulder lamb chops here; they are large, flavorful, and much less expensive than loin chops, which makes them quite satisfactory for serving to family. For a fancy party, make this recipe with small loin chops and serve two per person.

Although fresh spinach would be welcome, I use packaged frozen spinach because it is so convenient. I always have some on hand in the freezer, ready for recipes such as this.

*1 package (16 ounces) frozen
    leaf spinach*
2 tablespoons unsalted butter
*4 shoulder lamb chops (about
    1½ pounds total), about ½
    inch thick*
¾ teaspoon salt
*¾ teaspoon freshly ground
    black pepper*
¼ cup chopped onion
¼ teaspoon ground nutmeg

KEEP FROZEN SPINACH ON HAND FOR IMMEDIATE USE IN RECIPES SUCH AS THIS.

Place the frozen spinach in a sieve and rinse it under warm tap water to remove the ice crystals and partially defrost it. Set it aside to drain.

Meanwhile, heat the butter in a skillet. Sprinkle the chops with ¼ teaspoon each of the salt and pepper. When the butter is hot, add the chops and sauté over medium heat for about 3 minutes a side, until medium-rare. Transfer them to a platter and keep warm.

Add the onion to the drippings in the skillet, and sauté for 1 minute.

Press the spinach leaves between your palms to extract the excess water, and add the spinach to the skillet with the remaining ½ teaspoon each of salt and pepper and the nutmeg. Mix well and sauté for 2 to 3 minutes, until most of the water has evaporated from the spinach and the mixture is heated through.

Arrange the spinach on individual plates, place a lamb chop on top, and serve immediately.

4 SERVINGS

PIQUANT LAMB CURRY

This lamb curry is made in a pressure cooker, and for an informal family meal, can be served directly from it. After the pressure has built up, it takes 30 minutes—compared to at least 1 hour in a Dutch oven. You can make the curry ahead, either refrigerate or freeze it, and then reheat.

I have flavored this curry in the conventional way with onion, garlic, and ginger, but have also added banana and apple, for a somewhat different taste. I prefer to use a soft, white-fleshed apple, like a McIntosh or Rome Beauty, and I leave the skin on to lend some texture. Apple cider intensifies the flavor.

Serve this over rice, plain noodles, or potatoes.

2 tablespoons unsalted butter
2 pounds lean boneless lamb,
    cut into 1- to 2-inch cubes
1 tablespoon all-purpose flour
1½ tablespoons curry powder
1 teaspoon ground cumin
2 onions (6 ounces total),
    peeled and cut into 1-inch
    pieces (1½ cups)
4 cloves garlic, chopped (1
    tablespoon)
1 tablespoon chopped ginger
1 banana, peeled and sliced
2 small apples (about 8 ounces
    total), cored and cut into
    1-inch dice
1½ cups apple cider, chicken
    stock, or water
1½ teaspoons salt

Heat the butter in a pressure cooker, and when it is hot, add the meat. Cook over high heat for 15 minutes, stirring every 2 to 3 minutes, until the meat is seared and lightly browned on all sides. Add the flour, curry, and cumin and mix well. Then add the remainder of the ingredients, mix well, and bring to a boil, stirring. Cover with the lid and, following the manufacturer's instructions, bring up to the correct pressure. When proper pressure is reached, reduce the heat to very low and cook for 30 minutes.

4 SERVINGS

MAKING THIS CURRY IN A PRES-SURE COOKER CUTS THE COOKING TIME IN HALF.

VEAL CHOPS IN COGNAC AND MUSHROOM SAUCE

Composed of veal chops from the center loin in a rich sauce of cream and mushrooms, this dish is ideal for a special-occasion dinner. Although the chops are best prepared at the last moment, if you are careful not to overcook them, they can be cooked a few hours ahead and coated with the sauce. Reheat at the last minute in a microwave oven or on top of the stove for 3 to 4 minutes, just until the dish is heated through.

> **IF IT'S MORE CONVENIENT, COOK THE CHOPS AHEAD AND JUST RE-WARM THEM AT SERVING TIME.**

4 center-cut veal chops (10 to 12 ounces each), about 1¼ inches thick
½ teaspoon salt
½ teaspoon freshly ground black pepper
2 tablespoons unsalted butter
3 or 4 shallots, chopped (½ cup)
8 ounces mushrooms, sliced (about 3½ cups)
1 tablespoon cognac
⅔ cup heavy cream
¼ cup shredded basil leaves, for garnish

Sprinkle the chops with ¼ teaspoon each of the salt and pepper. Heat the butter in a heavy skillet or saucepan, and when it is hot, add the chops. Sauté, uncovered, over medium to high heat for 5 minutes, until nicely browned. Turn, cover, reduce the heat to low, and cook for 5 minutes on the other side. (At this point they should be medium-rare.) Place the chops on a serving platter and set it aside in a warm place while you make the sauce.

Add the shallots to the drippings in the pan, and sauté for about 30 seconds. Then add the mushrooms and cognac, and sauté for about 1 minute. Add the cream and simmer for about 1 minute longer. Stir in the remainder of the salt and pepper. Pour the sauce over the chops, sprinkle with the basil, and serve immediately.

4 SERVINGS

GRILLED THYME VEAL CHOPS

When cooking meat or fish on a barbecue grill, always be certain that the grill rack is very clean. This helps prevent the food from sticking. My grill has a lid, which makes it work like an oven and helps in the cooking.

The most common mistake in preparing veal chops is over-cooking—they take only a few minutes. When grilled, they should be well browned on the outside but still juicy and pink inside. The cooking time will be determined, of course, by the thickness of the chops.

Rib veal chops are usually less expensive than loin chops, which are like small porterhouse steaks with a fillet and the loin. Rib chops are more expensive than shoulder blade chops. All three cuts are quite good, so make your choice based on availability, preference, and price.

This goes well with most vegetables, from Green Beans and Shallots (page 204), to Peas and Lettuce (page 222), to most potato dishes.

---

2 tablespoons virgin olive oil
4 veal chops (8 ounces each),
    cut about ½ inch thick
    (bone in)
2 teaspoons fresh thyme leaves,
    or 1 teaspoon dried thyme
½ teaspoon freshly ground
    black pepper
¼ teaspoon salt

Heat your barbecue grill and place the rack (which should be very clean) 3 to 4 inches above the heat.

Place the olive oil on a large plate. Sprinkle the veal chops on both sides with the thyme, pep-per, and salt, and then dip them (both sides) in the olive oil. Place the chops on the hot grill, lower the lid, and cook for 2½ minutes per side. The meat should be brown on the outside, pink on the inside.

Transfer the chops to a plate and keep them warm, either in the grill (heat off) or in a 180-degree oven, for at least 5 but no more than 30 minutes, uncovered. The meat will relax and continue to cook slightly in its own heat.

4 SERVINGS

CALVES' LIVER LYONNAISE

I like calves' liver cooked medium-rare; if you like yours cooked more or less, adjust the cooking time accordingly.
When a dish is termed "Lyonnaise," it means it contains sautéed onions. Here, in addition to onions I use vinegar, which lends an acidity that works well with liver. Potatoes, pasta, or a rice dish would go well with this.

GOOD-QUALITY CALVES' LIVER IS PALE PINK IN COLOR AND HAS A MILD NUTTY FLAVOR.

2 tablespoons unsalted butter
2 tablespoons safflower or
    corn oil
4 slices calves' liver (6 ounces
    each), about ⅜ inch thick
1 teaspoon salt
½ teaspoon freshly ground
    black pepper
2 large onions (about 12 ounces
    total), peeled and sliced
    thin (about 4 cups)
2 tablespoons red wine vinegar
¼ cup chopped scallions
    (about 2)
⅓ cup water
1 tablespoon chopped chives,
    for garnish

Divide the butter and oil between two skillets, and place the skillets over medium to high heat. Meanwhile, sprinkle the liver with ½ teaspoon of the salt and ¼ teaspoon of the pepper.

When the butter and oil are hot, place the liver in the skillets and sauté over medium to high heat for about 1 minute on each side. Transfer the liver to a platter, and keep warm. Combine the drippings in one of the skillets.

Add the onions to the skillet, stir thoroughly, and sauté for 30 seconds. Then mix in the vinegar, scallions, water, and the remainder of the salt and pepper. Cover, and cook for 1 minute over high heat. Arrange the liver on warm plates, spoon the onion mixture on top, sprinkle with the chopped chives, and serve.

4 SERVINGS

YOU CAN MAKE THESE LIVER STEAKS AT THE LAST MINUTE, SINCE THEY TAKE ONLY ABOUT 2 MINUTES TO COOK.

STEAK A L'ORIENTALE

T he sauce for this dish is an interesting, exotic mixture of Oriental spices and sauces. I use five-spice powder, oyster sauce, chili sauce with garlic, sesame oil, and soy sauce—all of which I have on my pantry shelf.

Either sirloin tip or New York strip can be used here, but be sure the meat is completely cleaned of fat and sinew. If your steaks are a different weight and thickness than indicated below, adjust the cooking time accordingly to get the same good result.

4 sirloin tip or New York strip beef steaks (7 to 8 ounces each), ½ to ¾ inch thick, cleaned of all fat and sinew

1 teaspoon five-spice powder

2 tablespoons unsalted butter

2 tablespoons bottled oyster sauce

2 teaspoons chili sauce with garlic

2 teaspoons sesame oil

2 teaspoons soy sauce

⅓ cup water

8 scallions, trimmed (green tops removed), cleaned, and minced fine (about 1 cup)

THE INGREDIENTS FOR THIS DELICIOUS SAUCE SHOULD BE ON YOUR PANTRY SHELF.

Sprinkle the steaks on both sides with the five-spice powder. Heat the butter in a large heavy saucepan or skillet, and when it is foaming, add the steaks in one layer. Cook for about 2 minutes on each side.

Meanwhile, in a bowl combine the oyster sauce, chili sauce, sesame oil, soy sauce, and water.

When the steaks are cooked, remove them to a platter. Add the scallions to the drippings in the pan, and cook, stirring, for about 30 seconds. Then add the oyster sauce mixture, bring to a boil, and stir to dissolve all the solidified juices. Cook for about 45 seconds to 1 minute. Pour the sauce over the steaks and serve immediately.

4 SERVINGS

STEAK MARCHAND DE VIN

As the name *marchand de vin* (wine merchant) indicates, this steak is made with a red wine sauce. Traditionally a brown stock, or demi-glace, is used in the sauce; instead, I thicken it here with mustard and use a mixture of steak sauce, ketchup, and red wine to create a very satisfying, rich sauce. Since these steaks take only a few minutes, there is no reason to do them ahead.

2 tablespoons unsalted butter
4 chuck eye or New York strip steaks (about 6 ounces each), about ¾ inch thick, trimmed
½ teaspoon salt
½ teaspoon freshly ground black pepper
3 cloves garlic, peeled and chopped fine (about 1½ teaspoons)
½ teaspoon herbes de Provence (see Note, page 48)
⅓ cup dry red wine, such as Beaujolais
1 tablespoon bottled steak sauce
1 tablespoon ketchup
½ cup water
2 teaspoons Dijon-style mustard

Heat the butter in a large sturdy skillet. Sprinkle the steaks on both sides with the salt and pepper, and sauté in the hot butter over medium to high heat for about 3 minutes on each side for medium-rare. Remove the steaks to a platter and set it aside in a warm place while you make the sauce.

Add the garlic and herbes de Provence to the drippings in the skillet, and cook for about 30 seconds. Add the wine and cook until the moisture in the pan has almost completely evaporated; then stir in the steak sauce, ketchup, and water. Bring to a boil and cook for about 30 seconds. Mix in the mustard and just heat through (the mustard may break down if it boils).

Arrange the steaks on individual plates, coat with the sauce, and serve immediately.

4 SERVINGS

A WONDERFULLY RICH-TASTING SAUCE IS CREATED EASILY HERE WITH WINE, STEAK SAUCE, KETCHUP, AND MUSTARD.

BRAISED SHORT RIBS IN RED WINE SAUCE

This beef dish is particularly easy to make in a pressure cooker, and it takes only a few minutes to prepare the vegetables. Very little liquid—only 1 cup of red wine—is used because the meat releases a lot of its juice in the pressure cooker.

I use short ribs because they are so tender and flavorful. Try to choose ribs that are as lean, thick, and meaty as possible for a stew with an intense flavor and rich color. With the vegetables cooked alongside the meat, this makes a complete, generous meal.

4 to 6 well-trimmed short ribs, as lean as possible (about 2¾ pounds total)

3 onions (about 12 ounces total), peeled and cut into 1-inch pieces; or 12 ounces frozen pearl onions

4 or 5 carrots (about 12 ounces), peeled and cut into 1-inch pieces; or 12 ounces frozen baby carrots

12 cloves garlic (about 1 head), peeled

1 tablespoon all-purpose flour

2 teaspoons herbes de Provence (see Note, page 48)

1 teaspoon salt

½ teaspoon freshly ground black pepper

1 pound boiling potatoes, peeled and cut into 2-inch chunks; or 1 pound packaged frozen hash-brown potatoes

1 cup dry, robust red wine, such as Zinfandel, Merlot, or Cabernet Sauvignon

1 tablespoon chopped parsley, for garnish (optional)

THIS DISH IS EASILY MADE IN A PRESSURE COOKER. FOR A FAMILY DINNER, IT CAN BE SERVED DIRECTLY FROM THE COOKER.

Arrange the short ribs in a single layer in the bottom of a pressure cooker and cook, partially covered, over medium heat for 20 to 22 minutes, turning occasionally, until nicely browned on all sides. (No additional fat is needed since enough fat will emerge from the meat for it to brown well.)

Remove all but 1 tablespoon fat from the cooker, and add the onions, carrots, and garlic. Mix well and cook for about 5 minutes, until the vegetables are lightly browned. Add the flour, stir it in completely, and cook for about 2 minutes. Then stir in the herbes de Provence, salt, pepper, potatoes, and wine. Bring to a boil, cover, and bring up to correct pressure according to the manufacturer's instructions. Reduce the heat to very low, and cook for 40 to 45 minutes.

Release the pressure, following the manufacturer's instruc-

tions, and for a family dinner, sprinkle with the parsley and serve directly from the pot. For a more elegant presentation, pour the stew onto an attractive serving platter.

Note: It is important to use a good-quality pressure cooker, one made of thick, heavy metal, preferably stainless steel.

4 SERVINGS

FILLET OF BEEF AUX ECHALOTES

Trimmed slices of beef tenderloin are readily available at most supermarkets. Prepared as it is here—with shallots, garlic, and parsley—the meat is flavorful and cooks in a few minutes. Very tender, it goes well with most vegetables, from potatoes to carrots or green vegetables, as well as noodles or rice.

2 tablespoons unsalted butter
4 beef tenderloin steaks (6 ounces each), ¾ inch thick, completely trimmed of any fat or sinew
½ teaspoon freshly ground black pepper
½ teaspoon salt

10 shallots (6 ounces), peeled and sliced thin (about 1½ cups)
2 cloves garlic, chopped (1 teaspoon)
¼ cup water
2 tablespoons chopped parsley, for garnish

(continued)

Fillet of Beef aux Echalotes (continued)

Heat the butter in a sturdy saucepan. Sprinkle both sides of the steaks with the pepper and salt. When the butter is hot, sauté the steaks for about 3 minutes on each side for medium-rare (or cook them less or more, depending on how you like your steaks).

Transfer the steaks to a serving platter, and add the shallots and garlic to the drippings in the pan. Sauté for about 30 seconds. Then add the water and cook for 30 seconds to 1 minute, until most of the moisture has evaporated and the solidified glaze in the skillet has dissolved. Pour the sauce over the fillets, garnish with the parsley, and serve immediately.

4 SERVINGS

TRIPE RAGOUT

Beef tripe (cow's stomach) is available in most supermarkets. It looks like a honeycomb, and so is often called honeycomb tripe. Tripe has excellent nutritional value and is inexpensive, but it is not familiar to most Americans. However, it is a favorite of my daughter, Claudine, who likes it sautéed with onions and vinegar as well as in stew or soup. No matter how tripe is prepared, it requires long cooking to be tender, tasty, and digestible. Cooking it in a pressure cooker, as I've done here, reduces the time by at least half and helps seal in the flavor, making this the best cooking method. Because the tripe still takes a while to cook, I always prepare extra and freeze it in small containers for later use. Unfrozen, it will keep in the refrigerator for a week.

Serve this ragout with Basic Boiled Potatoes (page 224).

3½ pounds beef tripe
3 or 4 onions (1 pound total), peeled and cut into 1-inch pieces
3 or 4 carrots (8 ounces total),
peeled and cut into ½-inch dice (about 1½ cups)
2 small green bell peppers (8 ounces total), seeded and cut into ½-inch pieces

6 *cloves garlic, crushed, peeled,*
   and coarsely chopped
   (about 1½ tablespoons)
1 *or 2 celery ribs (4 ounces),*
   cut into ¼-inch dice
2 *tablespoons tomato paste*
1 *tablespoon herbes de Provence*
   (see Note, page 48)
1½ *tablespoons chopped ginger*
1 *medium-size jalapeño pepper*
½ *teaspoon freshly ground*
   black pepper
1 *cup dry white wine*
2 *teaspoons salt*

Rinse the tripe thoroughly under cool water, and cut it into 2- to 3-inch pieces. Place the tripe and all the remaining ingredients in a pressure cooker and bring to a boil over high heat. Cover

COOKING TRIPE IN A PRESSURE COOKER REDUCES THE TIME BY AT LEAST HALF AND SEALS IN THE FLAVOR.

tightly and continue cooking over high heat until the gauge indicates that the pressure is right. Then reduce the heat to very low and cook for 1¼ hours.

Release the pressure according to the manufacturer's instructions, and serve.

Note: If you freeze leftover ragout, reheat it in a microwave oven if possible.

6 SERVINGS

VEGETABLES

We could probably do without meat at my house, but we could never get along without vegetables. In addition to serving them as an accompaniment to meat, they are an important part of stews made with beef, ham, and sausage, like the Black-eyed Peas and Ham Stew or the Fricassee of Peas with Ham. Both of these dishes, as well as the Broccoli de Rabe with Sausage, use meat merely to flavor the vegetables.

Many of the vegetable dishes in this chapter can be served as a first course, among them the Corn Fritters in Beer Batter and the Broiled Eggplant Japonaise. Leeks Vinaigrette are an ideal first course, as are the Marinated Mushrooms and the Spicy Mushroom Toasts, which also make a great appetizer, a good luncheon main course, and are a delicious accompaniment to meat.

BLACK-EYED PEAS AND HAM

Black-eyed peas are one of my favorite legumes. (Black-eyed beans are the same thing—just more oval in shape).
   This is one of those earthy one-pot dishes that do not involve much work and can be served family-style, brought directly from the stove to the table. Any leftovers will freeze well.

3 tablespoons corn or canola oil
2 onions, peeled and coarsely chopped (about 2 cups)
2 carrots, peeled and cut into ½-inch pieces (1 cup)
2 teaspoons chili powder
1 teaspoon dried thyme
½ teaspoon crushed red pepper flakes
1 pound dried black-eyed peas
4 cloves garlic, peeled and sliced (about 2 tablespoons)
6 cups water
1½ teaspoons salt
12 ounces fully cooked ham, cut into 1-inch pieces
2 ripe tomatoes (about 10 ounces total), seeded and cut into 1-inch pieces (about 2 cups)
Tabasco sauce, to taste (optional)

Combine the oil, onions, carrots, chili powder, thyme, and red pepper flakes in a sturdy pot or large casserole. Stir well, and cook over medium heat for about 5 minutes, until the onions are cooked.

Meanwhile, put the black-eyed peas in a sieve, rinse thoroughly under cold water, and drain. Add them to the casserole along with the garlic, water, and salt. Bring to a boil, cover, and boil gently over very low heat for about 45 minutes, or until the peas are cooked through.

Mix in the ham and tomatoes, and cook for another 10 to 15 minutes. Serve as is or with Tabasco sauce to taste.

6 TO 8 SERVINGS

Creamy Black-eyed Pea Soup
Leftovers can be turned into a delicious soup: Simply purée the stew in a food processor, adding enough water to thin it to the desired consistency. Serve with croutons.

THIS EARTHY STEW CAN GO DIRECTLY FROM THE STOVE TO THE TABLE.

BOSTON BAKED BEANS

I love Boston baked beans and so does my wife, Gloria. They take 4 hours to cook but involve only 10 minutes of work when prepared this way.

I use plain canned small white beans, combining them in an earthenware crock with seasonings, bacon, and onion. The ingredients are mixed together cold, involving only ten minutes of work at the most, and then the dish is baked for several hours.

The earthenware container I use is 9 inches in diameter and 3 inches high. It takes more than an hour for the bean mixture to come to a boil in the oven. If you want to speed up the baking process, bring the mixture to a boil on top of the stove before putting it in the oven.

The beans are delicious reheated; do this in a microwave oven if possible.

3 cans (16 ounces each) small white beans
6 slices bacon (about 4 ounces total), cut into 1-inch pieces
1 large onion, peeled and coarsely chopped (about 1¼ cups)
¼ cup ketchup
2 teaspoons dry mustard
¼ teaspoon cayenne pepper
1 teaspoon dried oregano
¼ cup dark brown sugar
2 tablespoons molasses
¼ teaspoon salt

Place the beans with their liquid in an earthenware crock or casserole, and stir in all the remaining ingredients. The mixture should be at least ½ inch below the top of the crock. Set the crock on a baking sheet and place it in a 350-degree oven. Cook for about 2 hours.

Stir the crust that has formed on top of the beans down into the mixture. Continue cooking for 1 hour longer.

Again stir in the crust, and cook for 1 hour longer (4 hours total), until the mixture is glossy and most of the liquid has been absorbed.

Note: These beans are not as sweet as in most traditional recipes. If you like your beans sweeter, add more brown sugar or molasses.

8 SERVINGS

GREEN BEANS AND SHALLOTS

Frozen French-cut green beans are a time-saver—they can be defrosted quickly in a microwave oven or in a sieve under warm water. I like to cook them a little after defrosting because they are only blanched before freezing.

---

2 packages (10 ounces each) frozen French-cut green beans
4 tablespoons water
2 tablespoons unsalted butter
1 tablespoon canola or corn oil
About 2 shallots, coarsely chopped (2 tablespoons)
¼ teaspoon freshly ground black pepper
½ teaspoon salt

Defrost the beans in a microwave oven, or by holding them in a sieve under warm tap water.

Place the defrosted beans in a saucepan or skillet, add the water, and bring to a boil. Cover and cook for 3 to 4 minutes, until most of the moisture has evaporated. Then uncover, add the butter, oil, and shallots, and cook for 2 to 3 minutes, until the shallots have softened. Add the pepper and salt, toss to mix, and serve immediately.

4 SERVINGS

FRICASSEE OF LIMA BEANS

I always have packaged frozen lima beans on hand for use in quickly prepared fricassees like this one.

The beans are flavored with Canadian bacon, but ham would be good too. If you are using Canadian bacon, which tends to be salty, don't add any salt to the dish until you've tasted it near the end of the cooking period. This is ready to eat in about 15 minutes.

1 tablespoon unsalted butter
1 tablespoon safflower or
    corn oil
3 ounces Canadian bacon, cut
    into ½-inch pieces (about ¾
    cup)
1 onion (4 ounces), peeled and
    cut into ½-inch dice
½ teaspoon herbes de Provence
    (see Note, page 48)
1 package (10 ounces) frozen
    lima beans, preferably large
¼ teaspoon freshly ground
    black pepper
Salt to taste

Heat the butter and oil in a saucepan, add the Canadian bacon and onion, and sauté over medium to high heat for 3 to 4 minutes, until the bacon is nicely browned.

Meanwhile, place the frozen lima beans in a sieve and run them under warm tap water to thaw them slightly and to remove any "freezer taste" they may have acquired. Add the beans to the mixture in the saucepan, cover, and bring to a boil, stirring occasionally. Reduce the heat and cook, covered, over low heat for 8 to 10 minutes. Add the pepper and salt (if needed), and serve immediately.

4 SERVINGS

THIS DISH, MADE WITH FROZEN LIMA BEANS, IS READY TO EAT IN 15 MINUTES.

WHITE BEAN PUREE

You can make this creamy, delicious purée on short notice with canned white beans. It is a great side dish with sautéed chicken, roast veal, roast beef—and especially with lamb. It also makes a good dip!

1 tablespoon vegetable oil
1 onion (about 3 ounces),
*   peeled and sliced thin*
1 large clove garlic, peeled and
*   crushed*
1 can (16 ounces) small white
*   beans, drained*
¼ teaspoon freshly ground
*   black pepper*
½ teaspoon salt
1 tablespoon unsalted butter

Heat the oil in a skillet, then add the onions. Sauté over medium to high heat for about 1 minute. Add the garlic and cook, stirring, for 5 to 6 seconds. Then add the beans and cook for 2 to 3 minutes, until they are hot.

Transfer the mixture to the bowl of a food processor, and process for 8 to 10 seconds, until smooth. Add the pepper, salt, and butter, and process again briefly to incorporate.

Serve immediately, or set aside in a double boiler to keep warm.

Note: You can make this purée ahead of time, and then reheat it in a microwave oven.

4 SERVINGS

BROCCOLI DE RABE WITH SAUSAGE

Broccoli de rabe, a leafy, bitter broccoli with a thin stem and small yellow flowers, appears regularly in Chinese and Italian cooking. It is available almost year-round at most supermarkets. I like its slightly bitter and nutty taste, which goes particularly well with sausage. For this recipe use sweet Italian-style sausage meat (if necessary, buy links and remove the meat from the casing).

This dish is good as a first course or as a side dish with pasta, and should be served at room temperature. If it has been refrigerated, rewarm it to room temperature in a microwave oven for about 20 seconds.

2 pounds broccoli de rabe
1 pound sweet Italian-style
    sausage meat
4 cloves garlic, peeled and
    sliced (about 1½
    tablespoons)
¼ teaspoon red pepper flakes
½ teaspoon anise seeds
¼ teaspoon salt
2 tablespoons olive oil
Sprinkling of olive oil, for
    garnish (optional)

If the broccoli stems are tough and fibrous, remove the outer layer by pulling it off the stem. (This takes some time, but it is well worth the effort since the stems will be much more tender.) Discard the peelings.

Cut the broccoli into 2- to 3-inch chunks and rinse it thoroughly in a sieve under cold water.

Meanwhile, form the sausage meat into 1-ounce balls, each the size of a jumbo olive, and arrange them in one layer in a large saucepan. Cover, and cook over medium to low heat for about 10 minutes. (Liquid will emerge from the sausage pieces and they will begin frying after 6 or 7 minutes.) Turn the sausage and cook over low heat for another 10 minutes. Stir in the garlic, red pepper flakes, anise seeds, salt, and olive oil.

Add the broccoli, a handful at a time, to the sausage mixture, stirring it in under the sausage so it can steam. Cover and bring to a boil. Then lower the heat and cook, covered, for about 10 minutes. Uncover and cool to room temperature. Serve with a sprinkling of olive oil on top, if desired.

4 SERVINGS

MAKE THIS VERSATILE DISH AHEAD OF TIME AND SERVE IT AT ROOM TEMPERATURE AS A FIRST COURSE, SIDE DISH, OR EVEN AS AN HORS D'OEUVRE.

STEAMED CAULIFLOWER WITH LEMON BUTTER

I like cauliflower when it is firm and white, as it is near the end of the summer. It looks handsome when you serve it whole. This is a quick, delicious recipe that goes well with grilled meat, fish, or stew. Try the lemon butter sauce with other steamed vegetables as well, or with steamed or broiled fish.

1 head cauliflower (2 pounds), trimmed
1 cup water

LEMON BUTTER SAUCE
¼ cup water
4 tablespoons (½ stick) unsalted butter, cut into pieces
1 tablespoon lemon juice
1 tablespoon virgin olive oil
½ teaspoon salt
¼ teaspoon freshly ground black pepper

1 tablespoon chopped chives, for garnish

THIS EASY-TO-MAKE LEMON BUT-TER SAUCE GOES WELL WITH OTHER STEAMED VEGETABLES AND WITH STEAMED OR BROILED FISH.

Rinse the cauliflower carefully under cold water, and place it in a saucepan that is tall enough to hold the cauliflower in an upright position. (Trim the cauliflower at the root end if necessary.) Add the 1 cup water and bring it to a boil. Cover, and cook over high heat for 12 minutes, until the cauliflower is tender but still somewhat firm and most of the water has evaporated. Place the cauliflower on a round serving platter or in a gratin dish, and set aside in a warm place.

Bring the ¼ cup water to a boil in a saucepan (preferably stainless steel). Mix in the butter, lemon juice, olive oil, salt, and pepper. Bring to a strong boil, and when the mixture emulsifies (is thoroughly blended), pour it over the cauliflower.

Sprinkle with the chives and serve in wedges, cutting it as you would a pie.

6 SERVINGS

PUREE OF CARROTS AND POTATOES

This delicious purée can be made with fresh carrots and fresh potatoes, but it is excellent when done with frozen hash-brown potatoes and frozen baby carrots—and what a relief not to have to peel and cut vegetables when you're in a hurry! Just enough water is added to cook the vegetables; there should be no excess moisture remaining to be drained away at the end of the cooking time. This way, all the vitamins are retained.

4 cups packaged frozen hash-brown potatoes
4 cups (1 pound) baby carrots, frozen or fresh
1½ cups water
4 tablespoons (½ stick) unsalted butter, cut into pieces
¼ teaspoon freshly ground black pepper
1 teaspoon salt

Place the potatoes, carrots, and water in a stainless steel saucepan. Bring to a boil, cover, reduce the heat, and boil gently for about 5 minutes. The water should be almost gone; if there is still some remaining, remove the lid and cook over high heat for a few minutes until almost all the moisture has evaporated.

Transfer the potatoes and carrots to the bowl of a food processor, and add the rest of the ingredients. Process for 10 to 15 seconds (there should be pieces of carrot still visible in the mixture). Serve immediately, or allow to cool and then rewarm at serving time.

6 SERVINGS

IF YOU DON'T HAVE TIME TO PEEL FRESH VEGETABLES FOR THIS PUREE, USE FROZEN ONES; THEY WORK BEAUTIFULLY.

HONEYED CARROTS WITH PEPPER

You can use fresh carrots here—either baby carrots or larger carrots cut into 1-inch pieces—but making the dish with frozen baby carrots, which don't require peeling and cook in just a few minutes, simplifies it considerably. Cooked with honey, butter, and a dash of pepper, these carrots have a wonderful flavor.

4 cups (1 pound) baby carrots,
    fresh or frozen
½ cup water
2 tablespoons unsalted butter
¼ teaspoon salt
¼ teaspoon freshly ground
    black pepper
1 tablespoon honey

Place all the ingredients in a saucepan (preferably stainless steel), stir, and bring to a boil.

> FROZEN BABY CARROTS WORK WELL HERE—THEY DON'T REQUIRE PEELING AND COOK IN JUST A FEW MINUTES.

Cover, reduce the heat, and boil gently for 5 minutes. Serve immediately.

4 SERVINGS

CORN POELE

This tasty dish is made with either frozen or fresh corn kernels, both of which take only a few minutes to sauté. Some of the kernels become slightly carmelized and candied as they cook, producing an intense flavor. This is a perfect last-minute addition to a meal when you find you need another vegetable.

1 tablespoon unsalted butter
2 tablespoons corn oil
1 package (1 pound) frozen
    corn kernels, or 4 cups fresh
    corn kernels
¼ teaspoon freshly ground
    black pepper
¼ teaspoon salt

Heat the butter and oil in a large nonstick skillet. When it is hot, add the corn kernels and sauté, covered, over medium to high heat for about 4 to 5 min-utes. Remove the lid and cook for 1 or 2 minutes, shaking the pan, until the mixture is practically dry and some of the kernels are starting to brown a little. Add the pepper and salt and serve.

4 SERVINGS

EITHER FRESH OR FROZEN CORN CAN BE USED IN THIS FLAVORFUL DISH.

CREAM OF CORN PUDDING

Made with canned cream-style corn, this custardy mixture goes well with sautéed meats and with stews.

1 can (16½ ounces) cream-style
    sweet corn
2 eggs
¼ cup milk
½ cup all-purpose flour
¼ cup corn oil
½ teaspoon salt
¼ teaspoon freshly ground
    black pepper
1 tablespoon sugar

Place all the ingredients in the bowl of a food processor and pro-cess for 10 seconds. Lighty oil a 6-cup soufflé mold about 6 inches in diameter, and pour the pud-ding mixture into the mold. Bake in a 375-degree oven for 45 min-utes, until golden, puffy, and set.

4 SERVINGS

MADE WITH CANNED CREAM-STYLE CORN, THIS DELICIOUS PUDDING IS OVEN-READY IN JUST A FEW MIN-UTES.

CORN FRITTERS IN BEER BATTER

T his recipe takes only a few minutes to prepare. I use frozen corn but any type of fresh or frozen vegetable, from spinach to zucchini to carrots to peas—or even a mixture of these vegetables—can be used in these delicious little fritters that can be served with aperitifs, as a first course, or as a garnish for most meats. Although they are good eaten plain, they are especially flavorful served with a dollop of sour cream and a spoonful of caviar.

If you cook the fritters ahead, place them on a wire rack so the underside doesn't get soggy, and then reheat just before serving in a very hot oven, or place them under a hot broiler (5 or 6 inches from the heat) for a few minutes to recrisp. The fritters should be small—about 2 to 2½ inches in diameter—as they are best when very thin.

¾ cup all-purpose flour
1 cup beer
8 ounces frozen corn kernels
¼ teaspoon salt
About ½ cup canola or corn oil
Sour cream and caviar, for
     garnish (optional)

Place the flour in a mixing bowl. Pour about ¾ cup of the beer over the flour, and mix well with a whisk until smooth. Add the remainder of the beer and mix again. Place the frozen corn in a sieve, and run it under warm tap water to defrost. Add to the batter, along with the salt.

Heat 1½ to 2 tablespoons of the oil in each of two large skillets. When the oil is hot, spoon about 1½ tablespoons of the batter into each skillet, and spread it out with a spoon. Don't be concerned about a few holes here and there. Add more spoonfuls of batter to the skillets, so you are making three or four fritters at a time in each skillet, spreading the batter out for each fritter. Cook about 3 minutes per side over high heat,

IF YOU DON'T PLAN TO EAT THE FRITTERS IMMEDIATELY, COOL THEM ON A WIRE RACK SO THEY DON'T GET SOGGY ON THE UNDERSIDE.

until brown and crisp, and transfer to a wire rack. Continue making fritters, adding a little oil to the skillets as needed, until the batter is used up.

Serve the fritters immediately, or reheat them later in a hot oven or under a broiler. Serve topped with sour cream and caviar, if desired.

6 SERVINGS

EGGPLANT BORANI

This is inspired by a Russian recipe that features eggplant seasoned with cinnamon, coriander, and dill. Easy to do, it can be prepared ahead and then reheated at serving time.

1 eggplant (12 ounces), unpeeled, cut lengthwise into ½-inch-thick slices (about 12 slices)
1 onion (4 ounces), peeled and sliced thin
½ teaspoon salt
½ teaspoon dried basil
½ teaspoon ground cinnamon
½ teaspoon ground coriander
¼ teaspoon dill seeds
½ teaspoon freshly ground black pepper
3 tablespoons safflower or corn oil
1 tablespoon cider vinegar
⅓ cup water

Arrange the eggplant and onion slices alternately, overlapping them, in a gratin dish. Season with the salt, basil, cinnamon, coriander, dill, and pepper. Then sprinkle on the oil, vinegar, and water. Cover with aluminum foil, and place on a foil-lined cookie sheet. Bake in a 400-degree oven for about 25 minutes. Remove the foil cover and cook for 10 to 15 minutes, until most of the moisture has evaporated. Serve immediately, or set aside and reheat, covered, just before serving.

4 SERVINGS

YOU CAN PREPARE THIS DISH AHEAD AND REHEAT IT IN A MICROWAVE OVEN AT SERVING TIME.

BROILED EGGPLANT JAPONAISE

Make this quick, flavorful dish in the summer, when freshly picked eggplant is plentiful. Select the long, narrow "Japanese" eggplants, if they're available. Otherwise, a larger, fatter variety will work well, providing it is not too soft and seedy.

This makes a good first course, and it can also be served in place of salad with broiled or roasted meat or fish.

*2 tablespoons safflower or
    corn oil*
*2 small or 1 large eggplant (1
    pound), unpeeled, cut
    lengthwise into ½-inch-thick
    slices (about 8 slices)*
¼ teaspoon salt

EGGPLANT SOY SAUCE
*1 clove garlic, peeled, crushed,
    and chopped fine (½
    teaspoon)*
1½ tablespoons light soy sauce
1 teaspoon sugar
*1 tablespoon corn or safflower
    oil*
¼ teaspoon Tabasco sauce

Line a cookie sheet with aluminum foil (to facilitate cleanup), and pour the 2 tablespoons of corn oil onto it. Press the eggplant slices into the oil, turning them so they are coated on both sides, and arrange in one layer on the cookie sheet. Sprinkle with the salt. Place under a preheated broiler, about 5 to 6 inches from the heat, and broil for 5 minutes on one side, until the surface is bubbly and brown spots have appeared. Turn and broil for 5 minutes on the other side.

While the eggplant is broiling, mix the sauce ingredients together in a bowl. Transfer the broiled eggplant to a platter, and immediately pour the sauce over it. Set aside until cool, and serve at room temperature.

Note: The sauce is also good on salads, or with sushi or poached fish.

4 SERVINGS

LONG NARROW SLICES OF EGG-PLANT ARE BROILED JUST BRIEFLY AND SERVED AT ROOM TEMPERATURE WITH A DO-AHEAD SAUCE.

JARDINIERE OF VEGETABLES

T his vegetable stew is seasoned with lean salt pork. If possible, use *pancetta*, which is lean unsmoked Italian bacon. If it's not available, you can also use regular bacon, which will give the dish a slightly smoky taste.

Although you can use a mixture of fresh vegetables here—from carrots to turnips to peas to string beans—I use packaged frozen mixed vegetables as a time-saver. If you keep a 20-ounce bag of frozen mixed vegetables in your freezer and have bacon on hand, you can prepare this dish on the spur of the moment. It is hearty enough to serve as a brunch dish with a salad, or it can be a vegetable accompaniment for most roasted meats.

1 bag (20 ounces) frozen mixed vegetables
3 ounces pancetta *salt pork, or bacon, cut into ¼-inch pieces (about ½ cup)*
1 onion (about 5 ounces), peeled and chopped (1 cup)
1 tablespoon all-purpose flour
1 cup water
¼ teaspoon salt
¼ teaspoon freshly ground black pepper

Place the frozen vegetables in a sieve, and run them momentarily under hot tap water to partially defrost them. Set aside to drain.

Place the *pancetta* salt pork in a saucepan and cook it over medium heat for 6 to 8 minutes, until the pieces are brown and crisp. Add the onion and cook for 3 minutes. Then mix in the flour and cook for about 30 seconds. Add the water and bring to a boil, stirring. Mix in the vegetables, salt, and pepper and bring to a boil, stirring. Mix well again, cover, reduce the heat, and boil gently for 8 to 10 minutes. Serve immediately, or cool and then reheat at serving time.

4 SERVINGS

KEEP A FEW 20-OUNCE BAGS OF FROZEN VEGETABLES IN YOUR FREEZER FOR VEGETABLE STEWS AND SOUPS.

LEEKS VINAIGRETTE

L eeks, which are very inexpensive in Europe, are costly here—but they are so delicious served in a vinaigrette that they are worth the investment!

Even though in modern cuisine most vegetables are cooked only briefly, leeks are most flavorful when cooked until very tender when pierced with the point of a knife. People tend to trim leeks too much, discarding any part of the vegetable that is green. However, the leeks we buy at the supermarket are already trimmed. I remove the roots and the first layer of tough, fibrous leaves; then I trim selectively, removing only damaged or dark green leaf ends from the second layer and keeping all the tiny, tender center leaves. The trimmed leek has a shingled look, with the outer leaves closely cropped and the taller inner leaves intact.

After the leeks have been cooked, they are removed from the liquid and the juice is pressed out of them. The vinaigrette is added while the leeks are still lukewarm, so they can absorb it. Serve them immediately with some crusty French bread, or cover tightly and refrigerate—they will keep for a couple of days. Warm the leeks briefly in a microwave oven to bring them back to room temperature before serving.

Save the flavorful cooking liquid to use in Cream of Leek Soup (page 62).

AS A BONUS, CREAM OF LEEK SOUP (PAGE 62) CAN BE MADE WITH THE DELICIOUS COOKING LIQUID OBTAINED HERE.

6 leeks (1½ pounds), trimmed of roots and fibrous dark green outer leaves only (1¼ pounds trimmed)

5 cups water

VINAIGRETTE SAUCE
1½ tablespoons Dijon-style mustard (preferably "hot")
2 teaspoons red wine vinegar
⅓ cup oil, preferably a mixture of corn oil and olive oil
¼ teaspoon salt
¼ teaspoon freshly ground black pepper

Beginning about 1½ inches above the root end of the trimmed leeks, split the leeks lengthwise into four sections, leaving them still attached at the root end. Open and wash thoroughly to remove the sand that collects inside the leaves.

In a 9- to 10-inch-wide saucepan, bring the water to a boil. Add the leeks in a bunch, all facing the same direction, and bend the extending leaves back in so they fit in the saucepan. Press to position the leeks in one layer. Bring back to the boil, cover, and boil over medium to high heat for 8 to 9 minutes, until the leeks are tender when pierced with the point of a knife. Using a slotted spoon, remove the leeks to a flat gratin dish suitable for serving. (Reserve the cooking liquid for Cream of Leek Soup, page 62, adding water as needed to make about 4 cups.)

When the leeks have cooled to room temperature, press them, a few at a time, to remove additional juice (add the juice to the reserved cooking liquid). Arrange the leeks on a cutting board and cut into 2-inch pieces. Return the leeks to the gratin dish, alternating white and green pieces.

Prepare the vinaigrette: Using a spoon, mix together the mustard, vinegar, oil, salt, and pepper. Pour this over the leeks; then lift the leeks gently with a fork so the sauce can flow between the pieces and flavor them completely.

Serve at room temperature.

6 SERVINGS

ICEBERG AND GARLIC SAUTE

I like iceberg lettuce, not only raw in salads because of its crunchy, cool taste, but also cooked. It is convenient to use because it comes already washed and it keeps for a long time in the refrigerator.

In this recipe, I sauté the lettuce with garlic, olive oil, and red pepper flakes. Although the ultimate goal is to remove the

(continued)

Iceberg and Garlic Sauté (continued)

moisture from the lettuce, I do add some water at the beginning of the cooking time so the garlic doesn't burn; eventually, however, moisture emerges from the lettuce and it cooks in its own liquid. Prepared in a few minutes, this is a very simple, light vegetable that goes well with roasted and stewed meats.

2 tablespoons virgin olive oil
3 cloves garlic, peeled and
   chopped (about 2
   teaspoons)
¼ teaspoon crushed red pepper
   flakes
1 head (about 1 pound) iceberg
   lettuce, cut into 2-inch
   pieces and separated
¼ cup water
½ teaspoon salt

Heat the oil in a large skillet with a tight-fitting lid. When it is warm, add the garlic and red pepper flakes and cook for about 15 to 20 seconds. Then place 2 handfuls of the lettuce on top, and mix well so the garlic doesn't stick to the bottom of the pan.

Add the rest of the lettuce and the water, cover, and cook over medium to high heat for 2 to 3 minutes. Then mix well, add the salt, and continue cooking, covered, for 2 minutes longer, until completely wilted. Uncover, and if there is too much moisture, cook over high heat for 1 to 2 minutes, until most of the moisture has evaporated. There should be only enough moisture remaining so that the lettuce is wet. Serve immediately.

4 SERVINGS

> ICEBERG LETTUCE DOESN'T NEED WASHING AND IS GOOD COOKED AS WELL AS RAW.

MARINATED MUSHROOMS

This is a dish that you can prepare ahead in a few minutes and keep on hand in the refrigerator. It can be served as a first course or as part of a buffet, added to salads, or eaten with cold cuts or other types of meat. The mushrooms will keep, covered, in the refrigerator for two weeks.

Fresh button mushrooms often come prewashed these days, so you need only cook them briefly with the other ingredients. Frozen button mushrooms can be used as well.

*1½ pounds button mushrooms,
    prewashed if available*
*5 tablespoons extra-virgin
    olive oil*
½ teaspoon fennel seeds
1 teaspoon coriander seeds
*1 teaspoon coarsely ground
    black pepper*
1 teaspoon salt
2 teaspoons lemon juice
4 bay leaves
¼ cup dry white wine
¼ cup water

> **THESE WILL KEEP IN THE REFRIGERATOR FOR TWO WEEKS—GOOD TO HAVE ON HAND FOR UNEXPECTED GUESTS.**

Place all the ingredients in a stainless steel saucepan, and stir gently. Bring to a boil, cover, and boil over medium to high heat for 4 to 5 minutes. Pour into a crock or jar, and let cool. Serve warm, cold, or at room temperature.

6 SERVINGS

SPICY MUSHROOM TOASTS

When you can't think what to serve as a first course, try this simple dish—it is always satisfying. Just be sure to make the toasts at the last minute so they are crunchy, not soggy.

To simplify the preparation, use fresh presliced, prewashed mushrooms or frozen sliced mushrooms, both of which are available now at most supermarkets. The convenience of the frozen mushrooms is, of course, that you can have them on hand when unexpected guests drop in.

(continued)

Spicy Mushroom Toasts (continued)

2 tablespoons corn oil
1 pound mushrooms, sliced thin
    (about 6 cups)
½ teaspoon salt
¼ teaspoon freshly ground
    black pepper
About 2 tablespoons Hot Red
    Salsa (page 23), or to taste
½ cup sour cream
2 tablespoons coarsely chopped
    parsley
4 slices bread

Heat the oil in a skillet. When it is hot, add the mushrooms and sauté for about 5 minutes over high heat, until the liquid in the mushrooms has emerged and evaporated and there is just a little moisture remaining around them. Add the salt, pepper, hot salsa, and sour cream and bring to a boil. Stir in the parsley, and keep warm.

Toast the bread. Trim the crusts from the toasts, and cut the slices into diagonal quarters to form triangles (or whatever shape you prefer). Re-form the quarters on individual plates, forming 1 whole slice per serving. Spread with the mushroom mixture and serve.

4 SERVINGS

PEARL ONIONS AND PEAS IN CREAM SAUCE

This recipe is made with frozen tiny peas, which are of excellent quality, and fresh or frozen pearl onions, which are much better tasting than the canned variety.

1 package (10 ounces) frozen
    pearl onions
1 package (10 ounces) frozen
    petite peas
½ cup fresh or frozen
    homemade chicken stock
    (see Basic Chicken Stock,
    page 48) or canned chicken
    broth

½ cup heavy cream
½ teaspoon salt
¼ teaspoon freshly ground
    black pepper
⅛ teaspoon ground nutmeg
1 teaspoon potato starch
    dissolved in 2 tablespoons
    cold water

WHEN A RECIPE CALLS FOR PEAS, USE FROZEN PETITE PEAS, WHICH ARE OF EXCELLENT QUALITY.

Place the onions in a sieve and run warm tap water over them to partially defrost. (Washing away the frozen particles around the onions also helps eliminate the "freezer taste" these vegetables acquire.) Repeat with the peas.

Combine the onions, chicken stock, and cream in a saucepan, and bring to a boil over high heat. Reduce the heat, cover, and simmer over low heat for about 5 minutes, until the onions are cooked through. Add the salt, pepper, nutmeg, peas, and the dissolved potato starch. Mix well, return to the boil, and cook, covered, for about 1 minute. Serve.

6 SERVINGS

FRICASSEE OF PEAS WITH HAM

Frozen tiny peas are one of the best vegetables on the market. They are selected according to a procedure involving gravity: Freshly picked peas are dumped into a vat of salted water. The heavy ones drop to the bottom and the small, lighter ones, higher in sugar, float to the top. These are the tiny sweet peas, often labeled "petite," that we find in the freezer section.

1 package (10 ounces) frozen petite peas
2 tablespoons corn or canola oil
1 tablespoon unsalted butter
About 4 carrots (6 ounces total), peeled and cut into ½-inch dice (about 1¼ cups)
About 2 onions (4 ounces total), peeled and chopped fine

4 ounces cooked ham, cut into ½-inch dice (¾ cup)
¼ teaspoon dried thyme
2 teaspoons all-purpose flour
1 cup water
½ teaspoon salt
¼ teaspoon freshly ground black pepper

(continued)

Fricassee of Peas with Ham (continued)

If you like, defrost the peas by placing them in a sieve and running hot tap water over them; but it isn't necessary.

Heat the oil and butter in a saucepan, and when the mixture is hot, add the carrots, onions, ham, and thyme. Sauté over medium heat for 4 to 5 minutes, until the mixture is nicely browned.

Add the flour, mix well, and cook for about 30 seconds. Then stir in the water, salt, and pepper and bring the mixture to a boil.

> **THIS FLAVORFUL DISH IS READY TO EAT IN ABOUT HALF AN HOUR AND GOES WELL WITH MOST ROASTS OR GRILLED MEAT.**

Cover, reduce the heat, and cook for 3 to 4 minutes.

Add the peas (frozen or defrosted) and bring the mixture to a boil. Cover and boil gently for 2 to 3 minutes. Serve.

4 SERVINGS

PEAS AND LETTUCE

Use frozen peas for this recipe, being careful to select a variety marked "tiny" or "petite" peas.

I used Boston lettuce here, but any type—from iceberg to Romaine—would be fine. At my house we often serve this vegetable dish—or the Zucchini Flan (page 238), Sautéed Spinach with Nutmeg (page 235), or Corn Fritters in Beer Batter (page 212)—as the first course in a simple family dinner.

1 package (10 ounces) frozen
petite peas
1 small head (5 ounces) lettuce
2 tablespoons virgin olive oil
3 cloves garlic, peeled and
sliced thin (1 tablespoon)
¼ teaspoon red pepper flakes
¼ teaspoon sugar
½ teaspoon salt

Place the peas in a sieve, and run hot tap water over them to defrost them.

Cut the lettuce into 2-inch pieces, and wash it thoroughly in a sink filled with cold water. Lift the lettuce from the water and drain.

Heat the oil, garlic, and red

pepper flakes in a skillet or saucepan (preferably stainless steel). When the mixture is hot, sauté for about 1 minute, taking care not to burn the garlic. Add the drained lettuce, cover, and cook for about 1 minute, until the lettuce is wilted. Uncover, add the peas, and cook for 2 to 3 minutes, until most of the moisture has evaporated.

Stir in the sugar and salt, and serve.

4 SERVINGS

PUREE OF PEAS WITH MINT

This delicious purée can be made with either fresh, dried, or powdered mint, but it is imperative that frozen petite peas—the smallest, sweetest peas—be used. Make sure that, after draining, the hot peas go directly from the sieve into the food processor. If left longer before puréeing, their skin will shrivel and toughen, and consequently the purée will not be smooth.

3 cups water
2 packages (10 ounces each)
*   frozen petite peas*
½ teaspoon salt
1 teaspoon sugar
¼ teaspoon freshly ground
*   black pepper*
1 tablespoon chopped fresh
*   mint, or ½ teaspoon*
*   crumbled dried mint or*
*   mint tea powder*
3 tablespoons unsalted butter

> **THIS MAKES A GREAT GARNISH FOR POULTRY, FISH, OR ROAST VEAL.**

Bring the water to a boil in a saucepan. Add the peas, return the water to the boil, and cook for 2 minutes. Drain the peas in a colander, and immediately place

(continued)

Purée of Peas with Mint (continued)

them in the bowl of a food processor. Process for about 20 seconds. Using a rubber spatula, push any peas clinging to the sides of the bowl down to the bottom, and process for another 20 seconds.

Add the remainder of the ingredients and process for 10 to 15 seconds. The mixture should be smooth and bright green.

6 SERVINGS

BASIC BOILED POTATOES

I use a lot of potatoes at my house, and when I boil or steam them I usually make extra since I have several recipes that call for precooked potatoes—among them Potatoes Persillade (page 227) and Ragout of Potatoes (page 228). Boiled potatoes will keep, refrigerated, for a few days and are delicious in salad as well. This recipe calls for 1½ pounds of potatoes, but you can make double or triple this amount and use the remainder later in the week.

About 12 small boiling potatoes (1½ pounds total)

Wash the potatoes thoroughly and place them in a saucepan. Add enough tap water to extend about 1 inch above the surface of the potatoes. Cover the pan with a lid, bring the water to a boil, and boil gently for 18 to 22 minutes, until the potatoes are tender when pierced with the point of a sharp knife.

Pour out the water and set the potatoes aside to dry in the pan. (The residual heat in the potatoes will draw more moisture from them, making them firmer and creamier than if they were cooled under water.) When they are cool enough to handle, peel the potatoes for immediate use in other recipes, or cool completely and refrigerate (unpeeled) for later use.

4 SERVINGS

PARSLEY POTATOES WITH BUTTER

These go well with most poached, steamed, or grilled fish, as well as with light meats like veal.

1½ pounds cooked potatoes, peeled
2 tablespoons unsalted butter
⅛ teaspoon salt
2 tablespoons chopped parsley

Place the potatoes in a skillet with the butter and salt. Cover and heat for 3 to 4 minutes, until the potatoes are hot. Sprinkle with the parsley, and serve.

4 SERVINGS

POTATOES MAIRE

These creamed potatoes can be made with either fresh diced potatoes or frozen hash-brown potatoes. I use half-and-half, but this could be replaced with cream if you want the dish to be very rich, or with milk if you want it less rich. Either way, it is delicious with grilled meat or fish.

4 cups peeled, diced (½-inch) potatoes, or 4 cups packaged frozen hash-brown potatoes
1½ cups half-and-half
2 cloves garlic, peeled, crushed, and chopped fine (about 1 teaspoon)
½ teaspoon salt
¼ teaspoon freshly ground black pepper
1 tablespoon chopped chives

YOU CAN ELIMINATE PEELING AND DICING CHORES IF YOU USE FROZEN HASH-BROWNS INSTEAD OF FRESH POTATOES.

If you are using fresh potatoes, place the diced pieces in a saucepan, cover with water, bring to a boil, and boil until tender, about 3 minutes. Drain off the

(continued)

Potatoes Maire (continued)

liquid and return the potatoes to the pan. If you are using frozen hash-brown potatoes, place them in a saucepan.

Add the half-and-half, garlic, salt, and pepper to the potatoes. Bring to a boil, partially cover, reduce the heat to low, and cook for 8 to 10 minutes, until most of the liquid has been absorbed and the potatoes are just moist. Sprinkle with the chives, and serve.

4 SERVINGS

MASHED POTATOES AND GARLIC

When I was a child in France, each time my aunt cooked mashed potatoes—which I adored—she would put a couple of cloves of garlic in the cooking water. After the potatoes were cooked she would push them—garlic and all —through a food mill, and the resulting potato mixture would have a delicate garlic flavor, which I recall fondly and have tried to recapture in this simple recipe.

This can be made with fresh potatoes, peeled and cut into cubes, or if you are in a hurry, with an equal amount of packaged frozen hash-brown potatoes. Unlike my aunt's smooth mashed potatoes, these aren't pressed through a food mill after cooking and so are "rougher"; the larger chunks are merely broken with a whisk and beaten lightly with cream, so there may be some unmashed pieces for a more "country-style" result.

1¾ pounds potatoes, peeled and cut into 2-inch cubes (about 1½ pounds total, peeled), or packaged frozen hash-brown potatoes
2 large cloves garlic, peeled
2 tablespoons unsalted butter
1 cup half-and-half or a mixture of milk and cream

¼ teaspoon freshly ground black pepper
½ teaspoon salt

Place the potatoes and garlic in a saucepan, cover with water, and bring to a boil. Boil gently for 20 to 22 minutes, until tender; then drain. Add the butter, half-

> **NOTICE THE POTATOES ARE PU-REED BY WHISKING AND NOT BY RE-MOVING FROM THE PAN AND PUSH-ING THROUGH A FOOD MILL, MAKING CLEANUP A LOT SIMPLER.**

and-half, pepper, and salt. Mix with a whisk just until the potatoes are broken into pieces and the mixture is as smooth as you desire. Serve immediately.

Note: To prepare the potatoes ahead, cover the whisked mixture with 2 to 3 tablespoons milk (so the top remains moist and a "skin" doesn't form). Set aside, and reheat at serving time.

4 SERVINGS

POTATOES PERSILLADE

T his recipe is ready in a few minutes if the potatoes are cooked ahead. It goes well with everything from poached fish to sautéed meats and roasts.

1½ pounds small- to medium-size cooked potatoes (see Basic Boiled Potatoes, page 224), peeled or unpeeled
3 tablespoons vegetable oil
3 cloves garlic, peeled, crushed, and chopped (1½ teaspoons)
3 tablespoons chopped parsley, preferably flat-leaf
¼ teaspoon salt
1 tablespoon unsalted butter

Cut the cooked potatoes into slices ¼ inch thick.

Heat the oil in an 8-inch skillet (preferably nonstick), then add the potatoes and sauté over medium-to-high heat for 6 to 8 minutes, until they are browned.

Just before serving, add the garlic, parsley, salt, and butter. Cook, stirring, for 5 to 6 seconds. Serve immediately.

4 SERVINGS

> ***PERSILLADE,* A SIGNATURE OF PROVENÇAL COOKING, IS A MIXTURE OF EQUAL AMOUNTS OF CHOPPED PARSLEY AND GARLIC THAT IS ADDED AT THE END TO VEGETABLE AS WELL AS MEAT AND FISH DISHES.**

RAGOUT OF POTATOES

T his is another potato dish made with cooked potatoes. It can be prepared ahead and then warmed (preferably in a microwave oven) at the last minute.

1½ pounds cooked potatoes (see Basic Boiled Potatoes, page 224), peeled
2 tablespoons vegetable oil
2 medium-sized onions (about 10 ounces total), peeled and cut into ½-inch dice
4 cloves garlic, peeled and sliced (about 2 tablespoons)
2 teaspoons herbes de Provence (see Note, page 48)
2 tablespoons Hot Red Salsa (page 23)
1 cup fresh or frozen homemade chicken stock (see Basic Chicken Stock, page 48) or canned chicken broth
¼ teaspoon salt, or to taste
Chopped parsley or chives, for garnish

Cut the cooked potatoes into ½-inch cubes.

Heat the oil in a skillet. When it is hot, add the onions and sauté for 3 to 4 minutes, until they begin to soften and brown. Add the garlic, potatoes, herbes de Provence, salsa, stock, and salt if desired. Cover and bring to a boil. Then reduce the heat and simmer gently for 8 to 10 minutes, until most of the liquid has evaporated and the mixture is just slightly moist. Serve with a sprinkling of parsley or chives.

4 SERVINGS

HASH-BROWN POTATO CAKE

T hese hash-brown potatoes are pressed down to form a beautiful cakelike patty that is crisp and brown on the bottom. If you are proficient enough or daring enough, you can turn the patty and brown it on the other side. The potatoes are just as good, however, when cooked on one side only, as they are here, and then inverted onto a plate so they can be presented brown side up.

2 tablespoons unsalted butter
2 tablespoons corn or safflower
    oil
3 cups peeled, diced (½ inch)
    potatoes, or 3 cups packaged
    frozen hash-brown potatoes
¼ teaspoon salt
¼ teaspoon freshly ground
    black pepper
⅛ teaspoon ground nutmeg

Heat the butter and oil in a 9-inch nonstick skillet. When the mixture is hot, add the potatoes, salt, and pepper. Sauté, stirring occasionally, over medium to high heat for about 3 minutes, until the potatoes begin to soften. Cover, reduce the heat, and cook for about 5 minutes over medium heat.

Press on the potatoes with a spatula to compact them into a ½-inch-thick layer. Cover and cook over low heat for another 5 minutes. Then press down on the potatoes again, re-cover, and continue cooking for 5 more minutes. The underside should be nicely browned.

Invert the potato cake directly onto a serving platter, cut into wedges, and serve.

4 SERVINGS

A NONSTICK SKILLET IS ESSENTIAL WHEN MAKING THIS DISH.

POTATOES WITH WALNUTS AND CROUTONS

This is an interesting combination—potatoes, walnut pieces, and bread croutons. Although cubes of fresh potatoes are the conventional choice, I use frozen hash-brown potatoes. These usually come in ¾-inch cubes and are handy to have on hand in the freezer. (Walnut pieces should be stored in the freezer, too, so they don't get rancid.) An easy dish to prepare, it is delicious with fish, meat, or just a salad.

(continued)

Potatoes with Walnuts and Croutons (continued)

6 tablespoons corn or canola oil

4 cups (1 pound) packaged
  frozen hash-brown potatoes,
  partially defrosted

⅔ cup walnut, pecan, or other
  nut pieces

3 to 4 slices bread, cut into
  ½-inch croutons (about 1½
  cups)

1 tablespoon unsalted butter

2 tablespoons chopped chives or
  parsley

½ teaspoon salt

Heat the oil in a large non-stick skillet. When it is hot, add the potatoes and sauté for 6 to 8 minutes over high heat, stirring every few minutes, until lightly browned. Add the nuts and croutons and continue cooking, stirring every few seconds, for 3 to 4 minutes, until the nuts and bread have browned with the potatoes. Add the butter and allow it to melt into the mixture. Transfer to a serving platter, sprinkle with the chives and salt, and serve immediately.

4 SERVINGS

HASH-BROWN POTATOES BOULANGERE

You can, of course, peel and dice fresh potatoes for this recipe, but frozen hash-brown potatoes work very well. With a little beef stock and an onion on hand, you can make this gratin in a few minutes. Serve it with roast lamb, veal, or beef.

4 cups (about 20 ounces)
  peeled, diced (½ inch)
  potatoes, or 4 cups packaged
  frozen hash-brown potatoes

1 onion (about 5 ounces),
  peeled and sliced thin
  (1¼ cups)

1½ cups homemade beef stock
  or canned beef broth

½ teaspoon herbes de Provence
  (see Note, page 48)

2 bay leaves

2 tablespoons virgin olive oil

¼ teaspoon freshly ground
  black pepper

BOULANGERE REFERS TO A CLAS-
SIC DISH OF SLICED POTATOES,
SMOTHERED WITH ONIONS AND
STOCK.

Mix all the ingredients together in a 6-cup gratin dish. Set

the dish on a cookie sheet and bake
in a 400-degree oven for about 45
minutes, until most of the moisture has evaporated. Remove the
dish from the oven and let it rest
for about 15 minutes, until more
of the surrounding liquid has been
absorbed. Serve.

4 SERVINGS

POTATO OMELET

This is an ideal recipe for a last-minute meal when you have
unexpected guests. I always have potatoes and eggs on
hand, so all I need to make this delicious omelet are a
couple of scallions, which lend color to the dish and enhance its
flavor. Served with a salad, the omelet also makes a perfect main
dish for an informal dinner.

About 3 potatoes (1 pound),
    peeled and sliced thin
    (about 3 cups)
3 tablespoons safflower or
    corn oil
1 tablespoon unsalted butter
8 large eggs
½ teaspoon salt

¼ teaspoon freshly ground
    black pepper
3 scallions, peeled and minced
    fine (½ cup)

YOU PROBABLY ALREADY HAVE THE
BASIC INGREDIENTS—EGGS AND
POTATOES—ON HAND FOR THIS
GREAT LAST-MINUTE DISH.

Wash the potatoes in cool water,
drain, and dry thoroughly with
paper towels.

Heat the oil and butter in a
10-inch nonstick pan. When the
mixture is hot, add the potatoes,
cover (they tend to splatter), and
cook over medium to high heat
for 12 to 14 minutes, stirring every
3 to 4 minutes. The potatoes should

(continued)

Potato Omelet (continued)

be cooked through and lightly browned.

While the potatoes are cooking, break the eggs into a bowl and add the salt, pepper, and scallions. Mix well with a fork.

When the potatoes are cooked through, add the egg mixture, and using a rubber or wooden spatula, stir from the sides toward the center of the pan for 30 to 45 seconds, allowing the eggs to move between the potatoes and cook. By then most of the mixture will have

set, although it should still be quite wet in the center. Cover, reduce the heat, and cook over medium to low heat for 5 minutes at most, until a nice crust has formed on the underside. (There will still be some wetness on top.) Loosen the omelet around the edges by sliding a spatula underneath, and invert the omelet onto a serving plate. Cut it into six wedges, and serve.

4 SERVINGS

YAMS WITH MAPLE SYRUP AND BUTTER

This is a good recipe to serve with turkey or capon over the holidays. You can use fresh yams, of course, but the dish can be prepared much more quickly with canned yams, and they are very good this way.

1 can (1 pound) yams, drained
   (about 8 small yams)
⅛ teaspoon freshly ground
   black pepper
⅛ teaspoon salt
2 tablespoons maple syrup
1½ tablespoons unsalted butter,
   cut into small pieces

Arrange the yams in a single layer in a gratin dish, and sprin-

kle the remainder of the ingredients over them. Cover with aluminum foil, bake in a 400-degree oven for 25 to 30 minutes, until piping hot, and serve.

4 SERVINGS

CANNED YAMS WORK BEAUTIFULLY IN THIS QUICKLY PREPARED DISH.

SCALLIONS AU GRATIN

T his interesting, flavorful, and attractive dish goes well with roasted or grilled meat, and is elegant enough to serve as a first course for a formal dinner or as the main dish for a special lunch.

The dish can be assembled several hours ahead or even the night before, and then refrigerated until about 20 minutes before serving.

4 bunches (about 36) scallions
⅛ teaspoon salt
⅛ teaspoon freshly ground
 black pepper
½ cup heavy cream
2 tablespoons freshly grated
 Parmesan cheese

Cut off and discard the top 3 inches of the scallion leaves and any damaged outer leaves. Wash the scallions thoroughly under cool tap water and pat dry.

To cook in a microwave oven: Arrange the scallions in a 6-cup oval glass or china gratin dish, and cover with microwave-safe plastic wrap or a glass plate. Cook on high heat for about 2 minutes.

To cook on top of the stove: Place the scallions in a stainless steel skillet, add 1 cup of water, and bring to a boil. Cover, and boil over high heat for about 3 minutes, until the water has evaporated. Arrange in one layer in a 6-cup oval gratin dish.

Sprinkle the scallions with the salt and pepper; then pour the cream over them and sprinkle with the Parmesan cheese.

When you are ready to cook the gratin, bake it in a 400-degree oven for about 15 minutes. Then, to lightly brown the top, place the dish under the broiler, about 4 inches from the heat, and cook for about 2 minutes. Serve immediately.

4 SERVINGS

YOU CAN COOK THE SCALLIONS AND ASSEMBLE THIS DISH THE NIGHT BEFORE, AND REFRIGERATE IT UNTIL ABOUT 20 MINUTES BEFORE SERVING.

GRATIN OF PUMPKIN WITH CHEESE

I use canned unseasoned pumpkin purée here, combining it in the French style with salt, pepper, and cheese to make a vegetable gratin. This dish can be assembled and refrigerated hours ahead, but should be cooked in the last hour before serving.

1 can (16 ounces) natural
    pumpkin purée
2 eggs
1 cup light cream
¼ teaspoon freshly ground
    black pepper
¾ teaspoon salt
¼ teaspoon ground nutmeg
About 1 cup (2 ounces) grated
    Swiss cheese, preferably
    Gruyère or Emmenthaler
1 teaspoon unsalted butter

Place all the ingredients except the butter in a food processor and process for a few seconds until combined, or whisk together in a bowl by hand.

Grease a 5- to 6-cup gratin dish with the butter, and pour the pumpkin mixture into the dish. Cook immediately, or cover and refrigerate until about half an hour before serving.

Place the dish in a 375-degree oven and bake for 30 minutes, until set and lightly browned on top. Serve immediately.

4 SERVINGS

CANNED PUMPKIN PUREE IS PREPARED FRENCH-STYLE HERE, FOR SERVING AS A VEGETABLE.

SAUTEED SPINACH WITH NUTMEG

Another quick, easy dish, this one features nutmeg-flavored spinach that is stirred into a browned butter and oil mixture, giving it a wonderfully nutty taste.

Defrost the frozen spinach by setting it out for a few hours at room temperature, placing it in a microwave oven briefly, or running it under warm water. Be sure to press the defrosted spinach between your palms to extract most of the water so that the finished dish will not be watery.

2 packages (10 ounces each)
    frozen leaf spinach,
    defrosted
4 tablespoons (½ stick)
    unsalted butter
1 tablespoon corn or canola oil
¼ teaspoon ground nutmeg
¼ teaspoon freshly ground
    black pepper
½ teaspoon salt

Press the defrosted spinach between your palms to extract most of the liquid, and cut it into 1-inch pieces.

Combine the butter and oil in a skillet, and cook over medium to high heat until the mixture turns light brown. Sprinkle the spinach with the nutmeg, pepper, and salt, and add it to the hot butter and oil. Using a fork, spread out the spinach so that the flavorings are distributed evenly. Continue cooking for 2 minutes, then serve.

Note: To use fresh spinach for this dish, blanch it in boiling water until just wilted, then drain and allow to cool slightly. Press out the excess liquid as described, and proceed with the recipe.

6 SERVINGS

NUTMEG AND BROWNED BUTTER GIVE THIS QUICK, EASY DISH ITS NUTTY FLAVOR.

TOMATOES PROVENÇALE

This recipe is particularly good in late summer, when the large beefsteak tomatoes are ripe and very fleshy. The tomatoes can be partially cooked ahead of time, so it takes only five minutes to complete the dish just before serving—and they are precooked and then finished in a gratin dish that can go directly from the oven to the table.

2 pounds ripe, fleshy tomatoes
    (about 4)
3 tablespoons virgin olive oil
1½ slices bread
2 cloves garlic, peeled
½ cup loosely packed parsley
    leaves
1 teaspoon fresh thyme leaves,
    or ¼ teaspoon dried thyme
¼ teaspoon freshly ground
    black pepper
½ teaspoon salt

Cut the tomatoes in half parallel to the stem, and arrange them in a gratin dish that is attractive enough to bring to the table. Oil the tops of the tomatoes with 1 tablespoon of the olive oil, and place them under a preheated broiler, about 4 inches from the heat. Broil for 6 to 8 minutes. The tomatoes should be firm but tender when pierced gently with the point of a knife, and look slightly crusty and lightly brown on top.

Prepare the bread crumb mixture: Place the bread in the bowl of a food processor and pulse for about 10 seconds, until the bread is crumbed (you should have about ⅔ cup). Add the garlic, parsley, and thyme, and process for another 10 seconds, until the mixture is combined. Transfer it to a bowl, add the remaining 2 tablespoons oil and the pepper and salt, and toss gently. Spoon evenly over the tomatoes.

Just before serving, place the tomatoes under a preheated broiler, about 8 inches from the heat, and broil for 5 to 6 minutes, until they are heated through and brown on top. Serve immediately.

Note: To prepare this ahead of time, broil the tomatoes for 6 to 8 minutes; then let them cool to room temperature and refrigerate. About 10 minutes before serving time, prepare the bread crumb mixture and finish the tomatoes.

4 SERVINGS

MUSHROOM-AND-ANCHOVY-STUFFED TOMATOES

I love to make stuffed tomatoes, especially at the end of summer, when the tomatoes are ripe, flavorful, and inexpensive. This is the time when I also freeze or can tomatoes, or make tomato sauce or soup and freeze it for later use.

The tomatoes in this recipe are stuffed with a mixture of mushrooms (fresh or frozen), anchovy fillets, and onion. A substantial amount of juice is released as the tomatoes cook; spoon some of this natural juice over them, and serve either hot or cold. They can be served as a first course, or make an excellent luncheon entrée with a salad and a piece of cheese.

6 tomatoes (about 2½ pounds), of about equal size and as ripe as possible
¼ teaspoon salt

FILLING
3 tablespoons vegetable oil
2 onions (about 6 ounces total), peeled and chopped fine (1½ cups)
1 teaspoon Italian seasoning or herbes de Provence (see Note, page 48)

1 pound frozen sliced mushrooms; fresh presliced mushrooms; or fresh whole mushrooms, washed and sliced
1 can (2 ounces) anchovy fillets in oil, chopped (see Note, page 34)
1½ cups fresh bread crumbs, or ¾ cup dried bread crumbs
½ teaspoon freshly ground black pepper
½ teaspoon salt
2 tablespoons grated Parmesan cheese

NOTE THE DIFFERENCE IN VOLUME IN BREAD CRUMBS MADE FROM FRESH OR DRIED BREAD. ONE SLICE OF FRESH BREAD MAKES ½ CUP CRUMBS, WHILE 1 SLICE OF DRIED OR TOASTED BREAD MAKES ¼ CUP.

Cut a thin (⅜-inch) crosswise slice from the stem end of each tomato, and using a small spoon with a sharp edge, remove about 2 tablespoons of the tomato interior. Then, holding the tomatoes cut side down over the sink

(continued)

Mushroom-and-Anchovy-Stuffed Tomatoes (continued)

or a garbage can, press to extract most of the juice and seeds.

Arrange the tomatoes side by side in a gratin dish where they fit exactly. With your thumb, press around the inside wall of each tomato to smooth it and create a nice cavity. Sprinkle the inside of the tomatoes with the ¼ teaspoon salt.

Heat the oil in a saucepan. When it is hot, add the onions and Italian seasoning and cook for about 2 minutes. Add the mushrooms and cook for 5 minutes, until they render their juice. Then add the chopped anchovies and their oil (there will still be a lot of liquid in the pan at this point). Add the bread crumbs, and stir in the pepper and salt.

Stuff the tomatoes with the filling, dividing it evenly and mounding it so all of the stuffing is used. Sprinkle with the Parmesan cheese. Place the gratin dish in a 400-degree oven and bake for 35 to 40 minutes, until the tomatoes are well cooked and soft. Allow them to cool to lukewarm, basting occasionally with the natural juices released during cooking. Serve warm or cool.

Note: The tomatoes can be reheated; this is best done by placing them in a microwave oven for 1 to 2 minutes.

6 SERVINGS

ZUCCHINI FLAN

My mother makes a lot of gratins, flans, and custard-like dishes—this is one of her favorites. I prepare it often in the summer when I have an abundance of zucchini in the garden, although pumpkin or another type of squash could be used as well. It is an easy recipe because all the preparation is done in a food processor.

The flan can be served by itself or as an accompaniment to most roasted or grilled meat or fish. You will notice that a little liquid will seep out of the zucchini after the dish is baked. Pour it off or serve it with the gratin, as desired.

1 large or several small
  zucchini (2½ pounds total),
  washed and cut into ¾-inch-
  thick slices
1½ teaspoons salt
½ cup heavy cream
4 eggs
2 tablespoons cornstarch
½ teaspoon freshly ground
  black pepper
¼ cup grated Parmesan or
  Romano cheese
1 tablespoon unsalted butter

Arrange the zucchini slices on a foil-lined cookie sheet. Sprinkle with ½ teaspoon of the salt, and bake in a 400-degree oven for 10 minutes.

Transfer the softened zucchini to the bowl of a food processor, and process for a few seconds to purée. Using a rubber spatula, push down any zucchini clinging to the sides of the bowl, and process again, until very smooth (you should have approximately 4 cups). Add the cream, eggs, cornstarch, remaining 1 teaspoon salt, and pepper. Process until smooth. Add the cheese, and process a few seconds to incorporate.

Grease a 7-cup gratin dish (2 inches deep) with the butter. Pour the zucchini mixture into the dish, place it on a foil-lined cookie sheet, and bake in a 375-degree oven for about 45 minutes, until nicely set. If you want the top of the flan to be more browned, place it under the broiler for a few minutes at the end of the baking time.

Note: To prepare this dish ahead, assemble the ingredients in the gratin dish and refrigerate for up to 24 hours. Stir the mixture lightly just before baking.

6 SERVINGS

ALL THE WORK HERE IS DONE BY A FOOD PROCESSOR, SO THIS IS AN ESPECIALLY EASY RECIPE.

ZUCCHINI AND EGGPLANT GRATIN

I n summer, when zucchini and eggplant are plentiful, I often make this gratin at home. It only takes a few minutes to prepare, and the recipe can be varied by adding other vegetables, such as garlic and slices of tomato.

I arrange the slices of eggplant and zucchini alternately in a gratin dish, standing them almost upright like a deck of cards. As they cook, the slices sink down and flatten into the dish.

2 eggplants (about 1¾ pounds total), preferably narrow (3 to 4 inches in diameter)
1 large or 2 small zucchini (about 1¾ pounds total), as close in diameter to the eggplants as possible
1 teaspoon salt
½ teaspoon freshly ground black pepper
½ cup mixture of canola or corn oil and olive oil
2 slices bread
¼ cup grated Parmesan cheese

Wash (but do not peel) the eggplants and zucchini, and cut them into ½-inch-thick slices. You should have about 20 slices of each. Sprinkle with the salt and pep-per, and arrange alternate slices of eggplant and zucchini almost upright in a large gratin dish. Pour all but 1 tablespoon of the oil over the slices. Bake in a 400-degree oven for 30 minutes.

While the gratin is cooking, process the bread in a food processor to make 1 cup crumbs. Mix the bread crumbs with the Parmesan cheese and the remaining 1 tablespoon oil.

Press down on the vegetable slices so that they are flat in the dish. Sprinkle the bread crumb mixture evenly over the vegetables, and bake 30 minutes longer. Serve immediately.

6 SERVINGS

DESSERTS

We don't usually eat desserts at my house at the end of a family meal. However, when guests appear we always finish the meal with a dessert—most often one made with fruit. Sometimes these are simple concoctions, but on special occasions they are more elegant, like the Bartlett Pears in Puff Pastry, made with puff pastry from the supermarket.

When fruits are in season, use them fresh in recipes like the Blueberry Tart, made with a frozen pie shell, the Apple Brown Betty, and the Poached Fresh Figs with Campari, a spectacular dish when figs are at their peak in late summer. At other times of the year, use Individually Quick Frozen (IQF) fruits to create desserts like the Gratin of Raspberries or make Peach Tyler with canned fruit.

Throughout, I have used very simple ingredients, from store-bought cakes to commercial ice creams, all of which are readily available. Melted French ice cream—a mixture of milk, egg yolks, sugar, and vanilla—can even be used as sauce to serve with cakes or puddings. It makes a great batter for French toast. Or mix it with sour cream to serve with berries and other fruits.

APPLE AND GRAPE GRATIN

This delicious do-ahead dessert is made with unpeeled apples—the apple skin gives it a chewy texture. I use white grapes, but red grapes would be good too. The dish should be served at room temperature.

---

4 medium-size Russet or Golden Delicious apples (about 1¼ pounds total)
2 cups (12 ounces) white seedless grapes
⅓ cup apricot jam or preserves
⅓ cup maple syrup
4 tablespoons (½ stick, 2 ounces) unsalted butter
1 cup sour cream, for garnish (optional)

Cut the apples in half parallel to the stem, remove the cores, and cut each half into four wedges. Place them in a bowl and stir in the grapes, apricot jam, and maple syrup. Arrange the mixture in a gratin dish, and dot it with the butter. Place the dish on a foil-lined cookie sheet, and bake in a 375-degree oven for 1 hour, checking after 30 minutes to see if the liquid in the dish is caramelizing. If it is, add about 2 to 3 tablespoons water and continue cooking for the remainder of the hour. Serve lukewarm, with sour cream if desired.

6 SERVINGS

DON'T PEEL THE APPLES—THE SKINS GIVE THE DESSERT A WONDERFULLY CHEWY QUALITY.

APPLE BROWN BETTY

This dessert tastes great and is easy to make. I like to use soft, white, flavorful apples, like McIntosh, Rome Beauty, or Macoun, but any other variety to your liking would be good too. Notice that I don't peel the apples; the skin adds to the texture of the dish.

I like to cook the brown betty in a 6-cup gratin dish because its shallowness allows a lot of the mixture to be exposed. The surface will caramelize, producing a great intensity of taste.

6 McIntosh apples (about 1½ pounds total), halved, cored, and each half cut into 3 pieces

5 slices firm-textured white bread (about 5 ounces total), broken into 2-inch pieces

8 tablespoons (1 stick, 4 ounces) unsalted butter, melted

½ cup apricot preserves

2 teaspoons ground cinnamon

½ cup apple cider

¼ cup sugar

⅓ cup raisins

1 cup sour cream, for garnish (optional)

TO ELIMINATE LAST-MINUTE WORK, MAKE THIS DESSERT AHEAD AND JUST REWARM IT AT SERVING TIME.

In a bowl, mix together all the ingredients except the sour cream. Pack the mixture into a 6-cup oval gratin dish. Set the dish on a foil-lined cookie sheet and bake in a 400-degree oven for about 45 minutes, until nicely browned and caramelized on top. Cool until lukewarm, and serve as is or with sour cream.

6 SERVINGS

BANANAS FOSTER AND ICE CREAM

These sautéed bananas can be served cold with sour cream and a slice of pound cake, or they can be served, as they are here, while still warm with ice cream on top. I prefer vanilla ice cream with the bananas, but almost any flavor you like will be good served this way.

(continued)

Bananas Foster and Ice Cream (continued)·

4 very ripe bananas (1¾
    pounds total)
2 tablespoons unsalted butter
¼ cup sugar
2 tablespoons lemon juice
¼ cup water
¼ cup dark rum
1 pint vanilla ice cream, best
    possible quality

Peel the bananas and slice them crosswise.

Heat the butter and sugar in a skillet and cook over medium heat, stirring occasionally, for about 1 minute, until the sugar starts to brown lightly and the mixture begins to caramelize. Add the bananas and sauté, stirring, for about 1 minute. Then stir in the lemon juice, water, and rum.

Cover and cook over medium heat for about 1 minute, until a sauce has formed. Spoon the mixture onto dessert plates or into individual glass bowls or wine goblets, top each with a scoop of ice cream, and serve immediately.

Note: Use bananas that have black spots on their skin to ensure they are well ripened.

4 SERVINGS

THIS IS GOOD WAY TO USE UP THOSE BANANAS WITH SPOTTED BLACK SKIN.

CRISP OF BLUEBERRIES

Very often, frozen blueberries cannot replace fresh—in a soufflé or in a fruit mixture, for example—because they "bleed." Cooked as they are here with a crumbly dough topping, however, they work perfectly well. You don't need to wait for blueberry season to enjoy this dessert.

THE DOUGH TOPPING FOR THIS CRISP IS MADE QUICKLY IN A FOOD PROCESSOR.

⅓ cup sugar
1 tablespoon cornstarch
About 5 cups fresh or frozen
    blueberries (1½ pounds)

CRISP DOUGH
1 cup all-purpose flour
8 tablespoons (1 stick, 4
ounces) unsalted butter, cut
into pieces
½ cup walnut pieces
⅓ cup sugar
¼ cup half-and-half

1 cup lightly whipped heavy
cream, or 1 cup sour cream,
for garnish

Stir ⅓ cup sugar and the cornstarch together in a mixing bowl. Add the berries and toss gently to mix. Pour into a 6-cup gratin dish (the mixture should be about 1 inch deep).

Place the flour, butter, nuts, and ⅓ cup sugar in the bowl of a food processor and process for 15 to 20 seconds. Then add the half-and-half and process for another 5 to 10 seconds, just until the mixture holds together. Crumble the dough evenly over the berries, and bake in a 400-degree oven for 45 minutes, until nicely browned on top. Serve warm, with whipped heavy cream or sour cream.

6 SERVINGS

BLUEBERRY TART

You can make your own pie shell for this tart, but if you are pressed for time and have a packaged frozen shell in your freezer, you can assemble this dessert in a few minutes and even cook it ahead. It is best served at room temperature with a garnish of sour cream.

Fresh blueberries would be good here, but packaged Individually Quick Frozen (IQF) berries, which are unsweetened, work very well too.

¾ cup pecan pieces
¾ cup sugar
3 tablespoons all-purpose flour
1 pound frozen unsweetened
blueberries (preferably the
small wild variety)

1 frozen pie shell (9-inch)
1 cup sour cream

Place the pecan pieces, sugar, and flour in the bowl of a food processor and process until pow-

(continued)

Blueberry Tart (continued)

dered. Combine in a bowl with the frozen berries, and pour into the frozen pie shell.

YOU CAN ASSEMBLE THIS TART AND PUT IT IN THE OVEN WHILE THE BERRIES AND THE PIE SHELL ARE STILL FROZEN.

Place the tart on a foil-lined cookie sheet and bake in a 400-degree oven for 50 to 60 minutes, until the dough is well cooked and the mixture lightly browned on top. Cool for at least 1 hour before cutting.

To serve, cut into wedges and garnish with sour cream.

6 SERVINGS

CLAFOUTIS OF CHERRIES AMANDINE

A *clafoutis* is a French country dessert in which the cherries are coated with a batter of milk, eggs, and flour. In this version I add almonds and rum for a nice combination. A scoop of vanilla or coffee ice cream is good with this.

1¼ pounds pitted frozen cherries; or about 1½ pounds fresh cherries, pitted
⅔ cup cherry preserves

FRANGIPANE
1 cup almonds, unskinned
½ cup sugar
1 tablespoon cornstarch
2 tablespoons unsalted butter, softened
2 eggs
2 tablespoons dark rum

Confectioners' sugar for dusting (optional)

EITHER SWEET OR TART CHERRIES CAN BE USED IN THIS CLASSIC FRENCH DESSERT.

Place the pitted cherries in a gratin dish or in a round porcelain pie dish (suitable for serving) that is about 1½ inches deep and 10 inches across. Add the preserves, mix, and set aside.

Place the almonds, sugar, and cornstarch in the bowl of a food processor and process until powdered. Add the butter, eggs, and rum and process for a few seconds, until well mixed.

Pour the frangipane mixture over the cherries and mix lightly. Set the dish on a foil-lined cookie sheet and bake in a 375-degree oven for 40 minutes, until the top is brown and the mixture cooked through.

Allow the dish to cool to lukewarm. Sprinkle with powdered sugar if desired, and serve.

6 TO 8 SERVINGS

DAMSON PLUMS IN BLACK CURRANT SYRUP

At the end of the summer, Damson plums—the oval variety sometimes called prune plums or Italian plums—are available at the market. They are excellent poached and make an elegant dessert. Prepared ahead, they will keep in the refrigerator for about a week. I like to serve them garnished with a spoonful of sour cream and a slice of pound cake.

About 24 Damson or St. Clare plums (1½ pounds)
1 jar (12 ounces) cherry preserves
½ cup black currant syrup
1 pound cake (8 to 10 ounces)
1 cup sour cream

Place the plums, preserves, and syrup in a stainless steel pan. Stir gently and bring to a boil. Cover, lower the heat, and boil gently until tender, about 7 to 8 minutes, depending on the ripeness of the fruit. Set aside to cool, covered, in the poaching liquid.

When you are ready to serve, trim the pound cake, cut it into ½-inch-thick slices, and cut each slice in half to form two triangles. Arrange a few plums with some of the cooking liquid in each dessert dish and top with a large spoonful of sour cream. Serve with the pound cake triangles.

4 SERVINGS

REFRIGERATED IN THEIR POACHING LIQUID, THESE PLUMS WILL KEEP FOR ABOUT A WEEK.

POACHED FRESH FIGS WITH CAMPARI

I especially like to make this dessert when the tiny black Mission figs appear at the supermarket in midsummer. Of course you can use larger figs too—they'll be just as good. Whatever variety you select, the figs must be ripe. However, if they are so ripe that their skin is splitting, reduce the cooking time as necessary to prevent them from falling apart.

This delightful dessert can be made in only a few minutes, and it will keep and develop flavor for at least a week in the refrigerator. The juice of the figs turns it bright red, and the Campari gives it a slightly bitter, spicy taste. (If you are not fond of Campari, replace it with another liquor or eliminate it altogether.)

1 cup fruity white wine
⅓ cup sugar
¼ cup lime juice
About 20 small ripe Mission figs (1 pound)
2 teaspoons cornstarch dissolved in 2 tablespoons water
2 tablespoons Campari
1 cup sour cream
Pound cake (optional)

Combine the wine, sugar, and lime juice in a saucepan and bring to a boil. Add the figs, cover, and boil gently for 4 to 5 minutes, until the figs are tender when touched with a knife but are not bursting open and falling apart. Using a slotted spoon, transfer the figs to a bowl.

There should be about 1 cup liquid in the saucepan; if there is more, boil it down to reduce to 1 cup. Add the dissolved cornstarch, stir, and bring to a boil. Pour the sauce over the figs and allow to cool to room temperature. Then stir in the Campari.

Spoon 4 to 5 figs (or 2 or 3 larger figs) into individual deep dessert dishes. Spoon some sauce over the figs, place a dollop of sour cream in the center, and serve with a slice of pound cake if desired.

4 SERVINGS

GATEAU CLAUDINE

T his is a cake I've made many times for my daughter, Claudine. Even though I often make fancy multiple-layered cakes and decorate them elaborately with rich homemade buttercream frostings, Claudine likes this one—frosted with instant vanilla pudding and whipped cream—the best.

The cake can be one you made yourself or a store-bought sponge or pound cake. Decorate it as elaborately as you like; there is ample vanilla cream to cover the middle and outside of the cake, and enough left over to pipe on some additional decorations from a pastry bag fitted with a star tip. Candied fruit or violets also make an attractive and festive addition to the decorations.

1 cup heavy cream
1 package (3½ ounces) instant
   vanilla pudding
1 cup milk
1 sponge cake (8 ounces), about
   7 inches in diameter and 1½
   inches thick
2 tablespoons apricot preserves

Whip the cream until firm, and set aside.

Mix the instant pudding with the milk according to the instructions on the pudding box (using half the milk called for on the box) until combined, and fold in the whipped cream. Set the frosting aside. It will be ready to use within 10 to 15 minutes.

Cut the cake in half horizontally, and place one of the halves on a plate. Spread the jam over it, and cover the jam with a layer of the frosting. Place the second cake layer on top, and cover the top and sides with frosting. If desired, spoon any remaining frosting into a pastry bag fitted with a star tip, and add decorative touches to the cake. Cut into wedges and serve.

6 SERVINGS

ORANGE CAKE WITH GRAND MARNIER

I use a prepared sponge cake from the supermarket for this recipe, first trimming it to remove the outer surface, which tends to be dark, damp, and sugary. The Suzette butter, which I also use in the crepes recipe (see page 253), makes an easy and flavorful buttercream. The cake is served with a Grand Marnier sauce and garnished with thin slices of orange. Not much sugar is used in the Suzette butter or in the sauce because commercial cakes are quite sweet.

1 sponge cake (8 ounces), 1¼ to 1½ inches thick

SUZETTE BUTTER
4 tablespoons (½ stick, 2 ounces) unsalted butter, softened
1½ teaspoons grated orange rind
2 tablespoons orange juice
1 tablespoon confectioners' sugar

3 tablespoons orange juice

GRAND MARNIER SAUCE
8 ounces sour cream
1 tablespoon Grand Marnier liqueur
1 tablespoon confectioners' sugar

GARNISH
1 large seedless orange

Trim the gooey, sugary outer surface off the cake, and split the cake into two layers, each about ¾ inch thick.

Prepare the Suzette butter: Place the softened butter in the bowl of a food processor and add the orange rind, 2 tablespoons orange juice, and 1 tablespoon confectioners' sugar. Process until combined. (At first the mixture will not incorporate; keep processing until the liquid is absorbed.)

Spread the Suzette butter over the top of one of the cake layers, and place the other cake layer on top. Sprinkle it with the remaining 3 tablespoons orange juice. (At this point the cake can be wrapped in plastic wrap and stored in the refrigerator for up to 24 hours.)

Make the Grand Marnier sauce: Mix the sour cream, Grand Marnier, and 1 tablespoon confectioners' sugar. Set aside.

Completely remove the remaining skin, including the cottony part underneath, from the orange (previously grated for the orange rind), and cut the orange into about 12 thin or 6 thicker slices.

At serving time, place a spoonful of sauce on each dessert plate. Arrange two small wedges of cake on the sauce, and top with one or two orange slices. Serve immediately.

6 SERVINGS

> YOU CAN PREPARE THIS LAYER CAKE AHEAD OF TIME, AND THEN MAKE THE SAUCE IN JUST A FEW MINUTES BEFORE SERVING.

DRIED FRUITS ON ORANGES

The dried fruits for this easy, refreshing dessert can be mixed several days ahead, and the oranges prepared up to a day ahead. Buy the largest, best-quality seedless oranges available, or use large tangelos.

2½ cups dried mixed fruits
(pears, apricots, apples,
peaches, prunes, raisins, and
currants)
1 large lemon
1 large lime
2 tablespoons dark rum
⅓ cup honey
2 or 3 large seedless oranges
¼ cup Grand Marnier or
another orange liqueur
2 cups strawberries
Pound cake

Prepare the dried fruit mixture ahead of time so it can macerate. (If any of the fruit is extremely dry, as pears and peaches sometimes are, cover with boiling water and set aside for 5 to 10 minutes to soften.) Cut all the dried fruit into ¼-inch pieces, and place them in a plastic bag.

Using a vegetable peeler, remove the outermost peel of the lemon and the lime. Pile the strips together and cut them into a fine julienne. You need 1 tablespoon each of lemon and lime julienne. (You can also use a zester for this procedure.)

Squeeze the lemon and lime

(continued)

to extract the juice (you should have approximately ⅓ cup combined juices). Add the juice, julienned rind, rum, and honey to the dried fruit and mix thoroughly. Tightly seal the plastic bag and set it aside in a cool place for at least 2 hours or up to 2 weeks. (The close confinement of the fruit and liquid facilitates the maceration process.)

Remove the skin and white pith from the oranges, and trim them slightly at the base and top. Cut the oranges into ¾-inch-thick slices (you should get about 3 slices per orange). If the centers of the orange slices are seedy or tough, remove them with the blade of a serrated knife and discard.

Place the orange slices in a gratin dish, and pour the Grand Marnier over them. Cover with plastic wrap and set aside for up to 1 day.

On the day of serving, clean the strawberries, cut them into ¼- to ½-inch wedges, and refrigerate until serving time.

At serving time, arrange a slice of orange with some of the Grand Marnier liquid on each dessert plate. Cover with the medley of dried fruit, and sprinkle with the cut-up strawberries. Serve with a piece of your favorite pound cake.

6 TO 8 SERVINGS

ORANGE BAVARIAN CREAM

Instead of preparing a custard cream from scratch and combining it with gelatin to make a traditional Bavarian cream, I use vanilla ice cream and instant vanilla pudding to make this delicious dessert in only 30 minutes.

The dessert is particularly attractive when served in a glass bowl and garnished with thinly sliced seedless oranges sprinkled with Mandarin orange liqueur, Cointreau, or Grand Marnier. It goes well with pound cake, sponge cake, or plain cookies.

1 pint (2 cups) good-quality vanilla ice cream, defrosted (see Note)

1 cup half-and-half
1 package (3½ ounces) instant vanilla pudding

1 large seedless orange
2 tablespoons Cointreau, Grand
    Marnier, or Mandarin
    orange liqueur

**THIS RICH AND FESTIVE DESSERT IS
READY IN JUST 30 MINUTES.**

Combine the defrosted ice cream, half-and-half, and pudding mix in a bowl, and stir thoroughly. Pour into a glass serving bowl, and chill for 20 to 30 minutes in the refrigerator.

Meanwhile, peel the orange with a sharp knife, completely removing the peel and the cottony white membrane (pith) underneath. Cut the orange into very thin rounds (about twelve), and set aside until serving time.

Just before serving, arrange the orange slices on top of the Bavarian cream. Sprinkle with the liqueur and serve immediately.

Note: Defrost the ice cream at room temperature, or by placing it in a microwave oven for about 2 minutes.

6 SERVINGS

GRATIN OF CREPES SUZETTE

These crepes are large enough that two per person is a more than adequate serving. They can be cooked and even filled ahead, ready to go into the oven for heating at the last moment. I fill them with orange marmalade and the Suzette butter I use in the Orange Cake with Grand Marnier (see page 250).

The crepe batter is easily made in a food processor. The recipe should yield about ten 8-inch crepes; if you don't get that many, you are using more than the 2½ tablespoons of batter needed per crepe and your crepes are too thick. As soon as the batter touches the surface of the hot pan it will begin to set, so how fast you shake the pan and spread the batter will determine the thickness of the crepe. It's better to start with too little batter and then add some to the pan if necessary than to start with too much.

(continued)

Gratin of Crepes Suzette (continued)

CREPE BATTER
½ cup all-purpose flour
1 egg
1½ tablespoons corn oil
¾ cup whole milk
½ teaspoon sugar
Pinch of salt (about
    ¹⁄₁₆ teaspoon)

CREPE FILLING
1 recipe Suzette butter (see
    Orange Cake with Grand
    Marnier, page 250)
½ cup orange marmalade

1 tablespoon granulated sugar
1 or 2 tablespoons Grand
    Marnier or cognac
    (optional)

Prepare the crepes: Place all the batter ingredients in the bowl of a food processor and process for a few seconds, just until smooth.

Heat a nonstick skillet with an 8-inch base until hot. Place about 2½ tablespoons of the batter in the hot pan, and tilt the pan quickly one way and then the other to spread the batter thinly over the entire bottom of the pan. Cook for about 45 seconds over medium to high heat. Then, using a fork, lift up one edge of the crepe, grab it with your other hand, set aside the fork, and with both hands turn the crepe over. Cook about 30 seconds on the second side and then place on a plate, second side up. Repeat this procedure until all the batter is used, stacking the crepes on the plate as they are removed from the pan.

Prepare the crepe filling: Mix the Suzette butter with the orange marmalade in a food processor, or by hand with a whisk. It will separate initially but will eventually smooth out as you mix.

Dividing it evenly, spread the filling on the second browned side of each crepe, and fold the crepes into fourths. Arrange them in a gratin dish, slightly overlapping so that the folded point of each is visible. At this point the crepes can be refrigerated for up to 3 or 4 hours.

At serving time, sprinkle the crepes with the granulated sugar. Place the dish under the boiler, about 10 to 12 inches from the heat, for 7 to 8 minutes, until the crepes are heated through and nicely browned on top. For added flavor pour on the Grand Marnier and ignite it to flambé the crepes.

4 SERVINGS

THE CREPES CAN BE MADE AND EVEN FILLED AHEAD, SO AT SERVING TIME THEY NEED ONLY TO BE HEATED UNDER THE BROILER.

LEMON DELICE

If you like the flavor of lemon, you'll love this cake—which can be served on its own or in combination with ice cream or fruit. I use a good commercial pound cake, available fresh and frozen at most supermarkets, and fill and frost it with a buttercream made in a food processor. Serve strong black coffee with this dessert.

1 fresh or frozen pound cake
    (10 ounces), preferably
    whole-butter
4 tablespoons (½ stick, 2
    ounces) unsalted butter, at
    room temperature
2 ounces cream cheese
4 tablespoons lemon juice
⅓ cup confectioners' sugar

Remove the cake from its container and trim it evenly to remove the brown exterior from the top, sides, and bottom. Slice the cake horizontally to create three layers.

Combine the butter, cream cheese, 2 tablespoons lemon juice, and confectioners' sugar in the bowl of a food processor, and process until smooth. Sprinkle the cake layers with the remaining lemon juice and re-form the cake, coating each layer and the top and sides with buttercream. Refrigerate for 10 to 15 minutes before slicing and serving.

6 SERVINGS

A STORE-BOUGHT POUND CAKE IS TRANSFORMED INTO COMPANY FARE WITH A BUTTERCREAM MADE IN A FOOD PROCESSOR.

PEACH TYLER

Although this dessert is delicious when made with fresh peaches in the summer, it is also very good made with canned peaches, which I always have available in the event

(continued)

Peach Tyler (continued)

that unexpected guests appear. I season the juice from the peaches with white wine, peppercorns (for zestiness), and lime, and serve the dessert with plain yogurt.

1 can (1 pound) sliced peaches
    in syrup
½ cup dry white wine
½ teaspoon black peppercorns
½ teaspoon pure vanilla extract
6 strips of lime peel (removed
    with a vegetable peeler)
1 container (8 ounces) plain
    yogurt

Drain the peaches, reserving ½ cup of the syrup. Combine the reserved peach syrup with the wine, peppercorns, vanilla, and lime strips in a saucepan and bring to a boil. Cover, reduce the heat, and boil gently for 5 minutes. Then stir in the peaches and immediately set aside to cool, covered.

Serve cool (but not ice cold) on individual dessert dishes, garnishing each serving with about 2 heaping tablespoons of the yogurt.

4 SERVINGS

> CANNED PEACHES ARE GOOD SUBSTITUTES FOR FRESH ONES IN SIMPLE COMPOTES LIKE THIS.

BARTLETT PEARS IN PUFF PASTRY

In this easy dessert I cover pear halves with frozen puff pastry, and bake them right in the gratin dish in which they will be served. You could use apples instead of pears, although they tend to lose their shape more than the pears do as they cook.

6 tablespoons sugar
¾ teaspoon ground cinnamon
3 large ripe Bartlett pears
    (about 9 ounces each)

Juice of 1 lemon
1 sheet packaged frozen puff
    pastry (about 8 ounces, ½
    package), partially defrosted

2 tablespoons unsalted butter
⅓ cup water
Heavy cream or sour cream, for
garnish (optional)

Mix the sugar and cinnamon together and set aside.

Peel the pears and cut them in half lengthwise. Remove the core and seeds from each half and arrange them, cut side down, in one layer in a gratin dish. Sprinkle with the lemon juice and half the cinnamon-sugar mixture.

Unfold the sheet of puff pastry and divide it at the seams to form three pieces approximately 10 inches by 3 inches. Cut each of these in half to create six pastry pieces, each about 5 inches by 3 inches. Lay a pastry piece on top of each pear, and as the pastry defrosts a little more and relaxes slightly, press them gently around

PACKAGED PUFF PASTRY MAKES THIS A QUICK AND EASY DESSERT.

the pears so they take on the shape of the pear halves. Sprinkle with the remaining cinnamon-sugar mixture, and dot with the butter.

Place the gratin dish on a foil-lined cookie sheet and bake in a 375-degree oven for about 25 minutes, until the pastry is browning nicely and the mixture around the pears is bubbly and caramelized. Pour the water around the pears, and return them to the oven for 5 minutes. The water will melt the caramel and create a sauce. Serve the pears lukewarm, with heavy or sour cream if desired.

6 SERVINGS

CREAM CHEESE AND DRIED FRUIT WITH PEARS

This is an easy fall or winter dessert, and the cheese balls can be made ahead. I usually use whipped rather than regular block cream cheese, mixing into it different types of nuts and dried fruits and forming it into balls. You might like to add a piece of pound cake, sponge cake, or a cookie alongside.

(continued)

Cream Cheese and Dried Fruit with Pears (continued)

4 ripe Anjou or Bartlett pears
    (about 1¾ pounds total)
2 tablespoons lemon juice

CREAM CHEESE BALLS
⅓ cup pecan pieces
1 cup (8 ounces) whipped
    cream cheese
1¼ cups mixed dried fruit
    (apricots, prunes, apples,
    and pears), cut into ¼-inch
    dice

Pound cake, sponge cake, or
    cookies (optional)

Peel the pears, cut them in half, and remove the cores. Cut each half into thirds. Roll them in the lemon juice and set aside.

Spread the nuts out on a foil-lined baking sheet, and toast in a 400-degree oven for 5 to 6 minutes.

Mix the cream cheese, pecans, and dried fruit in a bowl. Using a spoon or dampened hands, form into six balls. At serving time, place one ball in the center of each dessert plate, and surround with four pear wedges.

6 SERVINGS

MAKE THE CREAM CHEESE BALLS AHEAD FOR THIS COOL-WEATHER DESSERT.

FROZEN PINEAPPLE PARFAIT

I make this dessert with frozen pineapple juice concentrate, which is a natural, pure reduction of juices, usually without sweeteners.

Soaking the ladyfingers in rum not only flavors them but prevents them from freezing in the dessert. You can use pieces of sponge cake or pound cake instead of ladyfingers, if you prefer.

12 small packaged ladyfingers
    (about 1½ ounces each)
2 tablespoons dark rum
1½ cups heavy cream
1 cup frozen pure pineapple
    juice concentrate

Break the ladyfingers into 1½- to 2-inch pieces into a glass serving bowl or soufflé mold, and sprinkle with the rum. Set aside.

Whip the cream until firm with an electric mixer or with a whisk.

When the concentrate is defrosted enough to be incorporated into the cream, place it in
a bowl and add the whipped
cream. Fold gently with a rubber
spatula until the concentrate is
combined with the cream. Pour
over the ladyfingers, mix lightly,
cover, and place in the freezer for
at least 3 hours. (The rum will
prevent the dessert from becom-

ing too firm.) Serve directly from
the freezer, spooning the parfait
into goblets or brandy snifters.

6 SERVINGS

> **SOAKING THE LADYFINGERS IN RUM KEEPS THEM FROM FREEZING IN THE PARFAIT.**

PINEAPPLE WITH KIRSCH

We have a warm and a cold version of the same recipe here: In the warm version, sugared slices of pineapple are broiled and served lukewarm with kirschwasser spooned over them and pound cake alongside. In the cold version, the pineapple is cut into chunks, marinated in a mixture of sugar and kirschwasser, and served cold with a dollop of sour cream and a slice of pound cake.

A very ripe fresh pineapple is the best choice for this recipe, but if that is unavailable, canned pineapple slices will do nicely. Kirschwasser, which is a cherry brandy, can be replaced with dark rum or cognac for different flavor.

1 very ripe pineapple (2½ pounds), or 2 cans (1 pound each) pineapple slices in unsweetened juice
2 tablespoons sugar
2 tablespoons kirschwasser

Sour cream, for cold version (optional)
Pound cake

> **FRESH PINEAPPLE IS THE BEST CHOICE, BUT CANNED PINEAPPLE SLICES ARE A FINE ALTERNATIVE.**

(continued)

Pineapple with Kirsch (continued)

Warm pineapple: If you are using fresh pineapple, peel off the thick skin and cut the fruit into six slices, each about ½ inch thick. If you like, remove the center or core, which tends to be tough, from each slice with a sharp knife or a small round cookie cutter. If you are using canned pineapple, drain the juice from the slices and reserve it for another use.

Sprinkle the slices with the sugar, and arrange them on a cookie sheet lined with aluminum foil. Place it under a broiler, about 4 inches from the heat, and broil for about 8 minutes, until the slices are sizzling on top. Arrange a slice on each dessert plate, and sprinkle with the kirschwasser. Serve immediately with pound cake.

Cold pineapple: If you are using canned pineapple, drain the slices, reserving ¼ cup of the juice. Cut the fresh or canned pineapple slices into 1-inch chunks, and mix them with the sugar and kirschwasser. If you are using canned pineapple, add the reserved juice. Set the mixture aside to macerate for a few minutes, or refrigerate for a few hours. Serve with sour cream, if desired, and a slice of pound cake.

6 SERVINGS

RASPBERRY TART

This tart is made with a store-bought frozen pie shell and packaged Individually Quick Frozen (IQF) berries, but you can, of course, make your own pie shell if you want to and use fresh raspberries if they are available.

This sweet-but-tart dessert is very good served with crème fraîche or sour cream.

1 pound frozen unsweetened raspberries
2 tablespoons cornstarch
1 jar (12 ounces) seedless raspberry preserves
¼ cup sugar

1 frozen 9-inch pie shell
1 cup crème fraîche or sour cream

In a bowl, mix the frozen berries with the cornstarch, preserves, and sugar. Pour into the frozen pie shell, place the shell on a foil-lined cookie sheet, and bake in a 400-degree oven for 50 to 60 minutes, until the dough is nicely browned and the filling is bubbly. Set aside to cool for 1 hour before cutting.

RASPBERRY PRESERVES HELP TO SWEETEN AND INTENSIFY THE FLAVOR OF THIS FILLING.

Serve in wedges, topped with crème fraîche or sour cream.

Note: The filling will be a little runny, but I find it much more flavorful this way than if a greater amount of cornstarch is added to make it thicker.

6 SERVINGS

GRATIN OF RASPBERRIES

This terrific, easy dessert can be made with either fresh berries or commercially packaged IQF (Individually Quick Frozen) berries. I always have a few packages of unsweetened frozen berries in my freezer so I can make this on short notice.

Serve the gratin lukewarm, with sour cream or crème fraîche (available in specialty food stores and some supermarkets).

1 pound IQF (Individually Quick Frozen) or fresh raspberries

KEEP A SUPPLY OF IQF (INDIVIDUALLY QUICK FROZEN) BERRIES IN YOUR FREEZER FOR USE IN FRUIT DESSERTS.

6 ounces pound cake
4 tablespoons (½ stick, 2 ounces) unsalted butter, cut into pieces
½ cup light brown sugar
Sour cream or crème fraîche, for garnish

(continued)

Gratin of Raspberries (continued)

Break the cake into chunks and process it in a food processor; you should have about 2 cups crumbs. Add the butter and brown sugar, and process until the mixture appears mealy. Sprinkle this on top of the berries.

Bake in a 400-degree oven for 25 to 30 minutes (20 to 25 min- utes for fresh berries), until nicely browned on top. Keep warm until serving time, or allow to cool and then reheat just before serving. Garnish each serving with a spoonful of sour cream or crème fraîche.

6 SERVINGS

STRAWBERRIES IN PEKOE TEA

This unusual, refreshing dessert is best made in summer when strawberries are at their peak. Flavored with tea and apricot preserves, the berries can be served cold in a parfait glass, plain or garnished with a little sour cream or whipped cream.

½ cup water
1 orange pekoe tea bag (or
    another tea to your liking)
½ cup apricot preserves
1 pint strawberries, cleaned and
    hulled
Sour cream or whipped heavy
    cream, for garnish

Bring the water to a boil, pour it over the tea bag in a mixing bowl, and allow the mixture to steep, covered, for 5 minutes. Re- move the tea bag and stir in the apricot preserves and the straw- berries. Set aside to macerate at room temperature for at least 1 hour, or as long as overnight in the refrigerator. Serve as is or garnished with sour cream or whipped cream.

4 SERVINGS

USE ONLY RIPE, FLAVORFUL STRAW-
BERRIES IN THIS QUICK DESSERT.

GRATIN OF MIXED FRUIT WITH CREAM

W hen you have to create a dessert quickly, buy frozen unsweetened mixed fruit (peaches, grapes, apricots, and melon), available in 1-pound packages at most supermarkets. The fruit makes a wonderful gratin when baked, as it is here, with a few flavor-enhancing ingredients. Serve it lukewarm or at room temperature.

1 pound frozen unsweetened
    mixed fruit
1 cup frozen berries
    (blueberries, raspberries, or
    strawberries)
4 ounces butter cookies,
    crumbled
2 tablespoons lemon juice
⅓ cup sugar
1 cup heavy cream
1 pint vanilla ice cream
    (optional)

In a bowl combine the mixed fruit, berries, cookie crumbs, lemon juice, sugar, and cream. Stir well, and transfer to a 6-cup gratin dish. Place the dish on a foil-lined baking sheet, and bake in a 400-degree oven for about 35 minutes, until cooked throughout. Cool until lukewarm (40 minutes to 1 hour) or to room temperature, and serve as is or with ice cream.

6 SERVINGS

FROZEN MIXED FRUIT AND BERRIES ARE THE FOUNDATION FOR THIS ELEGANT GRATIN.

VELVET HAMMER

I n this ice cream dessert, dark rum and coffee liqueur work well with vanilla ice cream to produce a smooth, rich, rewarding taste.

(continued)

Velvet Hammer (continued)

1 pint commercial vanilla ice
  cream, best quality available
2 tablespoons Kahlúa (coffee-
  flavored liqueur)
1½ tablespoons dark rum
1 tablespoon fresh coffee beans
  or chocolate coffee beans, for
  garnish

Spoon the ice cream into the bowl of a food processor, and add the Kahlúa and rum. Process until well blended (the ice cream will become quite soft). Transfer the mixture back to the ice cream container or to a bowl, cover, and

place in the freezer for at least 3 to 4 hours, until firm. (The liqueur and rum will prevent it from becoming too hard.)

When ready to serve, spoon into brandy snifters or dessert dishes, and garnish with the coffee beans.

4 SERVINGS

ASSEMBLE THIS QUICKLY IN A FOOD PROCESSOR AND FIRM IT UP IN THE FREEZER.

CRUMBLE COOKIE COFFEE ICE CREAM

Crumbled store-bought cookies form the base for this dessert featuring coffee ice cream. There are many terrific cookies on the market to choose from; I like to use whole-butter Danish-type cookies, which work particularly well in this context. This dessert looks especially attractive served in small goblets or glass dessert bowls.

4 ounces cookies
¼ cup golden raisins
2 tablespoons cognac
¼ cup orange juice
1 pint coffee ice cream, best
  quality available

Crumble the cookies coarsely into a bowl, and add the raisins, cognac, and orange juice. Toss lightly to mix, and set aside.

At serving time, arrange a layer of the cookie mixture in the

bottom of four goblets or glass
dessert dishes, and top each with
a scoop of the ice cream. Serve.

4 SERVINGS

> YOU CAN CREATE A SPECIAL DES-
> SERT WITH STORE-BOUGHT COOK-
> IES AND ICE CREAM.

VANILLA ICE CREAM AND CHOCOLATE SAUCE

This elegant but easy dessert consists of frozen vanilla ice cream served with a sauce made of defrosted deep chocolate ice cream.

The vanilla ice cream can be scooped directly out of its container at serving time, or for a fancier presentation, it can be formed into small balls and then refrozen until hard. Defrost the chocolate ice cream ahead of time, either at room temperature or in a microwave oven, so that the foam that appears as it melts (from the air whipped into the ice cream when it was made) has time to subside.

¼ cup sliced almonds
1 pint vanilla ice cream, best
    possible quality
½ pint deep, dark chocolate ice
    cream, defrosted
4 slices pound cake, ½ inch
    thick

> MELTED CHOCOLATE ICE CREAM
> MAKES A WONDERFUL SAUCE FOR
> VANILLA ICE CREAM BALLS.

Arrange the almonds on a foil-lined cookie sheet and toast in a 400-degree oven until nicely browned. Cut the pound cake slices in half and set them aside.

If you want to make ice cream balls, spoon equal amounts of vanilla ice cream into eight pieces of plastic wrap, and wrap tightly, molding the ice cream into balls about the size of a golf ball. Place in the freezer until solidly frozen.

At serving time, place a di-
(continued)

Vanilla Ice Cream and Chocolate Sauce (continued)

vided slice of pound cake (two pieces) on each dessert dish, and set an ice cream ball (or a scoop of ice cream) on each piece of cake.

Coat with the defrosted chocolate ice cream, and top with the toasted almonds. Serve immediately.

4 SERVINGS

CHOCOLATE ROCHER AND NUTS IN SOUR CREAM

Use good-quality commercial ice cream for this recipe. Served with a creamy vanilla sauce and pieces of pound cake, this is a luxurious dessert.

½ cup walnut halves
½ pint good-quality chocolate
  ice cream

VANILLA SAUCE
½ cup sour cream
2 tablespoons milk
1 tablespoon sugar
½ teaspoon pure vanilla extract

½ pound cake

> **CUT THE ICE CREAM WITH A SHARP KNIFE TO DIVIDE IT EQUALLY FOR SHAPING INTO BALLS.**

Spread the walnuts out on a cookie sheet, and toast them in a 400-degree oven for 10 to 12 minutes, until lightly browned. Set the nuts aside, and when they are cool enough to handle, crack them by hand or with a mortar and pestle, until coarsely chopped.

Divide the ice cream into four equal pieces, place each one on a piece of plastic wrap, and return to the freezer. When they are solidly frozen again, press the ice cream pieces to form four roundish balls, molding them with the plastic wrap. Working quickly so the ice cream doesn't melt, roll the balls in the chopped walnuts and return the balls to the freezer.

Prepare the vanilla sauce: Mix together the sour cream, milk, sugar, and vanilla extract. Set aside.

Trim the pound cake and cut it into ½-inch-thick slices. Stack the slices and cut them into sticks, or "fingers," approximately 4 inches long and 1 inch wide.

At serving time, place a spoonful of vanilla sauce on each plate and position an ice cream ball in the center. Serve with a few pound cake fingers.

4 SERVINGS

INSTANT CHOCOLATE MOUSSE

T his is the fastest way possible to make chocolate mousse —especially so if you have all the ingredients on hand. It is simply a mixture of melted chocolate and whipped cream flavored with a little Grand Marnier, which complements the chocolate well.

1 cup heavy cream
¾ cup milk
8 ounces bittersweet chocolate,
broken into ½-inch pieces
1 tablespoon Grand Marnier
1 ounce bittersweet or semi-
sweet chocolate, for garnish

Whip the cream with an electric mixer or with a whisk. Set aside.

Bring the milk to a boil in a small saucepan. Remove the pan from the heat, add the chocolate pieces, and stir with a whisk until the chocolate has melted and the mixture is smooth. Add the Grand Marnier and mix well. Cool to room temperature, testing by dipping your finger into the mixture periodically; when it has reached room temperature, it will feel neither hot nor cold. Transfer it to a bowl.

Add all the whipped cream to the melted chocolate in one stroke, and fold together with a large rubber spatula to incorporate it well. Cover, and refrigerate for about 2 hours to set before serving.

To serve, spoon the mousse into glass dessert bowls or goblets. For the garnish, run the blade of a vegetable peeler along the edge of the 1 ounce of chocolate, and let the shavings drop directly onto the servings of mousse.

4 SERVINGS

> **JUST FOLD WHIPPED CREAM INTO MELTED CHOCOLATE TO CREATE THIS SMOOTH, RICH MOUSSE.**

CINNAMON STICKS

T hese cinnamon sticks, like the savory Cheese Sticks on page 79, are made with packaged puff pastry from the supermarket. Each package contains two 10-inch-square sheets, each weighing about 8 ounces. The sheets are usually folded on themselves, with the layers separated by pieces of paper. Allow the pastry to defrost just enough so that it can be unfolded. It is easier to handle, to cut, and to arrange on the cookie sheet while it is still slightly frozen, before it softens and becomes sticky.

Store any leftovers in an airtight container to keep them from softening, or wrap them tightly and freeze them.

1 sheet (8 ounces, ½ package)
*   frozen puff pastry*
1 tablespoon unsalted butter,
*   softened*
⅓ cup sugar
2 teaspoons ground cinnamon

Place the frozen pastry dough on a cookie sheet. After 15 to 20 minutes, while it's still partially frozen, unfold the dough, even though it will tend to crack at the seams, and rub the surface with half the butter. Mix the sugar and cinnamon together, and spread half on the surface of the pastry, pushing it into the butter. Then turn the dough over and repeat the procedure with the remaining butter and cinnamon-sugar mixture. Cut the square into ten strips; then cut the strips in half to yield twenty strips of pastry, each approximately 1 inch wide and 5 inches long.

Arrange the strips about 1 inch apart on the cookie sheet, and bake in a 375-degree oven for 13 to 15 minutes, until dark brown. The sugar on the underside of the pastry will have melted and caramelized, so transfer the sticks to a wire rack while they are still hot; if they are allowed to cool, the sugar will stick and the pastry will be difficult to remove from the cookie sheet.

Serve as is or with your favorite fruit or ice cream dessert.

6 SERVINGS (ABOUT 20 STICKS)

> **WORK WITH PUFF PASTRY DOUGH WHILE IT IS STILL PARTIALLY FROZEN. AS IT THAWS IT BECOMES STICKY, MAKING IT DIFFICULT TO HANDLE.**

INDEX

vegetable(s) (*cont.*)
fricassee of peas with ham,
221–222
gratin of pumpkin with
cheese, 234
green beans and shallots, 204
hash-brown potato cake, 228–
229
hash-brown potatoes
boulangère, 230–231
honeyed carrots with pepper,
210
iceberg and garlic sauté, 217–
218
jardinière of, 215
leeks vinaigrette, 216–217
marinated mushrooms, 218–
219
mashed potatoes and garlic,
226–227
mushroom-and-anchovy-
stuffed tomatoes, 237–238
parsley potatoes with butter,
225
pearl onions and peas in
cream sauce, 220–221
peas and lettuce, 222–223
potatoes maire, 225–226
potatoes persillade, 227
potatoes with walnuts and
croutons, 229–230
potato omelet, 231–232
purée of carrots and potatoes,
209
purée of peas with mint, 223–
224
ragout of potatoes, 228
sautéed spinach with nutmeg,
235
scallions au gratin, 233

vegetable(s) (*cont.*)
soup, chunky, 54–55
spicy mushroom toasts, 219–
220
steamed cauliflower with
lemon butter, 208
tomatoes Provençale, 236
white bean purée, 206
yams with maple syrup and
butter, 232
zucchini and eggplant gratin,
240
zucchini flan, 238–239
see also salad(s); *specific
varieties*
velvet hammer, 263–264
vermicelle, soupe au, 53–54
vichyssoise, 62
vinaigrette:
asparagus, 147–148
leeks, 216–217
lemon, 155
mustard, 26–27
scallops, 138–139

walnuts, potatoes with croutons
and, 229–230
watercress au gratin, fish on,
148–149
white bean purée, 206
wine sauce, red, braised short
ribs in, 196–197
wonton:
beef pelminy in chicken broth,
122–123
ravioli, ricotta cheese, 121–
122
ravioli, shrimp, 119–121
wafers, crisp, 84–85

About the Author

Jacques Pepin is one of the country's foremost cooking teachers. A columnist for *The New York Times,* he is also dean of studies at the French Culinary Institute in New York and an instructor at Boston University. He is the author of *The Art of Cooking,* Volumes I and II, *Everyday Cooking with Jacques Pépin, La Technique,* and *La Méthode,* and has a new television series on national PBS-TV. Pépin lives in Connecticut with his wife and daughter.